Death and Discipleship

An Analysis of the Predictions of Jesus' Death in the Gospel of Mark

Wayne T. Slusser

Volume 3

DEATH AND DISCIPLESHIP

An Analysis of the Predictions of Jesus' Death in the Gospel of Mark

WAYNE T. SLUSSER

ACADEMIC THEOLOGICAL STUDIES

Death and Discipleship
An Analysis of the Predictions of Jesus' Death in the Gospel of Mark
Copyright © 2023 by Wayne T. Slusser

Published by Northeastern Baptist Press
       Post Office Box 4600
       Bennington, VT 05201

All rights reserved. No part of this book may be reproduced in any form without prior permission from Northeastern Baptist Press, except as provided for by USA copyright law.

All Scripture translations are the author's unless otherwise noted.

Cover design by Leason Stiles & Jared August

Hardcover ISBN: 978-1-953331-23-6

To Dr. Robert Baker,
Pastor, Dad, and Poppy.
Thank you for your godly example and ministry to me.
You are a Paul to this Timothy.

Contents

Series Introduction — i

Preface — iii

Chapter One
Introduction — 1

Chapter Two
Discourse Analysis as a Complement of Hermeneutics — 7

Chapter Three
Studying the Gospels as Literature — 49

Chapter Four
Studying the Gospel of Mark as Literature — 85

Chapter Five
Discourse Analysis of the Passion Predictions — 125

Chapter Six
Conclusion — 209

Bibliography — 217

Series Introduction

Northeastern Baptist Press publishes Christian books that inform, inspire, and encourage people to follow Jesus Christ. Realizing the need for an academic series that is tethered to the Baptist Faith and Message 2000, NEBP has developed the Academic Theological Studies (ATS) series.

The ATS series is comprised of doctoral dissertations as well as academic monographs that are carefully selected based on solid recommendations and rigorous peer review. Each study makes a unique and distinct contribution to the broader field of theology. Although all books in this series are specialized, they are not written for specialists. The ATS series provides the church at large with quality resources that have significant implications for practical issues. Toward this end, we publish within the fields of biblical studies, systematic and historical theology, Christian counseling, education, and pastoral ministry.

We foresee the ATS series growing into a significant collection of academic studies that provide the church with an accessible, yet academically rigorous avenue for theological inquiry.

Jared M. August
Ralph H. Slater
Series Editors

Preface

Discourse analysis is a complementary discipline of hermeneutics. Discourse analysis enables interpreters to show the relationship between the central section (8:22-10:52) and the Gospel of Mark as a whole, while also accounting for the various levels and features of the text within the central section itself. Two components of discourse analysis are discourse structure (genre and sub-genre) and discourse texture (text).

The analysis interprets two aspects of Mark's story, the theme. Mark declares, defines, and affirms Jesus' identity as the Son of God (formal aspect) and captures the significance for the reader through the disciples' role as committed followers of Jesus Christ (functional aspect). The analysis also explicates the relationship between Jesus' three passion predictions within the central section (8:22-10:52) and the Gospel of Mark.

Although Mark is narrative, it possesses unique features requiring a sub-genre of narrative. Mark is a theological narrative biography. This sub-genre accounts for three unique features of Mark's story: the literary medium (narrative); the episodic structure that emphasizes Jesus Christ (biography) as the central character; and the intended purpose, to awaken and subsequently to strengthen the faith of the reader (theology).

The analysis of the central section (8:22-10:52) points to the arrangement of Mark's story (1:14-8:21, Galilee; 8:22-10:52, on the way to Jerusalem; and 11:1-16:8, Jerusalem), while he portrays Jesus' identity as the Son of God. The central section looks back at the preceding declaration that Jesus is the Son of God (1:14-8:21) by further defining Jesus' role as the suffering and self-sacrificing Messiah and looks forward to the fulfillment of Jesus' predictions concerning his death and the affirmation, he is the Son of God (11:1-16:8).

DEATH AND DISCIPLESHIP:
An Analysis of the Predictions of Jesus' Death in the Gospel of Mark

The analysis of Jesus' three passion predictions (8:31-9:1; 9:30-37; 10:32-45) confirms the theme of Mark's story. Each consists of three events highlighting Jesus' role as Messiah and the disciples' role as committed followers of Jesus. Three analyses (Greek text, verb, and role) point to Mark's use of language (metafunctions), relationship of language (cohesion), emphasis of language (prominence), and limitations of language (discourse boundaries) to explain the discourse function of the various features of Jesus' three passion predictions.

Chapter One

Introduction

Discourse analysis is a complement to hermeneutics that seeks to understand the complexities of how language is used within a written text. It strives to account for the meaning and relationship of all levels of the text. This includes both the larger levels, such as the paragraph, episode, and the text as a whole (macro-structure) and the smaller levels such as the word, clause, and sentence (micro-structure). There are some New Testament scholars however, that question, even reject, discourse analysis as a viable sub-discipline in the exegetical process.[1] For example, Daniel Wallace limits his study of the New

---

1. Moisés Silva's comments, though a bit overstated, demonstrate the confusing character of discourse analysis leading one to question its viability. He states, "Indeed, the more I read the more lost I feel." He also writes, "Discourse analysis is about . . . *everything*!" ("Discourse Analysis and Philippians," In *Discourse Analysis and Other Topics in Biblical Greek* JSNTSS 113, eds. Stanley E. Porter and D. A. Carson [Sheffield: Sheffield Academic Press, 1995], 102-03). Robert L. Thomas also negatively and unnecessarily exaggerates the subjectivity of discourse analysis. He claims that to analyze a larger section of material without first probing the details of that section can breed a variety of understandings as to what the biblical author meant. He further claims that the subjective inclinations of those who implement discourse analysis become the authority for meaning and not the text. As a matter of fact, later in Thomas' book he characterizes discourse analysis as 'fickle' and possesses essentially the same methodological characteristics as open theism. He writes, "This hermeneutical innovation has given rise to what I have called 'hermeneutical hopscotch' (see pp. 153, 163). Discourse analysis hops from one carefully selected part of a larger section to another. By selecting only parts that contribute to supporting a predetermined opinion, the 'hopscotch' approach can prove just about anything the interpreter desires" (*Evangelical Hermeneutics: The New Versus the Old* [Grand Rapids: Kregel, 2002], 228, 486).

DEATH AND DISCIPLESHIP:
An Analysis of the Predictions of Jesus' Death in the Gospel of Mark

Testament to syntax because of the substantial disagreement among various schools of linguistics regarding terminology, methodology, and objectives.[2] Although he raises good concerns, there are certain common features of language use that discourse analysts point to as legitimate to determine the text as a whole. They are: "semantics, concerned with the conveyance of meaning through the forms of the language ('what the form means'); syntax, concerned with the organization of these forms into meaningful units; and pragmatics, concerned with the meanings of these forms in specific linguistic contexts ('what speakers mean when they use the forms')."[3] These common features,

---

Although Reed does not question the value of discourse analysis, he provides the potential reason for the confusion. He writes, "Because of its far-reaching impact, discourse analysis is one of the least well-defined areas of linguistics. Idiosyncratic models and terminological confusion proliferate as more linguists, as well as non-linguists, adopt discourse analysis as a theoretical framework for reading all kinds of texts" (*A Discourse Analysis of Philippians*, 16).

2. Daniel B. Wallace, *Greek Grammar Beyond the Basics: An Exegetical Syntax of the New Testament* (Grand Rapids: Zondervan, 1996), xv. See also P. H. Matthews, *Syntax* (Cambridge: Cambridge University Press, 1981), xix and Thomas, *Evangelical Hermeneutics: The New Versus the Old*, 228. Thomas' overall assessment of discourse analysis is that it "opposes the traditional method in so many crucial areas that it cannot do other than detract from interpretive analyses of the meaning of the biblical text. This system's use of the interpreter's preunderstanding as the starting point in exegesis forces the interpretive procedure into a subjective mold that inevitably steers conclusions away from an objective understanding of the author's meaning." Therefore, he claims that discourse analysis "hinders an accurate interpretation of the text" (233). He ultimately suggests that an understanding of the parts of the text is vital to traditional hermeneutics where more agreement among practitioners exists and less subjectivity occurs; and rightfully so. But this is only half of the method of discourse analysis. The author of this Book disagrees with Thomas' rejection of discourse analysis. The purpose and intent of discourse analysis is to probe *both at the micro (word) and macro-levels (paragraph)* in order to discover the biblical authorial intended meaning of the text. Thus, an incorporation of *both levels of text* provides the interpreter with a sense of the whole and its relationship to the parts that comprise the whole and not just an understanding of the parts of text in isolation. Further explanation of the benefits of discourse analysis in New Testament exegesis occurs later in chapter two.

3. Stanley E. Porter, "Discourse Analysis and New Testament Studies: An Introductory Survey," in *Discourse Analysis and Other Topics in Biblical Greek* JSNTSS, 113 ed. Stanley E. Porter and D. A. Carson (Sheffield: Sheffield Academic Press, 1995), 18.

for the most part, demonstrate the homogenous efforts of discourse analysts in the field of New Testament studies. When considered together, they seek to answer the question "how has the author organized his statements into a coherent whole to convey his intended meaning to his target audience?"[4]

Discourse analysis contributes to an understanding of how Mark communicates his intent to the reader. It does so in three ways. First, discourse analysis pays sufficient attention to all levels of the text as a unified whole. In other words, discourse analysis examines language at a level beyond the sentence. The discourse analyst moves from the text as a whole (macro-structure) to the word-level (micro-structure) and back again; thus, demonstrating the relationship and function of each level as it contributes to meaning.

Second, discourse analysis examines various grammatical features of the text that also contribute to meaning. These features include: metafunctions of language (function of language), cohesion (relationship of language), prominence (emphasis of language), and discourse boundaries (limitations of language). These textual features provide the reader with the author's rationale for meaning; that is, the textual features answer the question, how does the author organize his words, phrases, sentences, and episodes into a coherent whole so that his meaning is communicated to his readers?

---

4. Rodney J. Decker, *Temporal Deixis of the Greek Verb in the Gospel of Mark with Reference to Verbal Aspect*, Studies in Biblical Greek 10 (New York: Peter Lang, 2001), 53. Guthrie complements the goal in answering Decker's question. He writes, "Discourse analysis may be defined as a process of investigation by which one examines the form and function of all the parts and levels of a written discourse, with the aim of better understanding both the parts and the whole of that discourse" ("Discourse Analysis," 255). Reed also sees the text as a communicative whole. He writes, "There is a relationship grammatically, semantically and pragmatically between the various parts of a given text, and that there is a thematic element that flows through it, allows the listener/reader to recognize discourse as a cohesive piece of communication rather than a jumble of unrelated words and sentences. How is it, then, that speakers go about forming texts into a cohesive unit? How do they combine relatively unrelated words and sentences into a meaningful whole? Discourse analysts repeatedly seek answers to such questions, attempting to identify how a language is used to create cohesive communication" ("Discourse Analysis As A New Testament Hermeneutic," 234).

Third, discourse analysis utilizes objective evidence to examine the text.[5] The discourse analysis theory that best accounts for this objective evidence is the Systemic-Functional Linguistic theory. Discourse structure and discourse texture are the two components of this theory. The implementation of these two components provides the reader with the objective evidence necessary to account for the coherent representation of discourse through the use and function of language both at the macro and micro-structural levels respectively. These two components of discourse analysis examine the text to explicate the meaning.

Summary

This book is comprised of five chapters after the introduction. Chapters two and three provide the methodology necessary for the analysis in chapters four and five. The final chapter summarizes the results of the discourse analysis and evaluates the value of the research.

Chapter two explains the objective influence discourse analysis provides to examine the text at multiple levels. This writer argues that the Systemic-Functional Linguistic theory best accounts for the objective evidence necessary for such an examination. Chapter three contends that the Gospels fit into a sub-generic category of narrative; that is, theological narrative biography. This sub-generic category accounts for the unique nature of the Gospel accounts, for the Gospels are written as narrative explicating the life of Jesus Christ for the intended purpose of awakening and subsequently strengthening the reader's faith.

The two chapters regarding method are followed by two chapters that apply the method. Chapter four applies the first of two components of discourse analysis, discourse structure, specifically to the Gospel of Mark. It is concluded that Mark captures his narrative through the means of three geo-

---

5. Objective evidence refers to the biblical author's use of language in a given text or discourse. Language is examined at multiple levels. Discourse analysis takes the author's use of language and reports the function (metafunctions), relationship (cohesion), emphasis (prominence), and limitations (discourse boundaries) of language.

graphical locations all the while weaving his Christological emphasis through Jesus' journey to Jerusalem. His emphasis is to declare, define, and affirm Jesus' identity as the Son of God and subsequently to provide the reader with the importance of following Jesus because of knowing him.

Chapter five is the final stage of analysis. It is a detailed analysis of Jesus' passion predictions, thus applying the second of two components of discourse analysis, discourse texture. This final analysis points to the fact that Mark's central section (8:22-10:52) explicates his emphasis, thus demonstrating the contribution of discourse analysis to an understanding of the relationship and significance of this section to his whole story, as well as the impact the whole has on his central section. The conclusion, chapter six, summarizes the results of the analysis and assesses the value of discourse analysis as it pertains to the discipline of hermeneutics.

Limitations

The first limitation refers to genre. Discourse analysis is applied to the Gospel of Mark. Space does not permit an analysis of all the Gospel accounts. The second limitation refers to the text. Discourse analysis is only applied to the central section (8:22-10:52) of the Gospel of Mark, namely Jesus' three predictions of his death. As additional sections of Mark and other Gospel accounts are analyzed, the conclusions of this book will be tested.

Assumptions

There are two assumptions. The first assumption refers to the author of the Gospel of Mark. John Mark is the author. Although he was not an eyewitness, he obtained his information from Peter.[6] The second assumption refers to

---

6. For a more detailed analysis related to John Mark as author, see D. A. Carson and Douglas J. Moo, *An Introduction to the New Testament* (Grand Rapids: Zondervan, 2005), 172-77; Donald Guthrie, *New Testament Introduction*, rev ed (Downers Grove, Ill: InterVarsity Press, 1990), 81-84; Russell Small, "Mark," in *Approaching the New Testament: A Guide for Students*, gen. eds. Adam McClendon and John Cartwright (Nashville, TN: Broadman & Holman, 2022), 40-41.

the historicity of the Gospel of Mark. It is assumed that Mark is a revelatory historical account of his story.[7]

---

7. Moisés Silva states, "In the case of the Gospels, every indication we have is that the writers expected their statements to be taken as historical. Luke, in particular, as he begins both his gospel and the book of Acts, makes that purpose quite explicit (see Luke 1:1-4 and Acts 1:1-3), and the other writers give no clue that their intent is significantly different" ("But These Are Written That You May Believe, The Meaning of the Gospels," in *Introduction To Biblical Hermeneutics: The Search for Meaning* eds. Walter C. Kaiser Jr. and Moisés Silva [Grand Rapids: Zondervan, 2007], 158). Silva further states, "the denial or deletion of the historical referents in the narrative about Jesus' life and ministry were just as destructive of the truth-intentions of the writers as a denial or deletion of all historical contacts in the exodus narrative" ("I Will Remember the Deeds of the Lord," 134). See also See Craig Blomberg, *The Historical Reliability of the Gospels* (Downers Grove, Ill: InterVarsity Press, 1985) and *Jesus and the Gospels: An Introduction and Survey*, 2d ed (Nashville: Broadman and Holman, 2009), 138-40.

Chapter Two

Discourse Analysis as a Complement of Hermeneutics

The aim of this book is to answer one question: what contribution can discourse analysis make to the interpretation of the Gospel of Mark? Therefore, the focus of this chapter is to discuss the methodological approach that will be applied to the Gospel of Mark. Discourse analysis examines various levels of the text to show the relationship between the central section and the Gospel of Mark as a whole. The implication is that discourse analysis is a complement to New Testament exegesis.

There are four schools or approaches within discourse analysis. Each of these approaches possesses theoretical components to benefit New Testament exegesis. However, the Systemic Functional Linguistic theory is the one theory that is more closely implemented in the analysis of Jesus' three predictions of his death in the following chapters.

There are two components of discourse analysis which provides the basis for the analysis of the central section (8:22-10:52). The first component is discourse structure. The emphasis of this component examines Mark at the level of genre. The second component is discourse texture. The emphasis of this component examines the central section at the level of text; namely, the three predictions of Jesus' death.

DEATH AND DISCIPLESHIP:
An Analysis of the Predictions of Jesus' Death in the Gospel of Mark

Discourse analysis is defined as a language-based discipline that seeks to understand the complexities of the original context.[1] It is a branch of linguistic study that has emerged from the latter half of the twentieth century[2] and analyzes language in use.[3] It is primarily a linguistic approach that examines "how humans use language to communicate and, in particular, how addressers construct linguistic messages for addressees and how addressees work on linguistic messages in order to interpret them."[4] Jeffrey Reed agrees. He writes,

---

1. Stanley E. Porter writes, "The distinctiveness of discourse analysis and the concern of discourse analysts is to be able to provide as comprehensive a description as possible of the various components of a given discourse, including its meaning and structure, and the means by which these are created and conveyed" ("Discourse Analysis and New Testament Studies: An Introductory Survey," in *Discourse Analysis and Other Topics in Biblical Greek* JSNTSS, 113 ed. Stanley E. Porter and D. A. Carson [Sheffield: Sheffield Academic Press, 1995], 19). Jeffrey T. Reed explains the expansive scope of discourse analysis. He writes, "Discourse analysis is a way of reading. It is a framework with which the analyst approaches a text and explicates what it says and how it has been said in addition to what has been understood and how it has been understood. It may be classified under the rubric of hermeneutics" ("Discourse Analysis as New Testament Hermeneutic: A Retrospective and Prospective Appraisal," *JETS* 39, no. 2 [June 1996]: 224). For a definition of discourse, see 10n10.

2. H. A. Gleason observed that discourse analysis was just beginning and there are not many firm and substantive results (H. A. Gleason, "Contrastive Analysis in Discourse Structure," *Georgetown University Monograph Series on Languages and Linguistics* 21 (1968) 41).

3. Some worthy introductions to discourse analysis include, Gillian Brown and George Yule, *Discourse Analysis* (Cambridge: Cambridge University Press: 1983); Malcolm Coulthard, *An Introduction to Discourse Analysis* 2d ed. (London: Longman, 1985); Robert-Alain de Beaugrande and Wolfgang Ulrich Dressler, *Introduction to Text Linguistics* (London: Longman, 1981); Joseph E. Grimes, *The Thread of Discourse* Janua Linguarum 207 (Hague: Mouton, 1975); Robert E. Longacre, *The Grammar of Discourse* 2d ed. (New York and London: Plenum, 1996); Michael Stubbs, *Discourse Analysis: The Sociolinguistic Analysis of Natural Language* (Oxford: Basil Blackwell, 1983); T. A. van Dijk, *Text and Context: Explorations in the Semantics and Pragmatics of Discourse* (London: Longman, 1977).

4. Brown and Yule, *Discourse Analysis*, ix. de Beaugrande and Dressler label discourse analysis as 'the study of conversation' (*Introduction to Text Linguistics*, 19). Stanley E. Porter and Matthew Brook O'Donnell state that discourses involve the means of exchange, linguistic interaction. "Thus, a discourse or text can be defined in

"Discourse analysis is, therefore, an interdisciplinary approach to language and human communicative behavior."[5] Though discourse analysis examines the communication of human language, there is no reason to restrict the understanding of discourse to spoken language, for a written text is also discourse.[6]

This chapter considers the impact of discourse analysis on the field of New Testament studies, and therefore the relationship to the Gospel of Mark. Although discourse analysis originated in the field of linguistics, several scholars note its importance in biblical exegesis.[7] Discourse analysis and its impact on exegesis within the field of New Testament studies are both necessary and helpful. First, it is necessary because discourse analysis considers "units larger than the word, including not only immediate context but even larger units of discourse."[8] This is important because communication rarely occurs at the word level or simply in isolated sentences.[9] Rather, communica-

---

terms of any linguistic situation that involves this linguistic interaction, whether it is as short as a few words exchanged or as long as a major monograph" (*Discourse Analysis and the Greek New Testament: Theory, Application and Results* [Leiden: Brill, in preparation], 6).

5. Jeffrey T. Reed, "Discourse Analysis," in *A Handbook to the Exegesis of the New Testament*, ed. Stanley E. Porter (Leiden: Brill, 2002), 189.

6. George H. Guthrie contends "Thus a key to understanding an act of communication—we could say *any* act of communication—is to understand the organization of material as related to a given context, and this is a major objective of a form of inquiry known as 'discourse analysis'" ("Discourse Analysis," in *Interpreting the New Testament: Essays on Methods and Issues* ed. David Alan Black and David S. Dockery [Nashville: Broadman and Holman, 2001], 255).

7. See: Joseph D. Fantin, appendix "Modern Linguistics: Select History, Use in New Testament Studies and in this work, Evaluation, and Proposals for Future Work," in *The Greek Imperative Mood in the New Testament: A Cognitive and Communicative Approach*, Studies in Biblical Greek 12 (New York, NY: Peter Lang Publishing, 2010), 328-32; Guthrie, "Discourse Analysis," 267-68; Stanley E. Porter, "Greek Grammar and Syntax," in *The Face of New Testament Studies: A Survey of Recent Research*, ed. Scot McKnight and Grant R. Osborne (Grand Rapids: Baker, 2004), 87-88, 96-99.

8. Stanley E. Porter and Jeffrey T. Reed, "Greek Grammar Since BDF: A Retrospective and Prospective Analysis," *FN* 4, no. 7 (1991): 157.

9. Zellig S. Harris writes, "Language does not occur in stray words or sentences, but in connected discourse, from a one-word utterance to a ten-volume work, from a monolog to a Union Square argument. Arbitrary conglomerations of sentences

tion occurs in larger units called discourses.[10] Therefore, "discourse analysis shifts the focus of biblical exegesis from individual words, and even passages, and places it on whole discourses."[11] This shift in emphasis from words to

are indeed of no interest except as a check on grammatical description" ("Discourse Analysis," *Language* 28 [1952]: 3).

10. Peter Cotterell and Max Turner define a discourse as "any coherent sequence of strings, any coherent stretch of language" (*Linguistics and Biblical Interpretation* [Downers Grove, Ill: InterVarsity Press, 1989], 230). Jeffrey T. Reed states that "discourse, then, is probably best treated as whatever language users decide, . . . Speakers and listeners determine when a communicative event begins and when it ends. This encoded communicative event is what is referred to here as discourse" (*A Discourse Analysis of Philippians: Method and Rhetoric in the Debate over Literary Integrity*, JSNTSS 136 [Sheffield: Sheffield, 1997], 17-18).

William Klein, Craig Blomberg, and Robert Hubbard provide understanding as to how communication is developed. They state, "In one sense language consists of combining various elements, as building blocks, to construct meaningful communication. In simple terms, combining morphemes (minimal elements of meaning, like the plural –s in English) produces words; putting words together produces phrases, clauses, and sentences; and combining sentences results in texts, passages, or discourses" (*Introduction to Biblical Interpretation* [Nashville: Word, 1993], 201). See also the model of discourse analysis as it is viewed from the analogy of a pyramid by Stanley E. Porter. He writes, "The pinnacle of the pyramid represents the entire discourse, since it is at this level that singular topics or thematic structures can be stated and analyzed. The discourse is then broken down into an increasingly larger number of small units, its constituent elements. At the base of the pyramid are the formal units of language which comprise the larger structural and conceptual units" (*Idioms of the Greek New Testament*, 2d ed. Biblical Languages: Greek 2 [Sheffield: Sheffield Academic Press, 1999], 298-99).

11. Guthrie also states, "This does not mean that the individual words, sentences, and paragraphs are any less important than in traditional approaches to exegesis. Rather, discourse analysis moves the 'text' or 'discourse' from a place of ambiguity, and often obscurity, to a place of rigorous consideration and analysis" ("Discourse Analysis," 256). David Alan Black confirms Guthrie's point. He writes, "Just as we are seldom interested in isolated morphemes, so we are rarely concerned with words as separate entities. A spoken or written word in isolation may have many different possible meanings, but a discourse, which is the environment in which words exist, imposes limitations on the choice of possible meanings and tends to shape and define the meaning of each word" (*Linguistics For Students of New Testament Greek: A Survey of Basic Concepts and Applications*, 2d ed. [Grand Rapids: Baker, 1995], 138).

discourses provides the exegete with a better understanding of the text as a whole.[12] Second, it is helpful because, as Fantin rightly notes, "discourse analysis which focuses on higher-level aspects of the book (such as plot, theme, cohesion, etc.) may contribute in a broader way to exegesis (and hermeneutics) . . ."[13] Bergen agrees. He states, "Discourse criticism [discourse analysis] . . . aids the researcher in the tricky business of making judgments concerning authorial intention within the Biblical texts. As such it is establishing itself as another tool to be used at the workbench of Biblical exegesis."[14] The emphasis

---

12. Joel B. Green discusses the significance of discourse analysis for New Testament interpretation. He writes, "It is true that discourse analysis made its debut in NT study as NT interpretation was undergoing a paradigm shift from a primary focus on questions of a historical nature to approaches that privileged the NT text *qua* text. As a consequence, discourse analysis in NT study has largely been practiced in the form of *text-linguistics*, which works under the assumption that a close tie exists between the way a text is structured and the meaning of the text" ("Discourse Analysis and New Testament Interpretation," in *Hearing the New Testament: Strategies for Interpretation*, ed. Joel B. Green [Grand Rapids: Eerdmans, 1995], 176).

13. Fantin, appendix "Modern Linguistics," 328. Discourse analysis is a complementary discipline to hermeneutics. For example, traditional hermeneutics refers to a set of principles implemented to discover the truth intention of the author. These principles are "rules of interpretation to apply to all kinds of writing" (Elliott E. Johnson, *Expository Hermeneutics: An Introduction* [Grand Rapids: Zondervan, 1990], 8). Discourse analysis however goes beyond simply the implementation of hermeneutical principles, for it includes the study of how language works. For example, discourse analysis complements hermeneutics by showing the correlation between semantic and grammatical categories of the text. Discourse analysis does so not just at the word or sentence levels, but also at the paragraph and text level.

14. Robert D. Bergen, "Text As a Guide to Authorial Intention: An Introduction to Discourse Criticism," *JETS* 30, no. 3 (Sept 1987): 328. Bergen also states that "this approach to the Biblical text has potentially revolutionary implications for the field of Biblical hermeneutics. At the very least it will clarify as never before the semantic content of the structures themselves, not merely the semantic content in these structures. [Discourse analysis] has extended our awareness of what may be known about a text. It has taught us to ask new questions of the text. At the same time, it has suggested a means by which the answers may be known" (p. 336).

therefore of discourse analysis is not just its relationship to language, but also to hermeneutics.[15]

Schools of Discourse Analysis[16]

Discourse analysis is a relatively diverse discipline within New Testament studies. For some, the discipline holds an experimental status because there have been few applications of the discipline in New Testament studies.[17] The applications of discourse analysis that has been written vary in theory and method, thus pointing to the diversity[18] as well as the difficulty[19] in grasping the fundamental concepts of this discipline.

There are currently at least four major schools of discourse analysis in New Testament studies.[20] These include Summer Institute of Linguistics, Continental European Discourse Analysis, South African Discourse Analy-

---

15. For a helpful definition and extensive description of discourse analysis see Todd A. Scacewater, "Introduction – Discourse Analysis: History, Topics, and Applications" in *Discourse Analysis of the New Testament Writings* ed. Todd A. Scacewater (Dallas, TX: Fontes Press, 2020), 1-11.

16. Constantine R. Campbell provides a summary of these schools in *Advances in the Study of Greek: New Insights for Reading the New Testament*, Grand Rapids, Zondervan: 2015 (pp. 150-52).

17. Some examples are included throughout the discussion in which they relate.

18. Deborah Schiffrin, *Approaches to Discourse* (Oxford: Blackwell, 1994), 49-336.

19. Due to the diversity and difficulty, NT scholars are a bit skeptical of discourse analysis. Cotterell and Turner offer a critique. They write, "We must at least comment on the tentative nature of this particular aspect of linguistics. The fact is that at the present there are no firm conclusions, no generally accepted formulae, no fixed methodology, not even an agreed terminology" (*Linguistics and Biblical Interpretation*, 233).

20. Stanley E. Porter defines a linguistic school of thought as "the attemps to find conceptual structures by which to examine language without accepting what we have been told or what we assumed without further reflection and without imposing our own language upon another." ("Linguistic Schools," in *Linguistics and New Testament Greek: Key Issues in the Current Debate*, eds. David Alan Black and Benjamin L. Merkle [Grand Rapids: Baker, 2020], 12).

sis, and Systemic-Functional Linguistics. This Book will more closely follow the systemic-functional model. It is not the intent to provide a detailed analysis of each school; rather to simply introduce the basic concepts and impact upon New Testament studies.

Summer Institute of Linguistics (SIL)[21] Discourse Analysis

The Summer Institute of Linguistics was started in 1934 by William Cameron Townsend. SIL concentrates primarily upon Bible translation. Much of their interest lies in linguistic models that provide assistance to those interacting with ethnolinguistic people groups. SIL has been heavily influenced by the linguists Nida, Pike and Lamb, and Louw from the South African school.[22]

Although SIL is primarily engaged in Bible translation, there are two major models within SIL that have been involved in recent discourse analysis discussions. They are Pike's tagmemics[23] and Lamb's stratificational grammar.[24] Both functional models share the premise that language works in layers; that is, the smallest of layers (e.g. morpheme, word, and sentence) build upon the largest of layers (e.g. paragraphs, pericope) and increase to larger

---

21. Summer Institute of Linguistics (SIL) "is a faith-based nonprofit organization committed to serving language communities worldwide as they build capacity for sustainable language development. SIL does this primarily through research, translation, training and materials development" http://www.sil.org/sil/ (accessed July 19, 2011).

22. Some of the significant works include: Stephen H. Levinsohn, *Discourse Features of New Testament Greek: A Coursebook*, 2d ed (Dallas, Tex: Summer Institute of Linguistics, 1992); Robert E. Longacre, *The Grammar of Discourse*; Idem, "The Paragraph as a Grammatical Unit," in *Discourse and Syntax*, ed. Talmy Givón, 115-34 (New York: Academic Press, 1979); Eugene A. Nida, *Toward a Science of Translating: With Special Reference to Principles and Procedures Involved in Bible Translating* (Leiden: Brill, 1964); Idem, *Componential Analysis of Meaning: An Introduction to Semantic Structures* (Hague: Mouton, 1975).

23. Kenneth L. Pike, *Language in Relation to a Unified Theory of the Structure of Human Behavior* (Hague: Mouton, 1967).

24. Sydney M. Lamb, *Outline of Stratificational Grammar* (Washington, D.C: Georgetown U. Press, 1966).

structures or discourses.²⁵ In other words, this method aims to provide a systematic analysis of smaller units of language and to describe how they contribute to larger units of meaning within discourse.²⁶

---

25. Porter evaluates the method of SIL advocates because much of their work continues to focus on sentence-level grammar. As a result of this evaluation, Porter critiques the article by Stephen H. Levinsohn ("A Discourse Study of Constituent Order and the Article in Philippians," in *Discourse Analysis and Other Topics in Biblical Greek* JSNTSS 113, eds. Stanley E. Porter and D. A. Carson [Sheffield: Sheffield Academic Press, 1995], 60-74). He writes, "I have some question about what it means that this essay is an exercise in discourse analysis as opposed to a study in sentence grammar or syntax, since he essentially confines himself to the level of the clause or sentence. Other very important topics in discourse analysis are not considered, such as discourse boundaries, prominence, and coherence and cohesion" ("How Can Biblical Discourse Be Analyzed?: A Response to Several Attempts," in *Discourse Analysis and Other Topics in Biblical Greek*, JSNTSS 113, eds. Stanley E. Porter and D. A. Carson [Sheffield: Sheffield Academic Press, 1995],108).

26. Some of the significant works that emphasize the analysis of smaller units within larger units to demonstrate the contribution to meaning within discourse include: David L. Allen, "The Discourse Structure of Philemon: A Study in Textlinguistics," in *Scribes and Scripture: New Testament Essays in Honor of J. Harold Greenlee*, ed. David Alan Black (Winona Lake, Ind: Eisenbrauns, 1992), 77-96; Kathleen Callow, *Discourse Considerations in Translating the Word of God* (Grand Rapids: Zondervan, 1974); Gregory T. Christopher, "A Discourse Analysis of Colossians 2:16-3:17," *GTJ* 11 (1990): 205-20; Robert E. Longacre regarding his examination of micro- and macro-structures in "Building for the Worship of God: Exodus 25:1-30:10," in *Discourse Analysis of Biblical Literature*, ed. Walter Bodine, The Society of Biblical Literature Semeia Studies (Atlanta, GA: Scholars, 1995), 21-50; Linda L. Neely, "A Discourse Analysis of Hebrews," *Occasional Papers in Translation and Textlinguistics* 3-4 (1987): 1-146.

Continental European Discourse Analysis

This Continental European model was developed out of the German School of textlinguistics[27] and the Scandinavian School of New Testament studies.[28] The German group of discourse analysts concentrates upon the communicative and linguistic functions of the text in order to seek an understanding of the utilization of texts within human interaction through a beyond-the-sentence examination of the text.[29] The Scandinavian group concentrates upon modern rhetorical and communication theories in an attempt to "mediate the complex relationship between text and reader."[30] The aim of this group is to examine the macro-structure of discourse as it relates to the micro-structure.

---

27. de Beaugrande contends that Peter Hartmann is the father and founder of textlinguistics. http://www.beaugrande.com/GroundRulesTextLinguistics.htm (accessed July 26, 2011). Hartmann's two monumental works include: *Theorie der Grammatik* (Hague: Mouton, 1963) and *Zur Theorie Der Sprachwissenschaft* (Assen: Van Gorcum, 1961).

28. For a survey see Birger Olsson, "A Decade of Text-Linguistic Analyses of Biblical Texts at Uppsala," *ST* 39 (1985): 107-26.

29. Some examples that follow the insights of German textlinguistics include John G. Cook, *The Structure and Persuasive Power of Mark: A Linguistic Approach*, Semeia Studies, (Atlanta, Ga: Scholars Press, 1995); David Hellholm, *Das Visionenbuch des Hermas als Apokalypse: Formgeschichtliche und texttheoretische Studien zu einer literarischen Gattung. I. Methodologische Vorüberlegungen und makrostrukturelle Textanalyse* (ConBNT 13.1; Lund: Gleerup, 1980); Wolfgang Schenk, "The Testamental Disciple-Instruction of the Markan Jesus (Mark 13): Its Levels of Communication and its Rhetorical Structures," in *Discourse Analysis and the New Testament: Approaches and Results* JSNTSS 170, ed. Stanley E. Porter and Jeffrey T. Reed, 197-222 (Sheffield: Sheffield Academic Press, 1999).

Breytenbach and Olsson most clearly exemplify the German group and promote an attention to discourse rather than the sentence; they do so by examining the text as it relates to the meaning of the whole. See Cilliers Breytenbach, *Nachfolge und Zukunftserwartung nach Markus: Eine Methodenkritische Studie*, ATANT 71, (Zürich: Theologischer Verlag, 1984) and Birger Olsson, *Structure and Meaning in the Fourth Gospel: A Text-Linguistic Analysis of John 2:1-11 and 4:1-42* Coniectanea Biblica (Lund: Gleerup, 1974).

30. Porter and O'Donnell, *Discourse Analysis and the Greek New Testament*, 20. Two scholars representing the Scandinavian group are David Hellholm and Bruce

DEATH AND DISCIPLESHIP:
An Analysis of the Predictions of Jesus' Death in the Gospel of Mark

South African Discourse Analysis – J. P. Louw

The South African School consists of a group of New Testament scholars that are members of the New Testament Society of South Africa.[31] They understand that "meaningful relations not only exist between the words in a sentence, but also between larger parts of a text such as sentences, groups of sentences (clusters) and pericopae. It is therefore important to analyse the way a text is structured in order to grasp its meaning."[32] Louw initiated and was instrumental in the development of the South African approach to discourse analysis.[33]

C. Johanson. Hellholm draws upon rhetorical theory and Johanson attempts to see the discourse components and the interconnections between smaller and larger units through rhetorical theory. See David Hellholm, "Amplificatio in the Macro-Structure of Romans," in *Rhetoric and the New Testament: Essays from the 1992 Heidelberg Conference* JSNTSS 90, eds. Stanley E. Porter and Thomas H. Olbricht, (Sheffield: JSOT 1993), 123-51; Bruce C. Johanson, *To All the Brethren: A Text-Linguistic and Rhetorical Approach to 1 Thessalonians* Coniectanea Biblica (Stockholm: Almqvist & Wiksell, 1987).

Porter evaluates and critiques the method of the Continental European approach due to the independent treatment of various theories. How are these theories integrated? And do they fit together? See Porter and O'Donnell, *Discourse Analysis and the Greek New Testament*, 22. Porter also expresses concern with the work of David A. Black, "Discourse Structure of Philippians: A Study in Textlinguistics," *NovT* 37 (1995): 16-49.

31. Some of the scholars include Wessel J. Cronje, Eugene A. Nida, Johannes P. Louw, Andries H. Snyman, A B du Toit, and Ernst R. Wendlend. Their research of the discourse structure of the Greek New Testament was published. The first in this series is by Eugene A. Nida, Johannes P. Louw, Andries Snyman, and Wessel J. Cronje, *Style and Discourse: With Special Reference to the Text of the Greek New Testament* (Roggebaai, South Africa: Bible Society, 1983).

32. Snyman, "A Semantic Discourse Analysis of the Letter to Philemon," 88.

33. Louw's work is partially inspired by Nida's Bible translation theory. Some of Louw's more important works include Johannes P. Louw, *Semantics of New Testament Greek* (Philadelphia: Fortress Press; Chico, Calif: Scholars Press, 1982); idem, *A Semantic Discourse Anlysis of Romans* 2 vols, (Dept of Greek, Pretoria: University of Pretoria, 1987); "A Semiotic Approach to Discourse Analysis with Reference to Translation Theory," *BT* 39 (1988): 329-35. See others who implement Louw's method:

The defining feature of the South African school is Louw's colon analysis.³⁴ This analysis leads to a description of the cohesion of a text.³⁵

Systemic-Functional Linguistics (SFL) – Halliday and Hasan

Systemic-Functional Linguistics (SFL) developed primarily in England and Australia through the inspiration of Firth.³⁶ Two scholars in particular, Hal-

---

David A. Black, "Hebrews 1:1-4: A Study in Discourse Analysis," *WTJ* 49 (1987): 175-94; Cotterell and Turner, *Linguistics and Biblical Interpretation*, 230-92; Andries H. Snyman, "Hebrews 6:4-6: From A Semiotic Discourse Perspective," in *Discourse Analysis and the New Testament: Approaches and Results* JSNTSS 170, eds. Stanley E. Porter and Jeffrey T. Reed, 354-68 (Sheffield: Sheffield Academic Press, 1999).

34. Louw defines the colon. He states, "A colon is syntactically a stretch of language having a matrix which consists of a nominal and a verbal element along with additions linked to these two elements of the matrix, or additions which are in turn linked to other sadditions" (*A Semantic Discourse Anlysis of Romans*, 24). See also "South African Discourse Analysis in Theory and Practice," *VE* 29, no. 2 (2008): 387-406. Colon analysis is a syntactic unit that goes beyond a single word. It consists of a nominal unit (subject) and a verbal unit (predicate) that may either be a simple or complex sentence. The analysis continues by grouping the cola into clusters. The basis for these clusters is semantic considerations that possess structural markers that provide the analyst with criteria to then demarcate, or differentiate, the pericope. These structural markers that are based on semantic domains or traditional grammar (e.g. change in person, verb mood, transition in discourse), contribute to the demarcation. It is this demarcation then that cohesion is discovered. This leads to the principle objective of colon analysis, which is the determination of the cohesion of the text and the description of the relational aspects of the text.

35. The cohesion of the text refers to aspects of the text (participants/characters, or phrases/clauses/sentences) that provide the reader with how multiple texts are related together. In other words, the reader can see how the text conceptually 'hangs together.'

36. See also M. A. K. Halliday's discussion related to the history of SFL ("Dimensions of Discourse Analysis: Grammar," in *Handbook of Discourse Analysis* vol. 2 *Dimensions of Discourse*, ed. T. A. van Dijk (London: Academic Press, 1985), 30f. J. R. Firth was a British linguist and English professor who studied in the area of phonology and the study of meaning. See Siobhan Chapman and Christopher Routledge, eds., *Key Thinkers in Linguistics and the Philosophy of Language* (Edinburgh: Edinburgh University Press, 2005), 80-86 for more information regarding the life and work of John R. Firth. Works by Firth include: *Papers in Linguistics, 1934-51* (Oxford: Oxford

liday and Hasan, have taken the work of Firth and provided the school with theoretical and applicational momentum.[37] The SFL School with the influence of Halliday and Hasan strives to examine and understand language through a systemic-functional approach. By systemic, Halliday means "a theory of meaning as choice, by which a language, or any other semiotic sys-

---

University Press, 1951) and F. R. Palmer, ed., *Selected Papers of J. R. Firth 1952-59* (London: Longman, 1968).

37. Some of their works include: M. A. K. Halliday, *An Introduction to Functional Grammar* (London: Edward Arnold, 1985); idem, *Language as Social Semiotic: The Social Interpretation of Language and Meaning* (London: Edward Arnold, 1978); M. A. K. Halliday and R. Hasan, "Text and Context: Aspects of Language in a Social-Semiotic Perspective," *SL* 6 (1980): 4-91; idem, *Language, Context, and Text: Aspects of Language in a Social-Semiotic Perspective* (Geelong, Australia: Deakon University, 1985); M. A. K. Halliday and Christian M. I. M. Matthiessen, *Halliday's Introduction to Functional Grammar*, 4th rev. ed. (London: Routledge, 2014).

Some of those implementing the theories of Halliday and Hasan are known as the Birmingham school and are included in the following works: M. A. K. Halliday and Robin P. Fawcett, eds., *New Developments in Systemic Linguistics* Vol. 1: Theory and Description (London: Pinter, 1987) and Malcolm Coulthard and Martin Montgomery, eds., *Studies in Discourse Analysis* (London: Routledge and Kegan Paul, 1981).

Some of the scholars and their New Testament applications of SFL are listed here: Gustavo Martín-Asensio, "Participant Reference and Foregrounded Syntax in the Stephen Episode," in *Discourse Analysis and the New Testament: Approaches and Results* JSNTSS 170, eds. Stanley E. Porter and Jeffrey T. Reed (Sheffield: Sheffield Academic Press, 1999), 235-57, idem, *Transitivity-Based Foregrounding in the Acts of the Apostles: A Functional-Grammatical Approach to the Lucan Perspective* JSNTSS 202 (Sheffield: Sheffield Academic Press, 2000); Stephanie L. Black, *Sentence Conjunctions in the Gospel of Matthew: καί, δέ, τότε, γάρ, οὖν and Asyndeton in Narrative Discourse* (London: Sheffield Academic, 2002); Porter, *Idioms of the Greek New Testament*; idem, *Letter to the Romans: A Literary and Linguistic Commentary* (Sheffield: Sheffield Phoenix, 2016); Jeffrey T. Reed, "Cohesive Ties in 1 Timothy: In Defense of the Epistle's Unity," *Neot* 26 (1992)," idem, *A Discourse Analysis of Philippians*; "To Timothy or Not? A Discourse Analysis of 1 Timothy," in *Biblical Greek and Linguistics: Open Questions in Current Research* JSNTSS 80, eds. Stanley E. Porter and D. A. Carson (Sheffield: JSOT, 1993), 90-118; Porter and O'Donnell, *Discourse Analysis and the Greek New Testament: Theory and Application*; Porter and Reed, *Discourse Analysis and the New Testament*; Ray Van Neste, *Cohesion and Structure in the Pastoral Epistles* (London: T&T Clark, 2004).

tem, is interpreted as networks of interlocking options."[38] In other words, it is the choices that are available to the author/speaker as they fit within the grammar and lexicon of a language. By functional, Halliday views language as functioning in three dimensions; that is, how the language is used in situational contexts, the components of meaning in language that contribute to the function or metafunction, of the text (ideational, interpersonal, and textual),[39] and the elements of language and their function within the linguistic system. Each of these dimensions is examined and interpreted as functional with respect to the whole communicative act.[40] SFL advocates for a functional approach rather than a formal approach.[41] It is a comprehensive emphasis of examining the relationship of language in general to its function within dis-

---

38. Halliday, *An Introduction to Functional Grammar*, xiv.

39. Reed, *Discourse Analysis of Philippians*, provides understanding of Halliday's metafunction of the text as it relates to meaning within discourse. The ideational meanings "refer to what is 'going on' in the text with respect to what is going on outside of the text. . . . This is what people usually have in mind when they talk about what a word or sentence 'means' –namely, the 'content' of language," 62. The interpersonal meanings "are a form of *action*, that is, the speaker does something to the audience. Consequently, interpersonal meanings also reveal 'how the speaker defines how he sees the person, with whom he is communicating,'" 80. Textual meanings "relate an immediate linguistic context to both a preceding context and a context of situation," 88. He summarizes: "Ideational meanings concern 'the goings-on' in the text, . . . interpersonal meanings concern the social relationships between the participants . . . textual meanings concern the cohesive ties (organic and componential) and information flow (topicality and prominence) of discourse, that is, how the ideational (and interpersonal) meanings of the discourse are organized into a cohesive whole," 121-22.

40. Halliday, *An Introduction to Functional Grammar*, xv-xvi.

41. Reed defines the functional aspect of SFL. He writes, "Function not only concerns the semantic roles of linguistic forms, but the semantic roles of those forms in the immediate situation and the broader culture. . . . Function concerns the semantic organization of texts. Consequently, SFL attaches great importance to the sociological aspects of language—how people use language to 'do' things" (*A Discourse Analysis of Philippians*, 37). This approach to language is a social semiotic that is made up of the groupings of choices such that these groupings establish meaningful components of language. See Cynthia Long Westfall, *Discourse Analysis of the Letter to the Hebrews: The Relationship Between Form and Meaning*, Library of New Testament Studies (London: T&T Clark, 2006), 26.

course.[42] Its theory accounts for all the commonalities of discourse analysis (see below). Therefore, SFL has two aims; that is, to provide a comprehensive analysis through the understanding ("to show how, and why, the text means what it does")[43] and evaluation ("may enable one to say why the text is, or is not, an effective text for its own purposes")[44] of texts.

Summary of the Schools of Discourse Analysis

The four schools above provide an overview of the different approaches within discourse analysis. The SIL group mainly concentrates on issues of translation. However, it also examines the relationship between the smaller and larger units of language as they contribute to meaning within the discourse. The Continental European group analyzes discourse regarding syntax, semantics, and pragmatics noting the macro-structure of the text in relation to the micro-structure. The South African group seeks to view the text as cola and its inter-relations, thus illustrating the structure and description of the text leading to its cohesion. The SFL group analyzes the text through a systemic-functional approach that understands and evaluates language and its function as it relates to the context.[45]

---

42. Stephen Levinsohn (*Discourse Features of New Testament Greek: A Coursebook*, 2d ed) and Steven Runge (*Discourse Grammar of the Greek New Testament: A Practical Introduction for Teaching and Exegesis*, Peabody, Mass: Hendrickson, 2010) are two other scholars that represent the functional approach. Porter classifies their approaches as cognitive-functional linguistics. Levinsohn categorizes his approach as descriptive linguistics and "ascribes to the principle that 'choice implies meaning,' indicating that when authors exercise choice, they are also expressing a difference in meaning." Runge describes his approach as crosslinguistic, or eclectic. He espouses to three core principles: choice implies meaning, semantic meaning is to be differentiated from pragmatic effect, and default patterns of language should be distinguished from marked ones. See Porter's review and analysis: "Linguistic Schools," in *Linguistics and New Testament Greek*, 29-32.

43. Halliday, *An Introduction to Functional Grammar*, xv.

44. Ibid., xv.

45. Porter states, "Systemic Functional Linguistics, so far as I can determine, has been the most productive school of linguistics in New Testament Greek studies— apart from traditional grammar... The major reasons for its intensive utilization, how-

These schools demonstrate the importance of understanding and evaluating the relationship between the grammar, semantics, context, and structure of discourse, for "the text is a meaningful unit, and not simply a grammatical one."[46] The analysis of discourses then, is functional and semantic in its orientation; that is, "grammatical categories explained as the realization of semantic patterns."[47] Discourse is language in use. The goal of the discourse analyst is to study the language in use.[48] The fundamental objective for SFL discourse analysts is to demonstrate the relationship between the context of situation and the functions of language.[49] It requires the exegete to often re-

---

ever, appear to be its integrated model of meaning that encompasses the strata from expression to context. SFL is one of few linguistic models that has a robust concept of context. SFL connects language with social context and hence models context in an explicit fashion, thus lending SFL to itself being a discourse analytic model" ("Linguistic Schools," 35).

46. Porter and O'Donnell, *Discourse Analysis and the New Testament*, 27. Halliday states, "The term 'semantics' does not simply refer to the meaning of words; it is the entire system of meanings of a language, expressed by grammar as well as by vocabulary. . . . The relation between the meaning and the wording is not, however, an arbitrary one; the form of the grammar relates naturally to the meanings that are being encoded" (*An Introduction to Functional Grammar*, xvii).

47. Ibid., xvii. Porter and O'Donnell add, "This illustrates the importance of the linkage between grammar and semantics. One cannot isolate particular grammatical features and expect to be able to interpret them in their appropriate context without understanding both the code of the language and the levels of context in which it is used. . . . In other words, discourses are complex entities that are analyzable in terms of how the various features that are being analyzed as intertwined features hold the text together" (*Discourse Analysis and the New Testament*, 28).

48. Halliday agrees. He writes, "Discourse analysis has to be founded on a study of the system of the language. At the same time, the main reason for studying the system is to throw light on discourse – on what people say and write and listen to and read" (*An Introduction to Functional Grammar*, xxii).

49. Porter contends "This model is by far the most integrative . . . in the sense that it combines discussion of the discrete elements of language but in terms of the larger discourse structure, and it does these in terms of several terms of reference, including the correlation between grammatical forms and their meanings within particular linguistic contexts. Discussion begins with the discourse, rather than treating the discourse as merely an extended sentence. . . . The potential of the model can be seen in the fact

think how and in what ways the language of the New Testament is used. It also demands that grammatical and structural analyses occur at the smaller (sentence) and larger (paragraph/pericope) levels, for the understanding of the relationship of both levels culminates in meaningful configurations that too must be analyzed. This is discourse analysis.[50] Therefore the SFL theory provides the most comprehensive approach in understanding discourse as the text is analyzed and is the theory to be more closely followed.

COMMONALITIES OF DISCOURSE ANALYSIS

Although the four schools differ in the respective details, there are three commonalities of discourse analysis that are utilized to interpret the Gospel of Mark. The examination of language at a level beyond the sentence is the first commonality of discourse analysis. This is the most distinguishing aspect.[51] Fantin notes, "Although until recently, modern linguistics has focused upon sentence level and below (clause, phrase, word, phonology, etc.),"[52] linguistic investigation realized the importance of meaning beyond the sentence level and began to shift their attention above the sentence level. As a matter of fact, many scholars recognize that the article by Louw in the 1970's anticipated, and thus predicted, that linguistics would begin to direct its attention

---

that it is not merely an extension of sentence grammar but attempts to analyze discourse in context" (*Discourse Analysis and the New Testament*, 16-17).

    50. Jeffrey T. Reed specifically defines discourse analysis as it relates to SFL. He writes, "Studies in discourse analysis emphasize (a) the dynamic between intended meanings of speakers and variant responses of hearers, (b) the grammar of language beyond the level of the sentence, (c) the social and pragmatic functions of language, and (d) the ways in which language is used to create cohesiveness in discourse" ("Identifying Theme in the New Testament: Insights from Discourse Analysis," in *Discourse Analysis and Other Topics in Biblical Greek* JSNTSS 113, eds. Stanley E. Porter and D. A. Carson [Sheffield: Sheffield Academic Press, 1995], 75, n. 1).

    51. Porter, "Greek Grammar and Syntax," 96.

    52. Fantin, appendix "Modern Linguistics," 318.

to blocks of text larger than the sentence.[53] Porter and O'Donnell state, "As a result, whereas most linguistic investigation has treated the clause, often in linguistic isolation, as the largest unit of analysis, with much more concern being shown for smaller units, such as phrases; discourse analysis, while not neglecting such linguistic units, makes the clause in linguistic context the basic unit of analysis, extending analysis beyond this level."[54] As the reader considers this important shift from word to clause, clause to sentence, and from sentence to paragraph, he discovers a more coherent whole. Louw claims that the mere addition of the meaning of sentences is not satisfactory. Understanding therefore, is affected by more than a group of sentences; rather it is based on a whole discourse.[55]

However, discourse analysis does not just focus on the larger discourse unit, for it does not eliminate the necessity to examine words and clauses. Rather discourse analysts advocate both a 'bottom-up' and 'top-down' approach.[56] Discourse analysis moves from the micro-level (e.g., word) to the macro-level (e.g., paragraph) and back again. This helps to understand the intent of the discourse and therefore also enhances the understanding of the relationship between the unit and its parts.[57] On the one hand, the exegete

---

53. Johannes P. Louw, "Discourse Analysis and the Greek New Testament," *BT* 24, no. 1 (Jan 1973). Louw states, "The history of linguistics shows that for semantics *the word* was at first regarded as the practical unit of communication. . . . During the 1960's there was a definite move from *the word* to *the sentence* in practically every publication on semantics, and presently it seems that the 70's will direct its attention to larger units," 102. See James Barr, *Semantics of Biblical Language* (Oxford: Oxford University Press, 1961). His work utilizes linguistic principles to establish the importance of meaning beyond the word and sentence level.

54. Porter and O'Donnell, *Discourse Analysis and the Greek New Testament*, 5-6.

55. Louw, "Discourse Analysis and the Greek New Testament," 103. Robert Longacre challenged linguistics to consider language above the sentence. At that time, linguists were focused on the sentence. Though the study of the sentence is a legitimate sub-disciple of linguistics, he recognized that a sentence grammar has limitations. To overcome those limitations, linguists must consider the principles of language that operant above the sentence. ("Why We Need a Vertical Revolution in Linguistics," *The Fifth LACUS Forum* [Columbia, S.C.: Hornbeam, 1978] 247-70).

56. Brown and Yule, *Discourse Analysis*, 234-36.

57. J. L. Lemke contends, "Language is not simply used to produce word-mean-

must not forfeit the most basic level of exegesis (i.e., translation, word studies, analysis of sentence-level syntax, etc.). This is important. But on the other hand, the exegete must also consider the literary context of the whole and how the most basic parts impact it as well as how the whole impacts the parts. Therefore, discourse analysis seeks to examine language at all levels within a given context and to demonstrate the relationship between these levels as the author intended.

The second commonality examines the use of language in its context. There are two levels of discourse that shape meaning within a given context.[58] They are: co-text and context, both of which are necessary to examine because they help provide the structural, situational, and cultural insights regarding the act of communication; its social interaction.[59] Co-text refers to linguistic units within the text that create discourse (i.e., word, clause, sentence, and paragraph).[60] Reed contends that "with these co-textual levels of discourse in mind, the discourse analyst turns to the text at hand ready to inspect how the speaker/author has combined smaller linguistic forms (and their functions) to form a larger discourse."[61] Context refers to the outside or extra linguistic units "that influence discourse production and processing."[62] Context is often broken down into two broad terms, context of situation and context of culture. The context of situation refers to the historical situation of the discourse; whereas the context of culture refers to the cultural worldviews that are involved in the production of the discourse. Thus, each discourse is part of a historical context

---

ing or clause-meaning, it is used to produce text-meaning, and texts, by co-patterning many word-choices and clause formations, can make meanings that words and clauses cannot. That is why we make texts" ("Semantics and Social Values," *Word* 40 (1989): 48).

58. Stanley E. Porter and Andrew W. Pitts state, "Discourse analysis has come to be characterized by its emphasis on the way that large frames of context constrain meaning at multiple levels of language (word, word group or phrase, clause, and so on)" ("New Testament Greek Language and Linguistics in Recent Research," *CurBR* 2 [Feb 2008]: 235).

59. Stubbs, *Discourse Analysis: The Sociolinguistic Analysis of Natural Language*, 5-6.

60. Reed, *A Discourse Analysis of Philippians*, 42.

61. Ibid., 47.

62. Ibid., 42.

(context of situation) and also possesses words from a culture that influence the possible combination of other words, clauses, sentences, and paragraphs; all the way to the level of the discourse (context of culture).

The third commonality examines how language coheres together. Cohesion is a feature of the text that brings about unity. The text is typically a cohesive communicative act and is not a series of unrelated words and sentences. How then do speakers formulate such cohesive acts? This is a task of the discourse analyst; that is, "to identify how a language is used to create cohesive and coherent communication."[63]

Language is used for expression. For this to occur, Reed contends that the author organizes his thoughts and ideas and does so in a way that expresses his flow of thought.[64] Thus, the cohesive nature of an author's writing is tied to structure. A. B. du Toit states that "Anyone using language – except in the case of an unsuccessful expression of language – is naturally applying structure."[65] The analysis of a text, then, is a study of how the author arranges his argument at the paragraph level as it is presented into a coherent whole. Therefore, advocates of discourse analysis approach the structure of the text at the level of the discourse rather than the word or sentence, for it is at the discourse level that communication occurs.

In sum, one may view the commonalities of discourse analysis in the form of the following questions: What *format* does the reader/hearer communicate with others (language above the sentence level)? In what *context* does the reader/hearer communicate with others (language in its context)? How does the reader/hearer *arrange* his communication with others (language co-

---

63. Reed, *A Discourse Analysis of Philippians*, 31.

64. Jeffrey T. Reed, "Cohesive Ties in 1 Timothy," 131.

65. A. B. du Toit, "The Significance of Discourse Analysis for New Testament Interpretation and Translation: Introductory Remarks with Special Reference to 1 Peter 1:3-13," *Neot* 8 (1974): 55.

Cotterell and Turner state, "Any address, any conversation, any book, any discourse, has structure. . . . Discourse is not a random sequence of utterances, or an unrelated collection of sentences. In discourse we have sequences, words which are grammatically related and semantically connected, and this grammatical and semantic relatedness extends across sentence and paragraph boundaries to embrace the entire discourse" (*Linguistics and Bible Interpretation*, 247).

heres together)? Therefore, discourse analysis as a linguistic discipline asks a different set of questions than that of traditional grammars.[66] These questions involve the accounting for and establishing of components necessary to complement the hermeneutical process.

Components of Discourse Analysis

Discourse analysis is a sub-discipline, or complement to, New Testament hermeneutics. The study of the New Testament must be a textually-based discipline, for "the only direct access that we have into the world of the New Testament is through the text of the Greek New Testament."[67] The goal then of studying the New Testament is to discover the author's intended message.[68] In order to discover the intended message one needs to mediate and show the relationship between *what* the author says and *how* he says it. Discourse analysis examines such a relationship. In other words, the discourse analyst will need to analyze the text at multiple levels, from the word-level to the discourse-level and back again; examine the context in which the language is used, the function of language and discourse; and identify how the text is a coherent discourse.

The task of the discourse analyst is to utilize objective evidence to examine the text. Porter's contention is that many eclectic models of discourse analysis "are not coordinated and it is difficult to know what counts for evidence in them;"[69] thus advocating for the systemic-functional theory. The systemic-functional theory best utilizes components of discourse analysis to serve as objective evidence. The two components of the systemic-functional theory are discourse structure and discourse texture.[70]

---

66. Porter and Reed, "Greek Grammar since BDF," 156-62.

67. Porter and O'Donnell, *Discourse Analysis and the Greek New Testament*, 1.

68. Discourse analysis enables the interpreter to use the author's language and discover "authorial meaning by the means of the phenomena of the text" (Porter, "How Can Biblical Discourse be Analyzed?" 113).

69. Stanley E. Porter, "Dissertation information," e-mail message to author, April 2, 2009.

70. Two examples of discourse analysis that utilize the systemic-functional theory, as it pertains specifically to discourse structure and texture, are Reed's work in Phi-

Discourse Analysis as a Complement of Hermeneutics

This section explains the two components of the systemic-functional theory that are used to analyze the Gospel of Mark more objectively; namely the central section of the Gospel of Mark (8:22-10:52) and its relationship and function to the whole narrative.[71] Therefore, the SFL and its functional use in discourse relates to authorial meaning and the contribution to an understanding of the whole. The following two components of discourse analysis are used: discourse structure (genre and sub-genre) and discourse texture (metafunctions of language, cohesion, prominence, and discourse boundaries). They are used for the purpose of explicating the relationship, and therefore significance between the Gospel of Mark as a whole and the central section of Mark (8:22-10:52).

---

lippians and Westfall's work in Hebrews. These two examples draw heavily from the SFL model because of its functional use in discourse that accounts for all the commonalities of discourse analysis within an integrated system. Reed uses SFL to develop a methodology that addresses the debate over the literary integrity of Philippians. His approach implements Halliday and Hasan's understanding of the cohesiveness of discourse.

Discourse is cohesive because its structure (genre) and texture (metafunctions of language—ideational, interpersonal, and textual) are unified. Reed summarizes his contribution to the discourse analysis debate through the presentation of "a functional framework for doing discourse analysis. . . . The model emphasizes the role of genre or register, that is, the STRUCTURE of discourse, in the production and interpretation of discourses. It also underscores the ideational, interpersonal and textual meta-functions of language, that is, the TEXTURE of discourse, in the production and interpretation of texts" (*A Discourse Analysis of Philippians*, 403). He also discusses the structure of Philippians prior to the texture, thus implementing a top-down approach to discourse analysis; and he later relates the texture to the structure; exemplifying a bottom-up approach.

Westfall also uses SFL to "develop and apply methodology for constructing a conceptual representation of a given discourse" (*A Discourse Analysis of the Letter to the Hebrews*, 27). Her approach implements Halliday's method of determining the structure and meaning of a discourse through the integration of various components of the text that provides a coherent representation of discourse. The components of discourse analysis used by Westfall are structure, cohesion, prominence, and coherence.

71. Chapters three and four will implement discourse structure, while chapter five implements discourse texture to discover the function and significance of Jesus' three passion predictions as well as their relationship to the story of the Gospel of Mark as a whole.

DEATH AND DISCIPLESHIP:
An Analysis of the Predictions of Jesus' Death in the Gospel of Mark

Discourse Structure

The first component is discourse structure. Discourse structure involves an examination at the macro-structure level;[72] namely the level of genre. A top-down approach is implemented when beginning with discourse structure.[73] This approach examines the features of the text and depicts the genre (macro-structure) before examining the smaller linguistic units (micro-structure) and determining their relationship. As part of discourse structure, the focus is on both the literary genre (narrative) and sub-genre (theological narrative biography)[74] for this is unique to the Gospel accounts.

For example, this Book examines the relationship between the Gospel of Mark as a whole (macro-structure) and the three-fold pattern found in the central section of Mark (micro-structure). This examination delineates both the genre (narrative) and sub-genre (theological narrative biography) of the Gospel of Mark. The narrative is structured through the means of three geographical settings (Galilee, the way to Jerusalem, Jerusalem) to communicate Jesus' identity as the Son of God (cf. 1:1). Mark utilizes the central section (8:22-10:52) to awaken the faith of Jesus' followers based on knowing him as the Son of God (theological narrative biography); thus, explicating the function of the central section of Mark. Therefore, the discourse structure serves to help demonstrate the relationship, and thus function between the central section of the Gospel of Mark (8:22-10:52) and the book.

---

72. Black, *Linguistics for Students of New Testament Greek*, defines macro-structures as those "larger units of language such as paragraphs, sections, and entire texts," 171.

73. Reed states, "If possible, the analyst is better off identifying the genre of the text before moving to an analysis of its parts, that is, starting from the top and then working downwards. In this framework, the analysis of words and clauses is important, but only from the perspective of the larger discourse" (*A Discourse Analysis of Philippians*), 28.

74. It is proposed that the Gospels fit into a sub-genre of narrative and are defined as stories, or narratives, that catalogue events centered around one unifying character, Jesus Christ, and these events are structured and written in such a way that they serve to awaken and subsequently strengthen the faith of the reader.

Literary Genre: Narrative

Genre is defined in relationship to its literary character and form; therefore, it is the kind or type of literature by which a written text is depicted. Literary genre consists of social, cultural, and literary features that represent the time in which they were written.[75] Reed contends therefore that the readers can identify the time through the configuration of the elements of genre.[76] The elements that make-up genre are examined. Due to an examination of the elements of the Gospel of Mark (see chapter four), the genre classification of a Gospel is narrative.

A narrative "tells a story about particular people and their actions and contingencies in past time."[77] The narrative is constructed of episodes, or short stories that communicate the author's intended message. In essence, it is the narrative that serves as the vehicle by which the author carries the reader through his story within a given context or situation. Therefore, the discourse analyst examines the elements of narrative (structure, plot, setting, characters, and point of view) and through this examination, enables him to determine how the structure of the whole impacts the episodes. And then in turn, determine how the episodes relate to one another to impact the whole. In other words, it is the analysis of the narrative that provides the discourse analyst with a holistic understanding of *how* the author constructed the whole discourse.

---

75. Although a distinction will not be employed, M. A. K. Halliday and R. Hasan make a distinction between genre and register. They state that register refers to "a configuration of meanings that is associated with a particular situation" (*Language, Context, and Text: Aspects of Language in a Social-Semiotic Perspective* [Oxford: Oxford University Press, 1989], 38-39).

76. Reed, *A Discourse Analysis of Philippians*, 54.

77. Robert E. Longacre, "Discourse Perspective on the Hebrew Verb: Affirmation and Restatement," in *Linguistics and Biblical Hebrew*, ed. Walter R. Bodine (Winona Lake, Ind: Eisenbrauns, 1992), 178. See also the discussion by Longacre on narrative discourse, *The grammar of discourse*, 7-31. Callow defines narrative discourse. She writes, "Narrative discourse recounts a series of events ordered more or less chronologically, usually in the past" (*Discourse Considerations in Translating the Word of God*, 13).

DEATH AND DISCIPLESHIP:
An Analysis of the Predictions of Jesus' Death in the Gospel of Mark

Literary Sub-genre: Theological Narrative Biography

Gospel is defined as a story or narrative that is communicated through episodic elements explicating the biographical and historical account of Jesus Christ for, he is the central figure in the Gospels. The Gospels are both biographical and historical because they recount the life of a character, namely Jesus Christ, within a historical context, first-century Palestine. The Gospels, however, are more than narratives. They also explain and contain theology. Therefore, the Gospels have a theological purpose.

The purpose of the Gospel is not simply to inform the reader of the life of Jesus Christ. Rather they were written with the biographical, historical, and theological aspects intertwined to awaken faith. They were disciplinal; that is, geared to be disciple oriented. The reader learns who Jesus is and how-to live-in light of knowing him. Therefore, because the Gospel accounts possess unique features (biography, history, and theology) that are communicated within the narrative genre, form a distinct group of writings, a sub-genre. This book proposes the sub-genre of the Gospels as theological narrative biography.

The theological narrative biography serves as the unique sub-genre by which the biblical author facilitates his purposeful intention to the reader. As the discourse analyst examines the features of the theological narrative biography (biography, history, theology), a holistic understanding of the content of *what* the author's whole discourse is takes place.

Discourse structure consists of an examination of the features that make-up discourse as a whole; that is, the genre and sub-genre. Through this examination, discourse structure reveals the relationship and function between the discourse (the Gospel of Mark) with the smaller units of written text (central section of Mark). Discourse structure, therefore, uses the role of narrative (genre) and theological narrative biography (sub-genre) to explicate the production and interpretation of whole discourses.

Discourse Texture

The second component is discourse texture. The discourse texture involves an examination at the micro-structure level;[78] namely the level of the text. Therefore, the discourse analyst advocates a bottom-up approach. This approach examines the text through its grammatical and semantic function (micro-structure) before analyzing its relationship and function to the discourse as a whole (macro-structure). The discourse texture accounts for the following features of the text. They are: metafunctions of language (ideational, interpersonal, and textual), cohesion, prominence, and discourse boundaries.

For example, the examination involves showing the relationship between the three-fold pattern found in the central section of Mark (micro-structure) and the whole Gospel (macro-structure). The three-fold pattern refers to the repetition of three events in three separate chapters throughout the central section; that is, the three predictions of Jesus' death, the misunderstanding by the disciples and thus Jesus' teaching to the disciples. This examination involves the delineation of the metafunctions of language; that is, the involvement of characters and their actions (ideational), the interaction between characters (interpersonal), and the grammatical, semantic, and thematic organization of the three-fold pattern (textual).[79] The examination of the central section also demonstrates that this three-fold pattern is a cohesive whole (cohesion) that is highlighted through significant participants, their actions and sayings, and events (prominence) that are marked off by verbal-tense forms and geographical shifts in the text (discourse boundaries). Therefore, dis-

---

78. Black, *Linguistics for Students of New Testament Greek*, defines micro-structures as those "units such as phrases, clauses, and sentences," 171.

79. Callow's description and thus summary of Halliday's categories of the function of language is helpful. She writes, "1. The 'ideational' or content function: what a given utterance is about; participants and events in certain relationships. 2. The 'interpersonal' or social role function: the way in which the speaker is involved, whether as questioner, teacher, etc. 3. The 'textual' or discourse function: the value or significance attaching to the utterance in the discourse as a whole. Every utterance has all three functions simultaneously. It passes on information, implies a certain relationship between speaker and hearer, and fits into the discourse context in a certain way" (*Discourse Considerations in Translating the Word of God*, 12).

course texture serves to help demonstrate the relationship, and thus function between the central section of the Gospel of Mark (8:22-10:52) and the book.

Metafunctions of Language[80]

According to Halliday's systemic-functional theory, there are three features of language. They are ideational, interpersonal, and textual. As Callow notes, these features occur simultaneously within every discourse. It is through the lexis and grammar (lexico-grammar) of these features that the reader can understand the environment (ideational), social relations (interpersonal), and the cohesion of the features (textual). The third feature (textual) is most relevant to the discourse analyst, for it is through the textual feature that the ideational and interpersonal features come together in a coherent whole. Reed explains, "That there is a relationship both *semantically and grammatically* between the various parts of a text (cohesive ties) and that there is some *thematic element* which flows through it (information flow) results in cohesive discourse rather than a jumble of unrelated words and sentences."[81]

Ideational Feature

The ideational feature represents what is going on inside the world of the text; it is the actions and involvement of the characters. It represents the *meaning* of the word or sentence; "the 'representational content' of language."[82] This ideational feature primarily answers the question, how does the Greek lexical system represent meaning within the text? For example, Jesus' descriptive language serves as a play on words to inform the disciples of his mission ὁ υἱὸς τοῦ ἀνθρώπου παραδίδοται εἰς χεῖρας ἀνθρώπων ("the Son of Man *will be handed over* into the *hands* of men," Mk. 9:31) and represents the understanding of his future death experience.

---

80. Halliday describes metafunction as "The entire architecture of language is arranged along functional lines" (Halliday and Matthiessen, *Functional Grammar*, 31).

81. Reed, "Cohesive Ties in 1 Timothy," 133.

82. Reed, *A Discourse Analysis of Philippians*, 331. Campbell states, "We use language to encode our experience of the world. When someone describes a sunset, or talks about nuclear physics, or writes about jazz, she is encoding her understanding or experience of these things through language" (*Advances in the Study of Greek*, 64-65).

Interpersonal Feature

The interpersonal feature represents the social interaction between characters inside the world of the text. It can refer to the questions, statements, or commands of various characters that the author uses to interact with the reader. This interpersonal feature primarily answers the question, how does the author state the various responses of the characters within the text?[83] For example, Jesus' command to Peter ὕπαγέ ὀπίσω μου, σατανᾶ, ("get behind me Satan," Mk. 8:33) represents social interaction, an interpersonal feature of language.

Textual Feature

The textual feature represents the cohesiveness of the text. This feature enables the discourse analyst to not only examine the semantic content of the text (ideational and interpersonal), but also the organization (textual) of the text. Therefore, the textual feature primarily answers the question, how is the content of the text represented from beginning to end? For example, Jesus predicts his death three times to provide his disciples with a clear picture of his mission as Messiah. These three features of language will help to provide the reason for the biblical author's use of various characters and their interaction with one another.

Cohesion

Cohesion is about relationship; that is, the relationship between words, sentences, paragraphs, and discourses. Cohesion is what ties a text or a discourse together.[84] But cohesion does more than tie texts and discourses to-

---

83. Halliday and Matthiessen state, "If the ideational function of the grammar is 'language as reflection,' this is 'language as action'" (*Functional Grammar*, 30).

84. See M. A. K. Halliday and R. Hasan, *Cohesion in English* (London: Longman, 1976), 4-5; Robert A. Dooley and Stephen H. Levinsohn, *Analyzing Discourse: A Manual of Basic Concepts* (Dallas, Tex: SIL International, 2001), 27; Jeffrey T. Reed, "The Cohesiveness of Discourse: Towards A Model of Linguistic Criteria for Analyzing New Testament Discourse," in *Discourse Analysis and the New Testament* JSNTSS 170, eds. Stanley E. Porter and Jeffrey T. Reed, (Sheffield: Sheffield Academic Press, 1999), 28-46.

In Porter's intermediate grammar "Cohesion refers to grammatical, semantic

gether. It also relates them into a meaningful whole.[85] The cohesion of any given text in the New Testament appeals to the meaningful semantic and grammatical relationships between "elements of any extent, both smaller and larger than clauses, from single words to lengthy passages of text . . . which may hold across gaps of any extent."[86]

Cohesion can occur at the macro-structure and micro-structure levels. The intent is to utilize cohesion at both levels; that is, demonstrate how the central section of Mark coheres, or 'hangs together' as a section in and of itself and with the book into a meaningful whole; thus, demonstrating the function of the central section. This study then, uses cohesion to state the reason the biblical author places the central section of Mark within the story and why he places it where he does.[87] How are these cohesive relationships demonstrated? They will be examined through cohesive ties, or connectives.

According to Reed cohesive ties "refer to a language system's ability to form relations between linguistic items of the various levels of discourse."[88] Reed sees cohesive ties in two different categories. They are organic ties and componential ties. Organic ties refer to the units of language that bind the whole message together (e.g., conjunctions, prepositions, particles, use of the

---

and contextual factors which hold a discourse together" (*Idioms of the Greek New Testament*, 304).

85. This is typically the difference between cohesion and coherent. Dooley and Levinsohn state that cohesion refers to the "linguistic means to signal coherence. . ." and coherent refers to the conceptual signals within a text so the "hearer can make it 'hang together' conceptually, that is, interpret it within a single mental representation," (*Analyzing Discourse*, 27).

86. Jeffrey T. Reed, "Modern Linguistics and Historical Criticism: Using the Former for Doing the Latter," in *Linguistics and the New Testament: Critical Junctures* JSNTSS 168, eds. Stanley E. Porter and D. A. Carson (Sheffield: Sheffield Academic Press, 1999), 39.

87. David L. Mathewson and Elodie Ballantine Emig state, "Cohesion refers to the linguistic elements that an author uses to weave a discourse together. Cohesion links something in the text to something that has come before it. These linguistic elements provide signals for readers, showing how the discourse has been constructed and how readers should put it together" (*Intermediate Greek Grammar: Syntax for Students of the New Testament* [Grand Rapids: Baker, 2016], 272).

88. Reed, *A Discourse Analysis of Philippians*, 205.

genitive absolute).[89] Organic ties create links and set boundaries in the text. These cohesive ties can aid the reader regarding the development of the argument and use of language to create the argument.[90] Componential ties on the other hand, refer to various components of the text (e.g., lexical choices, choices of grammatical person, repetition of words). Componential ties express grammatical and lexical networks demonstrating how smaller parts of the text interrelate with one another.

The discourse analyst primarily discovers the cohesion of a text through an examination of the text, both grammatically and semantically. For example, there is a focus upon discourse connectives and repetition within discourse. The connectives or ties function within and between narrative episodes to hold the discourse together (e.g., Mark's use of καί,).[91] Repetition also

---

89. Westfall defines connectives as those ties "used by authors to create cohesion in the discourse and tend to indicate the logical relationships between sentences and units—cohesion and shifts are often determined by other factors" (*A Discourse Analysis of the Letter to the Hebrews*, 46).

90. Steven E. Runge states that "Greek connectives play a functional role in discourse by indicating how the writer intended one clause to relate to another, based on the connective used" (*Discourse Grammar of the Greek New Testament: A Practical Introduction for Teaching and Exegesis*, 18). See his full discussion (17-57).

91. The single discourse connective which holds the discourse together is καί. See the discussion of Stephen H. Levinsohn, *Discourse Features of New Testament Greek: A Coursebook on the Information Structure of New Testament Greek*, 2d ed (Dallas, Tex: SIL International, 2000), 71-93. Kermit Titrud understands καί as a connective for paragraphs. He claims, "Similarly, although καί (not καί τότε) may introduce a new paragraph in narrative, it does not do so nearly as often as, for example, δέ does. And when καί does introduce a new paragraph, the paragraphs are more closely linked semantically than when δέ introduces a new paragraph. In other words, there is a greater degree of cohesion between paragraphs linked by καί. A paragraph introduced by καί is very closely related to the preceding paragraph, continuing the same participant(s), setting, and often the same event.

On the other hand, a paragraph introduced by δέ is likely to be very loosely connected to the previous paragraph, having new participants and setting" ("The Function of καί in the Greek New Testament and an Application to 2 Peter," in *Linguistics and New Testament Interpretation: Essays on Discourse Analysis* ed David Alan Black with Katharine Barnwell and Stephen Levinsohn [Nashville: Broadman and Holman, 1992], 251).

holds the discourse together (e.g., Mark's use of a three-fold pattern; Jesus' death, misunderstanding by the disciples, and Jesus' teaching to disciples).

Prominence

Prominence is about drawing attention; that is, drawing the reader's attention to what the author is emphasizing.[92] In other words, prominence refers to that feature (events, participants, objects) within the text that is set aside by the author to grab the attention of the reader.[93] This is often referred to as emphasis.

The author uses various things to establish emphasis and importance.[94] Therefore, discourse analysts speak in terms of levels of prominence. These levels of prominence demonstrate which feature is more significant than other features within the same context. The levels of prominence are background, theme, and focus.[95]

In the case of narrative, background refers to those linguistic elements that carry the story forward. They serve as the support or backbone for the main storyline. These elements could refer to secondary participants or events, and scenery. The theme on the other hand, serves to emphasize the author's message. Thematic elements could refer to major participants and

---

92. Porter and O'Donnell state the importance of prominence. They write, "It is not only important, but necessary, that those using language indicate the relative degrees of prominence of various items in their discourses as a means of differentiating their importance for the discourse, and hence as a means of guiding interpreters in the best way to 'read' their discourse" (*Discourse Analysis and the Greek New Testament*, chapter on prominence, p. 1).

93. Reed defines prominence as "those semantic and grammatical elements of discourse that serve to set aside certain subjects, ideas or motifs of the author as more or less semantically and pragmatically significant than others" ("Identifying Theme in the New Testament: Insights from Discourse Analysis," 101). Richard A. Young (*Intermediate New Testament Greek* [Nashville: Broadman and Holman], 1994) states, "Prominence refers to the state of standing out from the surroundings so as to be easily noticed," 262.

94. Features authors use for prominence, see Andreas J. Köstenberger, Benjamin L. Merkle, and Robert L. Plummer, *Going Deeper with New Testament Greek*, rev. ed. (Nashville, TN: Broadman & Holman, 2020), 466-67.

95. Ibid., 77.

events that are often in chronological order and repeated throughout the story. The final level of prominence, focus, refers to linguistic elements that appear unexpectedly. Focus grabs the reader's attention and places this attention within the communicative process; thus, functioning in a more pragmatic way. There are several categories the discourse analyst can use to discover prominence; however, two are discussed here, semantic analysis (Greek text translation analysis – chapter 5) and verbal aspect (verb analysis – chapter 5).

Semantic Analysis

A semantic analysis of the text is an understanding of the meaning of various words, phrases, and even clauses. The discourse analyst can note words of emphasis (e.g., thinking, feeling, perceiving) as well as the presence of repeated words in the same semantic field that often lead to prominence by the author. Therefore, by examining these words and their semantic fields, one can begin to establish prominence. For example, there is a focus upon the different words and clauses used by Mark through the relationship of the presentation of Jesus as Messiah and the persecution of Jesus demonstrated by various groups involved (e.g., Mark's change regarding mode of betrayal; "rejected" versus "handed over"). The reader grabs the authorial emphasis of Jesus' death as it relates to the following episodes. This is just one aspect of discourse analysis that contributes to the meaning and thus significance, or prominence, of the text within a discourse.

The discourse analyst therefore discovers prominence by approaching the text with the assumption that the author wrote to communicate meaning. The words, clauses, paragraphs, and discourses function as either thematic or ground material. The author then uses his words to provide the theme (major participants or events) or background (elements to carry narrative forward) to his narrative. Prominence is therefore discovered within a text through an examination of the meaning of words, clauses, etc, or through the semantic analysis. The other way to discover prominence is using verbal aspect, or through a verb analysis.

Verbal Aspect[96]

One function of verbal aspect is to discover prominence within clauses of a text or discourse. Verbal aspect can function in three discourse aspects, or planes of discourse.[97] They are background, foreground, and frontground. The aorist tense-form (perfective aspect) often communicates the background prominence within a discourse. This is the principal tense-form used in narrative material to establish the backbone of the story.[98] The pres-

---

96. Porter defines verbal aspect as "The theory that tense-forms in Greek do not grammaticalize temporal relations, but another semantic category concerned with how a speaker or writer chooses to conceptualize and present a process. . . . The tense-forms grammaticalize verbal aspect and these morphologically-based verbal aspects serve the discourse function of indicating various levels of prominence" (*Discourse Analysis and the Greek New Testament*, chap 5, p. 15). See also Stanley E. Porter, *Verbal Aspect in the Greek of the New Testament with Reference to Tense and Mood*, Studies in Biblical Greek 1 (New York: Peter Lang, 1989), 75-108. For a brief history of verbal aspect see Constantine R. Campbell, *Basics of Verbal Aspect in Biblical Greek* (Grand Rapids: Zondervan, 2008), 26-33.

97. This Book follows the function of aspect at the discourse level proposed by Porter. However, as noted by Rodney Decker there is no standard as to the terminology in relation to the function of aspect in discourse. Though there is little agreement in terminology (see chart below), there is general consensus to function and meaning. ("The Function(s) of the Imperfect Tense in Mark's Gospel," Society of Biblical Literature Annual Meeting, Biblical Greek Language and Linguistics Section, New Orleans, LA, Nov 2009, 5n12).

	Porter	Hopper/Fanning	Campbell
Aorist	Background	Foreground	Foreground/mainline
Present	Foreground	Background	Background/offline
Imperfect	Foreground	Background	Background/offline

98. William Arp states the aorist (perfective aspect) "is the predominant narrative tense of Greek since it is the tense which carries a narrative along when no attention is being drawn to the events which are being spoken of" (Course notes for NT8, Seminar in Gospel Studies, Baptist Bible Seminary, Clarks Summit, Pa, fall 2005, 4). Campbell notes the narrative function of the perfective aspect. He states, "As a remote perfective tense-form, the aorist indicative plays an important role in narrative texts. Because the aorist indicative provides a bird's-eye view of an action (or a helicopter view) and portrays actions in summary it is often used to outline the skeletal structure of a narrative. . . . This basic outline, or skeletal structure, is called the mainline of a

ent and imperfect tense-forms (imperfective aspect) portray the thematic or foreground prominence. These tense-forms introduce significant characters or events within a discourse. The present (historical present)[99] is used typically to draw added attention to the action to which it refers, give prominence to the beginning of a paragraph or a change in setting, and highlight new scenes or participants.[100] The imperfect tense-form portrays the unfolding, progressive nature of a past event. It is used typically to dwell upon an action and to highlight the manner of the occurrence in a narrative.[101] The perfect tense-form (stative aspect) signals the frontground prominence. This tense-form typically introduces "elements in an even more discrete (separate and distinct), contoured, and complex way."[102] The perfect defines the given state of affairs in which the subject of the verb carries. Reed summarizes the aspectual categories in this way. He writes,

> The semantics of the aspectual categories lend themselves to discourse prominence. The perfective aspect lends itself to general descriptions of an event, whereas the imperfective aspect suggests that the author is

---

narrative" (*Basics of Verbal Aspect in Biblical Greek*, 38).

99. Wallace provides the reason for the historical present. He states, "It is normally to portray an event *vividly*, as though the reader were in the midst of the scene as it unfolds. Such vividness might be *rhetorical* (to focus on some aspect of the narrative) or literary (to indicate a change in topic)" (*Greek Grammar Beyond the Basics*, 526). See also Runge, *Discourse Grammar of the Greek New Testament*, 125-43.

100. Campbell notes that the present tense-form "portrays an actions with a view from the inside; we watch as the action unfolds before our eyes. . . . The present has the effect of drawing the readers into the story, as the discourse is presented before their eyes" (*Basics of Verbal Aspect*, 40, 42).

101. Arp, Course notes for NT8, 4. Young explains the difference between the aorist and imperfect tenses. He writes, "The imperfect paints a picture of the unfolding, progressive nature of a past event. The aorist tells the simple story; the imperfect draws the picture. It helps you to see the course of the act. It passes before the eye of the flowing stream of history" (*Intermediate New Testament Greek*, 113). Campbell adds, "Imperfects tend to provide supplemental information. This supplemental information contributes to narrative by giving information beyond the narrative mainline; . . . it puts flesh on the skeleton" (*Basics of Verbal Aspect*, 44).

102. Porter, *Idioms of the Greek New Testament*, 23.

focusing on the particulars of an event. The stative aspect is even more accented, since the attention is laid upon an event that has resulted from other circumstances (i.e., a stative event stands at the centre of activity).[103]

Through a verb analysis, the use of the categories of verbal aspect theory identifies prominence within the text and discourse. Verbal aspect views authorial choice not just at the word level in a group, but rather as part of the function of the sentence, paragraph, and discourse.[104] For example, an analysis of verbs throughout the central section (e.g., Mark's use of historical present) is done to discover how each episode/paragraph relates and functions with other texts, episodes, and discourses.

The semantic and verbal analyses will illustrate prominence. Prominence helps with the development of the text and discourse, for through these analyses the discourse analyst views prominence as that highlighted material that not only stands out within its text; but also helps to provide a relationship within its own text and adjacent texts or discourses.

Discourse Boundaries

Discourse boundaries are about limitations; that is, those various words and/or phrases that indicate when a paragraph or pericope begins and ends.[105] Some of the ways include: shifts in grammatical person (e.g. first to third person), shifts in verb-tense forms (e.g., aorist to present), shifts in topic (e.g., healing of blind man and the entrance into Jerusalem), and shifts in geography (e.g., desert and the synagogue). The focus is on two. They are shifts in verb-tense forms (e.g., Mark's use of historical present to distinguish a new paragraph)[106] and shifts in geography (e.g., Mark's change from 'on the way,'

---

103. Reed, "Identifying Theme in the New Testament," 85.

104. Porter states the purpose of verbal aspect. He writes, verbal aspect "is a morphologically-based semantic category which uses the grammatical forms of a language's verbal system to capture the speaker's reasoned subjective choice of conception of an action" (*Verbal Aspect*, 88).

105. Porter states, "Smaller units, such as clauses and sentences, have their own particular boundary markers, such as marks of punctuation and various connecting words (such as καί or δέ)" (*Idioms of the Greek New Testament*, 301).

106. Ibid., 302. Porter provides a similar analysis using verbal aspect to de-

Jericho to the 'entrance into Jerusalem'). In other words, a change in verb tense and geography will establish the discourse boundaries of the central section of Mark (8:22-10:52).

Discourse texture consists of an examination of the features that make-up the text; that is, the metafunctions of language, cohesion, prominence, and discourse boundaries. Through this examination, the discourse texture reveals the relationship and function between the smaller units of written text (central section of Mark) with the discourse. Therefore, discourse texture helps to explicate the role and function of language in the production and interpretation of texts.

Summary of Components of Discourse Analysis

The examination of the central section of Mark is based upon two components of discourse analysis. They are discourse structure and texture. On the one hand, this book employs a top-down approach. It examines the discourse structure, or genre and sub-genre, as it relates to the central section of the Gospel of Mark. This provides an understanding of the relationship between the macro-structure (Mark's narrative) and the micro-structure (central section). On the other hand, this book also employs a bottom-up approach. It examines the discourse texture, or the form and function of language within the three predictions of Jesus' death as it relates to the whole story of the Gospel of Mark. This provides an understanding of the relationship between the micro-structure (central section), and the macro-structure (Mark's narrative).

---

note discourse boundaries that is to be set forth in chapter five of this Book. He writes, "This pericope [Mark 11:1-11] is linked to the preceding one by Mark 10:52b, in which the author makes a transition out of the events regarding the healing of blind Bartimaeus by stating <And immediately Bartimaeus received his sight (ἀνέβλεψεν, aorist) and then followed (ἠκολούθει, imperfect) Jesus on the path.> This compound clause shifts the focus of the discourse from one event to another, the aorist being used as the background tense to conclude the previous pericope and the imperfect being used to introduce (i.e., foreground) a new stage in the discourse. . . . Mark 11:1 opens the new pericope, which details the events of Jesus' kingly entrance into Jerusalem, with three present tense-form verbs to highlight (foreground) new events in the narrative" ("Greek Grammar Since BDF," 155).

DEATH AND DISCIPLESHIP:
AN ANALYSIS OF THE PREDICTIONS OF JESUS' DEATH IN THE GOSPEL OF MARK

These two components explicate the category of the whole story; that is, how it is told (narrative) and what and why it is told (theological narrative biography). This is discourse structure. They also explicate the form and function of language (metafunctions of language), the relationship of language (cohesion), the emphasis of language (prominence), and the limitations of language (discourse boundaries) of the text within the discourse. This is discourse texture. Chapter five does such an analysis. The central section of Mark (8:22-10:52) is examined using discourse analysis to establish its relationship, and therefore its significance, with the rest of Mark's story.

BENEFITS OF DISCOURSE ANALYSIS TO NEW TESTAMENT EXEGESIS

Discourse analysis is a complementing discipline to exegesis.[107] It does not replace the hard work of exegesis that occurs at the word, phrase, and sentence level. Gregory Christopher has shown that the principles at the sentence level are not the same at the discourse level. He contends that one may study the sentence as a legitimate sub-discipline of linguistics. However, language has a larger context than the sentence.[108] The implications are clear. The study of the Passion Predictions within the Gospel of Mark must go beyond the study of the sentence to understand its significance to the Gospel as a whole.

Discourse analysis promotes a thorough understanding of the authorial intention of the biblical writers.[109] Though an analysis of the words and sen-

---

107. Discourse analysis accompanies the exegetical process. It does so however by shifting the focus beyond the word level and placing the focus on clauses, paragraphs, and even whole discourses. The discourse analyst is still an exegete; the task at hand is to interpret the text and only the text. The analyst examines both the smaller units of the text (word, sentence, etc.) and the larger units (clause, paragraph, etc.) so as to discover the relationship and function of each within the text.

108. Gregory T. Christopher, "Linguistics and Literary Theory: Redefining the Disciplinary Boundaries," PhD diss., U. of Texas at Arlington, 2000, 157-58.

109. Benjamin L. Merkle agrees. He writes, "Discourse analysis is analyzing a text (or any organized communicative act) with the goal of understanding how it relates to its surrounding context in order to elucidate the author's intended message" (*Exe-*

tences is important, a rigorous consideration of the paragraph and discourse is fundamentally important to the biblical exegete. It is through this hermeneutical endeavor that the interpreter can better mediate the historical, grammatical, and structural distance called for by the author of the text.[110]

Essentially as one applies discourse analysis, he is advocating a method of hermeneutics that benefits New Testament studies in three ways.[111] The first benefit that discourse analysis offers New Testament exegesis is the important focus on the *structure* of the text. In other words, discourse analysis pays sufficient attention to all the levels of the text beyond the sentence level; thus, helping the exegete chart the course (structure) of the whole message and its relationship to parts of the whole, not just verse by verse.[112]

Discourse analysis considers and examines the author's structure through a shift in emphasis from words to discourses and thus provides the exegete with a better understanding of the text as a whole.[113] It is also an un-

---

getical Gems from Biblical Greek: A Refreshing Guide to Grammar and Interpretation [Grand Rapids: Baker, 2019], 157).

110. Reed claims that discourse analysis "is a way of reading. It is a framework with which the analyst approaches a text and explicates what it says and how it has been understood. It may be classified under the rubric of hermeneutics" (*A Discourse Analysis of Philippians*, 16).

111. Fantin rightly cautions the discourse analyst. He writes, "There is a danger of viewing the use of linguistics in biblical studies as some type of magical key to unlocking the meaning of the biblical text. Or, more subdued, the use of linguistics gives one's interpretation more authority than another" (appendix "Modern Linguistics," 329).

112. Johannes P. Louw, "Reading A Text As Discourse," in *Linguistics and New Testament Interpretation: Essays on Discourse Analysis*, ed. David Alan Black with Katharine Barnwell and Stephen Levinsohn (Nashville: Broadman and Holman, 1992), 21. Reed states, "One benefit of such study is that we may gain a better understanding of how an author builds an argument from one clause to the next or how a story develops from one section to the other" ("Discourse Analysis," 206).

113. Kathleen Callow writes, "The aim of discourse analysis is obviously, in the long term, the analysis of discourses, i.e., whole passages. To do this, we often have to start by analysing low-level surface-structure signals which have discourse significance, such as connectives, word order, and verb mood. Such analysis is essential in order to have good, objective evidence for their function on any particular occasion of use, but it is not our only aim: our future purpose is to see how a whole passage

derstanding "of the organization of material as related to a given context."[114] The emphasis on the relationship between words and phrases and paragraphs brings about an analysis of discourses; thus, providing the exegete with a better understanding of how to structure and outline the author's message.[115]

The second benefit discourse analysis offers New Testament exegesis is the focus on the *cohesion* of the text. Cohesion establishes the meaning of the author's argument at the level of the whole discourse rather than as separate units.[116] Discourse analysis "attempts to see how a text coheres, how it fits together as a unified whole, and how the relationship between its sentences constitutes the 'text.'"[117] Traditional grammars however focus much of their atten-

---

fits together to express the intended meaning of the writer and what contribution each constituent element makes to the whole" ("Patterns of Thematic Development in 1 Corinthians 5:1-13," in *Linguistics and New Testament Interpretation: Essays on Discourse Analysis*, eds. David Alan Black with Katharine Barnwell and Stephen Levinsohn [Nashville: Broadman and Holman, 1992], 194).

114. Guthrie, "Discourse Analysis," 255.

115. Ibid., "Currently, little consensus exists concerning how to determine a proper outline for a book or section of a book of the New Testament—perhaps that is why the outlines vary so widely from scholar to scholar. Discourse analysis offers means of discussing unit boundaries and the functions of units on the discourse level. It moves the discussion from merely thematic and even literary grounds to broader considerations such as transitions, cohesion, semantic patterns, and logical relationships between paragraphs or sections" (268).

116. Green rightly notes that one of the positive hermeneutical developments of discourse analysis "is the move away from a concentration of the interpretive agenda *behind the text* to a greater interest in the text itself" ("Discourse Analysis and New Testament Interpretation," 178).

117. David Alan Black, "Introduction," in *Linguistics and New Testament Interpretation: Essays on Discourse Analysis* ed. David Alan Black with Katharine Barnwell and Stephen Levinsohn (Nashville: Broadman and Holman, 1992), 12. A. H. Snyman states, "Meaningful relations not only exist between the words in a sentence, but also between larger parts of a text such as sentences, groups of sentences (clusters) and pericopes. It is therefore important to analyse the way a text is structured in order to grasp its meaning" ("Discourse Analysis: A Semantic Discourse Analysis of the Letter to Philemon," in *Text and Interpretation: New Approaches in the Criticism of the New Testament*, ed. P. J. Hartin and J. H. Petzer [Leiden: Brill, 1991], 88).

tion at the sentence or word level.[118] Some exegetes tend to analyze passages at the level of the sentence, others in an incomplete manner, analyze at the word level.[119] However, Carson suggests that responsible exegesis is that which focuses on "linguistic analysis, both lexis (analysis of the vocabulary) and syntax (analysis of the way words are related to each other) .... It will also analyze the text at the level of the clause, the level of the sentence, the level of the discourse, and the level of the genre."[120] Although discourse can refer to the word, sentence, and paragraph levels, typically discourse consists of more than one

---

118. Some examples are A. T. Robertson, *A Grammar of the Greek New Testament in the Light of Historical Research* (Nashville: Broadman and Holman, 1934); F. Blass, A. Debrunner, and Robert W. Funk, *A Greek Grammar of the New Testament and Other Early Christian Literature*, 9th-10th ed (Chicago: U of Chicago Press), 1961; and Wallace, *Greek Grammar Beyond the Basics*.

Cotterell and Turner, *Linguistics and Biblical Interpretation*, state, "English exegesis in the past has excelled in the study of the meaning of words, lexical semantics, rather than in the study of chunks of text, because of the assumed precision of such studies," 18. Guthrie states, "Commentaries move section by section through a book, treating each section in a verse-by-verse, clause-by-clause, and sometimes word-by-word manner. Yet often there is little attempt to demonstrate how the words, clauses, and sentences in a paragraph work together to accomplish the author's goal for that paragraph in relation to the whole book or section of the book" ("Discourse Analysis," 256-57).

119. Young states that this is unfortunate. "This calls our attention to an inherent weakness of traditional sentence grammars for exegetical purposes. Because they focus only on isolated sentences, they cannot possibly be considered definitive to analyze meaning" (*Intermediate New Testament Greek*, 247).

Wallace is a proponent of sentence-level exegesis. He does not include a discussion regarding discourse analysis in his grammar. See his grammar for reasons as to why there is no discourse analysis discussion. *Greek Grammar Beyond the Basics*, xv.

120. D. A. Carson, "Systematic Theology and Biblical Theology," in *New Dictionary of Biblical Theology: Exploring the Unity & Diversity of Scripture*, eds. Brian S. Rosner, T. Desmond Alexander, and Carson Goldsworthy (Downers Grove: InterVarsity Press, 2001), 91.

Talmy Givón boldly states, "It has become obvious to a growing number of linguists that the study of the syntax of isolated sentences, extracted, without natural context from the purposeful constructions of speakers is a methodology that has outlived its usefulness" (Preface, *Discourse and Syntax*, vol. 12 Syntax and Semantics, ed. T. Givón [New York: Academic, 1979], xiii).

sentence and more frequently refers to the paragraph level. According to Black, the emphasis for the discourse analyst is the text. He writes,

> It is rarely legitimate to draw conclusions simply on the basis of a word count, since concepts often involve more elaborate structures than just single words. It is at this crucial point that textlinguistics performs a valuable service. By inquiring after the *whole* meaning of the text rather than just the meaning of its parts, textlinguistics offers a major interpretive key for our understanding.... Unless one moves constantly between the parts and the whole, the particular and the general, what appears to be a thorough and detailed interpretation may in fact be nothing more than a systematic refusal to confront the primary questions of meaning?[121]

The third benefit discourse analysis offers New Testament exegesis is the focus on the *context*. Language is used by groups of people in various cultures and social functions; thus, it is language as it is structured by the speaker/hearer and writer/reader, which determines how the construction of discourses occurs. There are multiple features of a text. Discourse analysis accounts for these features in and through the text. But it does not just examine the grammatical and semantic relation of language within a text; but also examines the form and function of language as it is communicated and chosen by the author.

In sum, discourse analysis examines the text as a communicative act between humans through the medium of language. Because language is developed and therefore written as social interaction through various cultures, it must be studied at the level of discourse, for rarely is communication done at the word and sentence level. The advantage of discourse analysis is its ability to examine *how* the text is put together (structure), and *what* the relationship is between the smallest (word, sentence) and the largest of units (paragraph/pericope, book) as it is developed by the author. Although discourse analysis

---

121. David Alan Black, *Linguistics for Students of New Testament Greek: A Survey of Basic Concepts and Applications*, 2d ed. (Grand Rapids: Baker, 1995), 173. See also Christopher, "A Discourse Analysis of Colossians 2:16-3:17," 205-20.

does not forfeit the most basic of exegetical endeavors (semantics, lexical – the meaning of words); its primary intent is to analyze the authorial organization of units (syntax – relationship between the words) to explicate his intention (pragmatics – explanation & interpretation of the words) in each context. It is the importance, and thus examination of all levels of the text itself and their cohesive relationship to the whole that captures the essence of discourse analysis. Therefore, the benefit discourse analysis offers New Testament exegesis is its ability to relate the whole to the parts and the parts to the whole.

Conclusion

This book uses a sub-discipline or complementing method of hermeneutics to examine and thus demonstrate the significance of Jesus' three passion predictions within the central section (8:22-10:52) as they relate to the Gospel of Mark as a whole. This method is called discourse analysis. The goal of discourse analysis is to examine the text at multiple levels (e.g., word, sentence, paragraph, and discourse). Discourse analysis provides a better investigation and thus conclusion to the authorial intention and cohesion of the text as it relates to meaning.

The discourse theory that is more closely followed is the systemic-functional theory, for this more objectively analyzes the relationship and thus function between the discourse (the Gospel of Mark as a whole) and text (central section of Mark). It also serves to more completely account for the use and function of language at all levels of discourse; thus, incorporating all the commonalities of discourse analysis (i.e., language at a level beyond the sentence, use of language in its context, and cohesion of language). To incorporate all the commonalities of discourse analysis, the systemic-functional theory utilizes two components. These components are discourse structure and discourse texture. This examination therefore implements these two components of discourse analysis: thus, advocating a top-down (discourse structure) and bottom-up approach (discourse texture). This enables the reader/interpreter to view the text holistically.

Chapter Three

Studying the Gospels as Literature

Introduction

This book incorporates two key components of discourse analysis. They help to provide a proper interpretation of the intended message of the Passion predictions and their function within the Gospel of Mark. These key components are discourse structure and discourse texture. The focus of this chapter is discourse structure.

Discourse analysis is applied to the central section (8:22-10:52) of the Gospel of Mark (see chapter 5). The application of discourse analysis explicates the function of the central section within the Gospel in relationship to its genre. Therefore, how does the central section function within the Gospel as a whole? Discourse structure helps to answer this question because it examines the whole discourse at the level of genre, or macro-structure. Therefore, an understanding of the genre of the Gospel of Mark is important. It is important because the understanding of genre provides the interpreter with the big picture; that is, Mark's intended message to his audience.

Discourse structure is an examination of macro-structure. Macro-structure can refer to genre, or in this case, genre, and sub-genre.[1] The Gospel ac-

---

1. Discourse structure also "refers to the fundamental interpretation of the

DEATH AND DISCIPLESHIP:
An Analysis of the Predictions of Jesus' Death in the Gospel of Mark

counts are a sub-genre of the larger genre narrative because they are unique. The Gospels are unique due to their biographical *and* theological emphasis. In other words, the Gospels do not just communicate the life of a central figure, Jesus Christ, but they also provide the reader with a theological emphasis, that is, they awaken and subsequently strengthen the faith of Christ's followers.

Genre is the basic framework in which communication occurs. Written communication or literature is not packaged in neutral containers but reflects the social and cultural conventions of the time in which the text is written. Literary genre therefore affects how writing is to be interpreted.[2] Literary

---

whole book based on its genre. It is concerned with the interpretation of a book as a whole" (William Arp, Course notes for NT1, Seminar in New Testament Hermeneutics and Exegetical Method, Baptist Bible Seminary, Clarks Summit, Pa, summer 2002, 3.) See also the view of Elliott E. Johnson as it pertains to the 'sense of the whole,' "Author's Intention and Biblical Interpretation," in *Hermeneutics, Inerrancy and the Bible: Papers from ICBI Summit II*, eds. Earl D. Radmacher and Robert D. Preus (Grand Rapids: Zondervan, 1984), 408-29; Idem., *Expository Hermeneutics: An Introduction* (Grand Rapids: Zondervan, 1990), 9-12.

2. The interpreter is to keep in mind however that genre is simply a guide or framework for interpretation, never is it to impose a rigid set of requirements to one's exegetical study.

For example, Paul's letters are often interpreted by scholars through the application of categories from classic rhetoric (see Charles A. Wanamaker, *The Epistles to the Thessalonians*, The New International Greek Testament Commentary [Grand Rapids: Eerdmans, 1990]; James D. G. Dunn, *The Epistles to the Colossians and to Philemon*, The New International Greek Testament Commentary [Grand Rapids: Eerdmans, 1996]; and F. F. Forrester Church, "Rhetorical Structure and Design in Paul's Letter to Philemon," *HTR* 71 [Jan-April 1978]: 17-33). The suppositions that underlie this interpretation are twofold; that is, the ancients themselves would have been familiar with and recognized these categories of rhetoric and Paul would have intended to use them. Porter's contention is "Thus, although categories of ancient rhetoric may have been 'in the air' of the Greco-Roman world, their use in the writing or analysis of letters cannot be substantiated. . . . The above conclusion does not preclude exegeting the Pauline letters in terms of the categories of ancient rhetoric, however, as long as it is kept in mind that these categories, especially those regarding the arrangement of the parts of the speech, probably did not consciously influence the writing of the letters and almost assuredly did not figure significantly in their earliest interpretation (Stanley E.

genre of all kinds is interpreted differently (e.g., epistles versus Gospels), for each possesses genuinely unique features.

Sub-genre on the other hand, is a sub-category of the larger genre framework in which the text is to be understood. A sub-genre, therefore, facilitates a more distinct category that possesses similarities to the genre category yet does not possess all the defining characteristics of the larger category. It is its own unique category. Thus, the interpreter of literature must identify the literary genre and in the case of the Gospel accounts, the literary sub-genre, and then analyze how the elements of both provide an understanding of the whole.[3] David E. Aune emphasizes that "the original significance that a literary text had for both author and reader is tied to the genre of that text, so that the meaning of the part is dependent upon the meaning of the whole."[4]

Porter, "Exegesis of the Pauline Letters, Including the Deutero-Pauline Letters," in *A Handbook to the Exegesis of the New Testament*, ed. Stanley E. Porter [Leiden: Brill, 2002], 542-43). Although this is an example of Pauline literature, it serves to simply demonstrate the value of genre in the interpretive process without imposing outside guidelines to determine meaning; rather genre provides help to discover meaning.

3. Grant R. Osborne sees the significance of genre identification for interpretation because "all writers couch their messages in a certain genre in order to give the reader sufficient rules by which to decode that message. These hints guide the reader (or hearer) and provide clues for interpretation" (*The Hermeneutical Spiral: A Comprehensive Introduction to Biblical Interpretation*, rev and exp. [Downers Grove, Ill: InterVarsity Press, 2006], 26). Early E. D. Hirsch Jr. claims that "an understanding of all verbal meaning is necessarily genre-bound" (*Validity in Interpretation* [New Haven, Conn: Yale U. Press, 1967], 76).

Richard A. Burridge, *What Are the Gospels? A Comparison with Graeco-Roman Biography* (SNTSMS 70, Cambridge: Cambridge University Press, 1992) states, "We have seen that genre functions by providing a set of expectations as a sort of contract between author and reader. It is constituted and mediated through a variety of different generic features, none of which need be peculiar to the genre; however, when they are taken all together, they reveal a particular pattern, which enables us to recognize the genre" 109.

4. Aune, *The New Testament in Its Literary Environment*, (Philadelphia, Pa: Westminster Press, 1987), 13.

DEATH AND DISCIPLESHIP:
AN ANALYSIS OF THE PREDICTIONS OF JESUS' DEATH IN THE GOSPEL OF MARK

LITERARY GENRE: AN OVERVIEW

Literature requires interpretation because it is a presentation of human expression. However, it is not just human expression, but it is also an art form. This art form is characterized by technique, structure, and beauty. The commonest way of defining literature is through its kind and type, or literary genres. The New Testament is not unique. The authors communicate their meaning through literary genres. This literary approach pays close attention to what the author expresses through content and the way in which he expresses his content. The influence of culture and historical conditions upon the writing of the Bible is important to its understanding.[5]

The various cultural and historical influences on the writing of the New Testament include, but are not limited to, the Greco-Roman world.[6] The types of texts that comprise the New Testament are culture-specific; that is, each text will have a variety of linguistic elements that can only be specific and distinctive to that culture.[7] The culture-specific features of the Greco-Roman world provide understanding as one classifies the text into literary genre.

---

5. Aune states, "Even though the New Testament is published between two covers like any other book, it is not quite as homogeneous as it first appears. Actually, it is not a 'book' in the usual sense but a collection of twenty-seven compositions in various literary genres by roughly a dozen authors written over a hundred-year period (c.a. A.D. 50 to 150) in an ancient language (Greek) and within an alien culture (the ancient Mediterranean world)" (*The New Testament in its Literary Environment*, 13).

6. There is not a discussion regarding the influence of the Old Testament upon the writing of the New Testament. The Old Testament does not possess the similarities as that of the Greco-Roman biographies. Therefore, it is the understanding of Hellenism that more closely relates to the Gospel accounts and are used in the proposed definition of the sub-genre of narrative, theological narrative biography.

7. Robert A. Dooley and Stephen H. Levinsohn *Analyzing Discourse: A Manual of Basic Concepts* (Dallas, Tex: SIL International, 2001), 7. It is important to understand that genre is tied to its era and literary milieu. See also Anthony R. Cross, "Genres of the New Testament," in *Dictionary of New Testament Background*, ed. Craig A. Evans and Stanley E. Porter (Downers Grove, Ill: InterVarsity Press, 2000), 402.

Definition of Literary Genre

Literary genre is simply defined as the kind or type of literature by which a written text is classified.[8] Literary genres consist of related texts that have "coherent and recurring configuration of literary features involving form (including structure and style), content, and function."[9] They have both external (compositional form) and internal (contents) components that are uniquely assembled by the author that assists the reader with interpretation. The external components are "the overall structural pattern, the form . . . style, interrelationships, and content. Internal factors include the cohesive plot, action, narrative voice, setting and language."[10]

Literary genre is distinct from literary forms.[11] The composite whole, of which constituent parts are made, is literary genre; whereas the parts or smaller units are the literary forms.[12] For example, the parable is a literary

---

8. David L. Turner states, "Genre as an English lexeme derives from French, and in turn from the Latin *genus*. Typical glosses for the word genre include 'type,' 'sort,' 'kind,' or 'class'" (*Interpreting the Gospels and Acts: An Exegetical Handbook*, series ed. John D. Harvey, Handbooks for New Testament Exegesis [Grand Rapids: Kregel, 2019], 27).

9. Aune, *The New Testament in Its Literary Environment*, 13. See also Craig L. Blomberg, "The Diversity of Literary Genres in the New Testament," in *Interpreting the New Testament: Essays on Methods and Issues*, ed. David Alan Black and David S. Dockery (Nashville: Broadman and Holman, 2001), 272; John Barton, *Reading the Old Testament: Method in Biblical Study* (London: Darton, Longman and Todd, 1984), 16; and J. J. Collins, "Introduction: Towards the Morphology of a Genre," *Semeia* 14 (1979): 1.

10. Osborne, *The Hermeneutical Spiral*, 182. The basic glossary definition offered by Walter C. Kaiser Jr. and Moisés Silva includes both components (*Introduction to Biblical Hermeneutics: The Search for Meaning*, rev and exp ed [Grand Rapids: Zondervan, 2007], 335). See also René Wellek and Austin Warren, *Theory of Literature*, 3d ed. (New York: Harcourt, Brace and World, 1956), 231.

11. See discussions on this distinction by Craig L. Blomberg with Jennifer Foutz Markley, *A Handbook of New Testament Exegesis* (Grand Rapids: Baker, 2010), 102-11; Campbell, *Advances in the Study of Greek*, 140-44.

12. Some authors do not distinguish between these. See J. L. Bailey and L. D. Vander Broek, *Literary Forms in the New Testament* (London: SPCK, 1992) and D.

form which works of many genres may include. Due to the complexities with the discipline of genre criticism, this distinction is necessary so as not to confuse the whole and parts of a given text.

Literary genre therefore is discovered through the discipline known as genre criticism, one of several sub-disciplines of New Testament studies. Genre criticism is "probably best understood simply as a tool to discover the situational circumstances within which the document came into being."[13] It is the discovering of unique features that make the text one type of genre as opposed to another type. It works with the canonical form of the text as it is written and not any form before or after that.[14] Genre criticism identifies and analyzes the text as it is; it does not do so without paying attention to the form, style, and function of the text.[15] Genre "becomes a mediator between form and content; it constructs and responds to recurring situation. . . .. Genre is truly, therefore, a marker of meaning . . . a dynamic rather than a static concept."[16]

Brent Sandy and Ronald L. Giese (*Cracking Old Testament Codes: A Guide to Interpreting the Literary Genres of the Old Testament* (Nashville: Broadman and Holman, 1995), 5-27. The purpose of this distinction is to provide clarification regarding the definition of literary genre.

13. Brook W. R. Pearson and Stanley E. Porter, "The Genres of the New Testament," in *A Handbook to the Exegesis of the New Testament*, ed. Stanley E. Porter, (Leiden: Brill, 2002), 133.

14. Tremper Longman III uses the term genre analysis as opposed to genre criticism. He wishes to communicate the necessity of the text and its content along a synchronic analysis rather than diachronic to substantiate that it is the written text and its form that necessitates a given genre classification. He states, "What I label genre analysis bears a close resemblance to form criticism. The major difference is that form criticism is a diachronic analysis, whereas genre analysis is synchronic, concerned to identify the type of literature, not its prehistory" ("Literary Approaches to Biblical Interpretation," in *Foundations of Contemporary Interpretation*, ed. Moisés Silva [Grand Rapids: Zondervan, 1996], 141).

15. See these helpful resources, V. Philips Long, "The Art of Biblical History," in *Foundations of Contemporary Interpretation*, ed. Moisés Silva (Grand Rapids: Zondervan, 1996), 306; Grant R. Osborne, "Genre Criticism—Sensus Literalis," *TrinJ* 4, no. 2 (1983).

16. Amy Devitt, "Generalizing about Genre: New Conceptions of an Old Concept," *College Composition and Communication* 44 (Dec 1993): 578-80.

Thus, it is important to note that though genre criticism is essential to interpretation, "the idea of genre . . . is not one that is drawn from *outside* the text . . . but rather something that is drawn from reading the work itself."[17] This is critical because all communication is genre-bound.[18] If indeed genre captures the context of written communication, then it is essential for the interpretation of written texts.

Role of Literary Genre in Interpretation

Literary genre is essential to interpretation, for it is part and parcel of the grammatical-historical method of exegesis. Literary genre is not just for the mere classification of texts, though literary genre provides this, but it provides the literary context for a given sentence or paragraph. In short, it is not just to classify but also clarify. The concept and classifications of literary genre is important for interpretation, for it is this "that describes the broad contours and features of a particular literary work."[19] Literary genre is the epistemological tool for discovering the intended meaning.[20]

Literary genre is that framework by which the author accepts and shapes his text in adherence to it. It is a literary convention that communicates not

---

17. Pearson and Porter, "The Genres of the New Testament," state, "For example, in the case of the one who suggests that, as *Hamlet* is a tragedy, all of the characteristics of tragedy, ancient and modern, must be understood before one can appreciate the significance of the action in the play." [Whereas the correct use of genre is] "understanding that the action in *Hamlet*, while similar to other works often labeled as tragedies, is unique to itself and can only be understood by a thorough examination thereof," 133.

18. Edgar V. McKnight states, "The question of genre cannot be avoided, for every reader reads a text in the light of its presumed purpose and nature as a representation of reality and/or a work of art, and in light of the conventions of that particular sort of writing" ("Literary Criticism," in *Dictionary of Jesus and the Gospels*, eds. Joel B. Green, Scot McKnight, and I. Howard Marshall [Downers Grove, Ill: InterVarsity Press, 1992], 478).

19. Michael H. Burer, "Narrative Genre: Studying the Story," in *Interpreting the New Testament Text: Introduction to the Art and Science of Exegesis*, ed. Darrell L. Bock and Buist M. Fanning (Wheaton, Ill: Crossway, 2006), 198.

20. Osborne, "Genre Criticism—Sensus Literalis," 1-27.

only the text, but also meaning to its readers or hearers.[21] At the same time, literary genre is not a self-imposed structure that determines meaning. Literary genre is simply how an author expresses his content to the audience. It is the style and medium by which communication takes place. Whatever literary genre the author chooses to communicate cannot be separated from the content within this medium. Any interpretation of a written text therefore requires the analysis of genre, for it is impossible to separate *what* is said from *how* it is said.[22] The role of literary genre for interpretation is critical to an understanding of the text since the choice of genre complements the meaning of the text.[23]

---

21. Kevin J. Vanhoozer states, "Genre thus enables the reader to interpret meaning and to recognize what kinds of truth claims are being made in and by a text" ("The Semantics of Biblical Literature: Truth and Scripture's Diverse Literary Forms," in *Hermeneutics, Authority, and Canon*, ed. D. A. Carson and John D. Woodbridge [Grand Rapids: Zondervan, 1986], 80).

Leland Ryken states that literary genre is nothing more than "a norm or expectation to guide the reader in his encounter with the text" (*How to Read the Bible As Literature* [Grand Rapids: Zondervan, 1984], 25).

22. Sandy and Giese, states, "To read generically is to sign a rhetorical contract with the author to understand his work in the terms that he shared within his intended audience. The task of hermeneutics is not to develop new procedures of understanding but to clarify the conditions in which understanding occurs" (*Cracking Old Testament Codes*, 38)

Richard A. Burridge, (*What Are the Gospels? A Comparison with Graeco-Roman Biography*, 109) states, "We have seen that genre functions by providing a set of expectations as a sort of contract between author and reader. It is constituted and mediated through a variety of different generic features, none of which need be peculiar to the genre; however, when they are taken all together, they reveal a particular pattern, which enables us to recognize the genre."

23. J. Scott Duvall and J. Daniel Hays state, "Even though the author and reader cannot have a face-to-face conversation, they meet in the text where they are able to communicate because they subscribe to a common set of rules—the rules of the particular genre . . . we must let the author's choice of genre determine the rules we use to understand his or her words" (*Grasping God's Word: A Hands-On Approach to Reading, Interpreting, and Applying the Bible*, 4th ed. [Grand Rapids: Zondervan, 2020], 152).

Misuse of Literary Genre in Interpretation

Literary genre is the guide or framework the author implements to communicate a given passage and the interpreter uses to understand the author's intended meaning of a given passage. Though genre identification is indispensable to interpretation; that is, meaning is genre-bound, it is also important for the interpreter to know that genres are not absolute and mutually distinctive categories. With this in mind, the interpreter must always be aware of the context that surrounds the passage. In other words, it is critical the interpreter use literary genre in two ways. The first is related to classification and the second to methodology.

First, the interpreter is to remember that literary genres are convenient categories to help with the interpretation process, but he must recognize that these genres are not rigid, final forms in which the author fits his text. Literary genres possess family resemblances or a composite of features that individual texts share with other texts. The misuse of literary genre occurs when the interpreter is too dogmatic either in classification of genre or the use of this classification as a means for interpretation.[24] The use of literary genre must be understood according to its flexibility and functionality, not its rigidity and formality. The Gospels are a case in point. The Gospels are more than history or biography. They are a unique synthesis of three characteristics: theology, narrative, and biography.

Second, the interpreter is to use literary genre alongside of the "exegesis and historical and biographical theologies . . . .. For one without the other would provide an imbalanced, imprecise understanding of a text."[25] The misuse of literary genre occurs when the interpreter only uses the generic classification as the means of interpretation; that is, a presuppositional gener-

---

24. William G. Doty explains using Paul's writings. "I argue . . . that in his letters a genre or subgenre was created, and that our task is that of identifying the stages and steps in generic construction. Instead of arguing that there is one clearly identified Pauline form, I argue that there is a basic understanding of structure by which Paul wrote, but that this basic understanding could be modified on occasion, and that the basic understanding itself was something that came into being only gradually" (*Letters in Primitive Christianity* [Philadelphia: Fortress Press, 1973], 21).

25. Sandy and Giese, *Cracking Old Testament Codes*, 42-43.

ic approach to the text. Literary genre is not to be used independently of the literal-grammatical-historical method of interpretation.

Summary of Literary Genre

A written text is classified based on its common literary features, form, content, and function. The texts that share common literary features are classified into literary genres. Literary genres guide the reader. They are the basic framework used by the author to communicate his story. Genre enables the reader to treat the text as a whole, a unified communicative act. Through this unified whole, genre can join the author, text, and reader. Genre facilitates *what* the text is and *how* the text is to be understood.

Narrative as a Genre

The interpretation of any written text involves the author, text, and reader. This written text is a form of language communicated (author) that is portrayed in each situation (text) and is then interpreted (reader). Written texts can be classified into genre, or as Robert Longacre posits, "every language has a system of discourse types (e.g., narrative)"[26] and it is through these discourse types that written communication takes place. Narrative is a discourse type. It is the dominant form of discourse in the Bible.[27]

---

26. Robert E. Longacre, *Joseph, A Story of Divine Providence: A Text Theoretical and Textlinguistic Analysis of Genesis 37 and 39-48* (Winona Lake, Ind: Eisenbrauns, 1989), 59. A discourse is a linguistic term indicating *how* a written text is communicated.

27. Walter C. Kaiser, Jr. "I Will Remember the Deeds of the Lord: The Meaning of Narrative," in *An Introduction to Biblical Hermeneutics: The Search for Meaning*, rev & exp ed. eds. Walter C. Kaiser Jr and Moisés Silva (Grand Rapids: Zondervan, 2007), 122-23.

Definition of Narrative

Narrative is communication in which the author organizes the sequence of episodes within a specified context.[28] These communicative episodes along with participants (characters) are written literary texts that form the plot of the story. It is the story then that both presents episodes and reveals the essence of the characters.[29] The power of the story is the unique ability to involve the reader in what is happening.[30] According to Perrin, the function of the story "is to help the reader hear the voices, take part in the action, get involved in the plot."[31] Therefore, narrative is the product of a composition that

---

28. Kaiser, "Remember the Deeds," "Narrative in its broadest sense is an account of specific space-time events and participants whose stories are recorded with a beginning, a middle, and an end" (123-24).

29. Osborne notes, "The biblical narratives contain both history and theology, and I would add that these are brought together via a 'story' format. The historical basis for the stories is crucial, but the representation of that story in the text is the actual object of interpretation" (*The Hermeneutical Spiral*, 200). Sydney Greidanus agrees with Osborne. He notes, "Although there is much to be said for the power of story and how it works apart from the question of historicity, it must also be said that treating all biblical narratives like parables is a gross oversimplification, for not all biblical narratives are non-historical. . . . The issue here again is the intent or purpose of the text. If that intent . . . entails relating historical events, then sidestepping that intent in one's interpretation fails to do full justice to that narrative's meaning" (*The Modern Preacher and the Ancient Text: Interpreting and Preaching Biblical Literature* [Grand Rapids: Eerdmans, 1988], 199).

See also the contribution of Michael H. Burer, "Narrative Genre," 198-202. Contra Hans Frei who understands narrative as not containing history; rather was 'history-like' (*Eclipse of Biblical Narrative* [New Haven, Conn: Yale University Press, 1974], chap 1).

30. Meir Sternberg calls narrative "a functional structure, a means to a communicative end, a transaction between the narrator and the audience on whom he wishes to produce a certain effect by way of certain strategies" (*The Poetics of Biblical Narrative, Ideological Literature and the Drama of Reading* [Bloomington, Ind: Indiana University Press], 1985), 1.

31. Norman Perrin, *The New Testament: An Introduction* (New York: Harcourt Brace Jovanovich, 1974), 165.

communicates a message in which its meaning is ascertained by a reader who encounters characters acting within certain settings in sequential order.[32]

Elements of Narrative

Narratives are built around basic elements. These elements include structure, plot, setting, characters, and point-of-view. They provide a focus on the work, not just the individual paragraph. The assumption is that each narrative consists of individual paragraphs.[33] In order to understand narrative, the reader must seek to appreciate each of the elements individually and then conclude how each contributes to the whole.[34]

Structure

The structure of the narrative refers to the order of episodes; that is, the sequential order the reader views as he reads the story. These episodes[35] can

---

32. Robert C. Tannehill states the importance of the reader's understanding of the composition of a Gospel as a whole, and especially as narrative. He writes, "The outline of a Gospel has also been a subject of frequent study. This usually results in a topical outline with neat divisions. Such an outline may be appropriate to a well-constructed essay, but it is not necessarily appropriate to a narrative. There are special aspects of *narrative* composition which biblical scholars will continue to ignore if there is not greater awareness of how stories are told and how they communicate" ("The Disciples in Mark: The Function of a Narrative Role," *JRel* 57 [1977]: 387).

33. Robert J. Banks, "Narrative Exegesis," in *Dictionary of Jesus and the Gospels*, eds. Joel B. Green, Scot McKnight, and I. Howard Marshall (Downers Grove, Ill: InterVarsity Press, 1992), 570.

34. Tannehill, "The Disciples in Mark," clarifies that a story is a representation of a narrator. It is through the choice of the narrator that the reader understands *how* the story is told and that these choices reflect his emphases and values (387).

35. Mark Alan Powell uses the term event rather than episode. He defines an event as "Incidents or happenings that occur within a story, and a story cannot exist without them. . . . Simply to consider events as the content of the narrative or as definitive of what we have called the story is not enough. One must also consider the 'story-as-discoursed,' the manner in which the events are presented" (*What Is Narrative Criticism*, [Minneapolis, Minn: Fortress Press, 1990], 35).

be ordered in several ways; chronological, topical, or geographical. This ordering is known as redaction; that is, the arranging of episodes in such a way to communicate the theology of the narrative.[36]

The structure of the narrative is communicated through episodes or paragraphs that are interrelated forming a whole. The structure is patterned through literary devices that ultimately organize the text into clauses, sentences, and paragraphs. These literary devices include, but are not limited to, repetition, inclusion, and chiasm.[37] It is therefore important for the reader to note the structure or patterns of narrative for they help to assist with the apprehension of the story through the author's decisions regarding organization and arrangement of material. Structure answers the *how* of the story and illustrates the *why*.

Plot

The plot of a narrative is like the structure in that it too communicates a coherent arrangement of episodes that are interrelated; thus, it is a complete communicative act or whole story.[38] The difference between plot and structure is that the plot is concerned more with the linking between episodes, or the movement from one episode to another and its cause[39] and not just the order or arrangement of episodes. Plot answers the *what* of the story.

---

36. The author's use of redaction here is distinguished from the critical methodology redaction criticism. Here it is assumed that the biblical author arranges his text to communicate meaning. However, this work does not assume that Mark has done so using outside sources such as Q, L, etc. Scholars recognize that these sources are hypothetical and allow them to become the basis for the composition of the Gospel account. This necessarily follows because some of them deny the traditional authorship of the Gospel accounts.

37. See the list in Powell, 32-33; also, David Bauer, *The Structure of Matthew's Gospel: A Study in Literary Design*, JSNTSS 31 (Sheffield: Almond Press, 1988), 13-20.

38. Ryken, *How to Read the Bible As Literature*, 40.

39. Walter C. Kaiser and Moisés Silva, *Introduction to Biblical Hermeneutics*, 126.

DEATH AND DISCIPLESHIP:
AN ANALYSIS OF THE PREDICTIONS OF JESUS' DEATH IN THE GOSPEL OF MARK

Setting

The setting of the narrative "refers to the where and when or the spatial, temporal and social locations of narrative events."[40] The setting however does not just include the events of the narrative but can also include the characters of the narrative. In other words, the characters themselves can speak throughout the narrative or they can simply blend into the background, thus becoming part of the setting.

There are three types of settings in narrative. They include spatial, temporal, and social. A spatial setting pertains to the location in which the story is told (e.g., Jesus questioning his disciples as to his identity in Caesarea Philippi, Mk. 8:27). It refers to any "physical environment in which the characters of the story live as well as the 'props' and 'furniture' that make up that environment."[41] A temporal setting can refer to either chronological or typological time. The chronological reference is either a point in time or duration of time in which an action takes place. The typological time references on the other hand, indicate the kind of time within which an action transpires[42] (e.g., evening as opposed to daylight).

Last, social setting is a cultural climate. It is "a set of beliefs, attitudes, and customs that prevail in the world of the story (e.g., Jesus' presentation of the contrasting roles of leadership in the first century, Mk. 10:42-44)."[43] Especially given the time in which the Bible was written, the reader must familiarize himself with the social and cultural customs of the time. The notation of the setting provides a conceptualization of the world around a character within the story that may otherwise be restricted due to the cultural and tem-

---

40. Stamps, "Rhetorical and Narratological Criticism," 232. Powell states, "Settings are the adverbs of literary structure: they designate when, where, and how the action occurs" (*What Is Narrative Criticism*, 69).

41. Powell, *What Is Narrative Criticism*, 70.

42. Ibid., 73.

43. Ryken, *How To Read the Bible As Literature*, 36. Powell states that a social setting concerns "social circumstances. These include political institutions, class structures, economic systems, social customs, and general cultural context assumed to be operative in the work," (*What Is Narrative Criticism*, 74).

poral gap between reader and text. The setting answers the *when* and *where* of the story.

Characters

The characters of the narrative are those who perform the various activities that are "generally crucial to the development of the story."[44] The majority of the time these characters are people, however they can also be animals or non-human entities. A group of people can also serve as a single character (e.g., the crowds/multitudes in the Gospels). Typically, it is the characters within a narrative that produce actions; thus, communicating the plot of the story. Sometimes however, the author uses the identity and personality of his characters to show what the characters themselves are like in the narrative. For example, the author either makes direct statements about the characters (e.g., Matthew states that Joseph is a just man, 1:19) or uses the characters' points of view about other characters (e.g., John the Baptist calls the religious leaders a 'brood of vipers,' Matt 3:7).[45]

It is clear throughout narrative that the characters are essential. They often provide how an author may tell the story. They also offer responses and attitudes throughout the story giving the reader a point-of-view that would not have been otherwise provided, and characters, due to their traits and personalities, also bring the reader into a worldview that would not have been otherwise present. The characters answer the *who* of any story.

Point-of-view

The point-of-view of a narrative refers to the reference point an author uses to organize the story. The point-of-view is told from some reference point within which has an evaluative consequence. Most narratives are dominated by the narrator, who is considered to have a reliable perspective. As the narrator communicates his story, he may communicate it as one of the characters. The author's reference point provides the reader with a reliable point-

---

44. Stamps, "Rhetorical and Narratological Criticism," 231.
45. Powell, *What Is Narrative Criticism*, 52-53.

of-view.[46] Grant Osborne claims that point-of-view is a perspective taken by the narrator and characters of a story. This perspective provides the force or significance of the story for the reader (e.g., the disciples' fear and concern for their life as the boat was about to sink, Mk. 4:37-38). In other words, "every author has a certain message that he or she wishes to get across to the reader. . . . This point of view guides the reader to the significance of the story and determines the actual 'shape' that the author gives to the narrative."[47] The *basis* or *reason* for the episodes within the narrative is established through the point-of-view.

The Study of Narrative: Narrative Criticism

Traditionally New Testament scholars have discussed narrative in terms of three related schools of thought. They are source, form, and redaction criticism. In the eighteenth-century scholars spent their efforts finding the earliest sources that underlie the Synoptic Gospels.[48] Source criticism is defined as the "attempt to identify the written traditions behind the Gospels in order to determine the relationship of the Synoptics."[49] This method provided

---

46. Powell calls this the evaluative point-of-view and "may be defined as the standards of judgment by which readers are led to evaluate the events, characters, and settings that comprise the story" (*What Is Narrative Criticism*, 24). Ryken states that the reader is determining the perspective by which he is to share with the storyteller, *How To Read the Bible As Literature*, 61.

47. Osborne, *The Hermeneutical Spiral*, 204. See also Adele Berlin, *Poetics and Interpretation of Biblical Narrative* (Sheffield: Almond, 1983), 43-55.

48. See the following for introductions: Robert H. Stein, *Studying the Synoptic Gospels: Origin and Interpretation*, 2d ed. (Grand Rapids: Baker, 2001); Darrell L. Bock, *Studying the Historical Jesus: A Guide to Sources and Methods* (Grand Rapids: Baker, 2002); and D. A. Carson and Douglas J. Moo, *An Introduction to the New Testament*, 2d ed. (Grand Rapids: Zondervan, 2005), 85-103.

Burer defines synoptic as "the first three Gospels—Matthew, Mark, and Luke. This is due to fact that they share common material and a common order, and thus can be profitably studied when viewed together" ("Narrative Genre," 204).

49. Scot McKnight, *Interpreting the Synoptic Gospels* (Grand Rapids: Baker, 1988), 34.

the scholar with an understanding of the materials used in the creation of the Gospels.

Before the end of the nineteenth and the beginning of the twentieth centuries, scholars went another direction. The goal was to no longer study the Gospels as whole discourses, but to study the individual units that make up the Gospels. Form criticism represents the endeavor to determine the oral form of written documents or sources and to classify the material according to the various forms or categories or narrative, or discourse.[50] In other words, form criticism helped the scholar to determine how the Gospel was compiled and then use this information to determine the historical accuracy of its form.

Although the holistic approach to the Gospels was left behind in the early twentieth century, it re-surfaced again during the second half of the twentieth century through a critical method known as redaction criticism. Redaction criticism "seeks to uncover the theology and setting of a writing by studying the ways the redactor or editor changed the traditions he inherited and the seams or transitions that the redactor used to link those traditions together."[51] It was through this method that scholars argued the Gospel writers were more than editors. They were now considered authors who edited,

---

50. See also Darrell L. Bock, "Form Criticism," in *Interpreting the New Testament: Essays on Methods and Issues*, ed. David Alan Black and David S. Dockery (Nashville: Broadman and Holman, 2001), 106-27; Carson and Moo, *An Introduction to the New Testament*, 79-85; Edgar V. McKnight, *What Is Form Criticism?* (Philadelphia: Fortress Press, 1969).

Burer provides the seminal works on form criticism (see "Narrative Genre," 204n24). They are: Karl Ludwig Schmidt, *Der Rahmen der Geschichte Jesu: Literarkritische Untersuchungen zur ältesten Jesusüberlieferung* (Berlin: Trowitzsch, 1919); Martin Dibelius, *From Tradition to Gospel,* Library of Theological Translations (New York: Scribner, 1971); Rudolf Bultmann, *The History of the Synoptic Tradition*, trans. John Marsh (New York: Harper & Row, 1963); and Vincent Taylor, *The Formation of the Gospel Tradition* (London: Macmillan, 1933).

51. Grant R. Osborne, "Redaction Criticism," in *Interpreting the New Testament: Essays on Methods and Issues*, eds. David Alan Black and David S. Dockery (Nashville: Broadman and Holman, 2001), 128. See also Carson and Moo, *An Introduction to the New Testament*, 103-12; Norman Perrin, *What Is Redaction Criticism* (Philadelphia: Fortress Press, 1970).

arranged, and shaped the accounts of Jesus' life in such a way that specific theological purposes were conveyed.

As a result, the authorial purpose was rediscovered and scholars began to emphasize a holistic approach through the totality of the narrative of Gospel, for the narrative would now become the literary medium by which the Gospel accounts could be studied. This reemphasis is what led to literary analysis.[52] A more recent development however is narrative criticism.[53] Because of the underlying assumptions of the aforementioned critical methodologies (source, form, and redaction criticism), the focus here is narrative criticism.[54]

---

52. Carson and Moo define literary criticism "as a catchall designation for contemporary approaches to the gospels that focus on careful study of the way the gospels function as pieces of literature," *An Introduction to the New Testament*, 115.

53. For a detailed description of this method, see Jeannine K. Brown, "Narrative Criticism," in *Dictionary of Jesus and the Gospels*, 2d ed, eds. Joel B. Green, Jeannine K. Brown, and Nicholas Perrin, 619-24 (Downers Grove, IL: InterVarsity, 2013).

54. One assumption of the critical methodologies, (source, form, and redaction criticism), is that they undermine the historicity of the Gospel accounts. In an edition of *Interpretation*, Mark A. Powell demonstrates that several scholars, both of secular and biblical literature, reject redaction criticism and related approaches and propose a narrative analysis of the Gospel of Mark. For example, Norman R. Petersen claims that the Gospel of Mark ought to be read as a narrative and not as a redaction ("Point of View in Mark's Narrative," *Semeia* 12 (1978): 119). David Rhoads understands the Gospel of Mark in terms of literary-critical concerns, not historical-critical concerns (*Mark As Story: An Introduction to the Narrative of a Gospel*, 2d ed [Minneapolis: Fortress Press, 1999]).

Mark Powell claims the intent of narrative criticism provides a better interpretation because the historical-critical method (redaction criticism and others) does not take the interpretation of Mark as historically accurate ("Toward A Narrative-Critical Understanding of Mark," *Interpretation* 47, n. 4 [Oct 1993]: 342). Although some proponents of narrative criticism may not always assume historicity of the text (e.g. Rhoads, Dewey, and Michie, see 18n51), the Markan scholars (Powell, Peterson, and Perrin) do assume the historicity of the Gospel of Mark. This Book approaches the Gospel of Mark as a revelatory historical account of the details of Jesus' life and the surrounding events. It was written by John Mark.

See also Steven L. McKenzie and Stephen R. Haynes eds. who state in the introduction, "Increasingly over the last twenty years the hegemony of historical methods for interpreting the Bible has been challenged by biblical critics unhappy with either

The reason for the study, and therefore consideration of narrative criticism, is because this method focuses upon the coherence of the text and its final form.⁵⁵ It examines the elements of a narrative (structure, plot, setting, characters, and point-of-view) and understands the relationship of these elements as a unified whole.⁵⁶ In other words, "narrative criticism assists the exegetical task by providing an interpretive perspective which can evaluate the purpose or significance of the 'what' and 'why' (structure and plot), the 'who' (characters), the 'when' and 'where' (setting), and the 'wherefore' (point-of-view) of the events in a biblical narrative."⁵⁷

the results or the very assumptions of historical-critical scholarship" (*To Each Its Own Meaning: An Introduction to Biblical Criticisms and Their Application* [Louisville, Ky: Westminster John Knox Press, 1993], 2). The purpose of their book is to introduce the most important methods of biblical criticism and their application.

55. James L. Resseguie states narrative criticism is "The 'what' of a text (its content) and the 'how' of a text (its rhetoric and structure) are analyzed as a complete tapestry, an organic whole" (*Narrative Criticism of the New Testament: An Introduction* [Grand Rapids: Baker, 2005], 18-19).

David M. Gunn stresses the literary importance of narrative criticism. He states that what is meant by narrative criticism is, "interpreting the existing text (in its 'final form') in terms primarily of its own story world, seen as replete with meaning, rather than understanding the text by attempting to reconstruct its sources and editorial history . . . Here meaning is to be found by close reading that identifies formal and conventional structures of the narrative, determines plot, develops characterization, distinguishes point of view, exposes language play, and relates all to some overarching, encapsulating theme. Unlike historical criticism, which in practice has segmented the text" ("Narrative Criticism," in *To Each Its Own Meaning: An Introduction to Biblical Criticisms and Their Application*, eds. Steven L. McKenzie and Stephen R. Haynes [Louisville, Ky: Westminster John Knox Press, 1993], 171).

56. Rhoads, Dewey, and Michie, *Mark As Story*, 3-4. Though these scholars question the historic reliability of the Gospel of Mark, their method demonstrates the unity and coherence of narrative by emphasizing the unity of the final text. Thus, by understanding the story as a unified whole, the reader is able then to better appreciate its impact.

The author of this work disagrees with the position of Rhoads, Dewey, and Michie regarding their view on the historicity of the Gospel of Mark (see chapter one of this book for the author's view as to the historicity of the Gospel of Mark). See also the discussion by Resseguie, *Narrative Criticism of the New Testament*, 22-23.

57. Stamps, "Rhetorical and Narratological Criticism," 232. David A. DeSil-

DEATH AND DISCIPLESHIP:
An Analysis of the Predictions of Jesus' Death in the Gospel of Mark

Some are cautious about narrative criticism.[58] For example, Stein claims that narrative criticism and its principles are primarily from the study of fictional literature and narrative criticism seems to have too close a connection with reader-response criticism.[59] While appropriate, Powell balances Stein's critique. His contention is that "this movement [narrative criticism] developed within the field of biblical studies without an exact counterpart in the

---

va states, "It invites precisely this attention to the story—the characters, plot and other literary features an author uses to create a story world—and to the effects the text invites and encourages in its readers" (*An Introduction to the New Testament: Contexts, Methods and Ministry Formation* [Downers Grove, Ill: InterVarsity Press, 2004], 395). See also Francis J. Moloney, "Narrative Criticism of the Gospels," in *A Hard Saying: The Gospel and Culture* (Collegeville, Minn: Liturgical Press, 2001), 85-105.

58. Osborne notes seven weaknesses. Though they are not intended to be a rejection of narrative criticism, he lists these weaknesses as a caution against excessive use. The weaknesses are: a dehistoricizing tendency (a denial of any historical element in the text); setting aside the author (the present reader becomes the author of meaning rather than the 'past' author of the text); a denial of intended meaning (present reader becomes the author and produces his own meaning); reductionistic thinking (assuming meaning is only in narrative elements and not also in the exegetical & historical-research); imposition of modern literary categories on ancient genres (derivation of the text's character through modern fiction); preoccupation of obscure theories (use of technical language that is difficult to comprehend); and ignoring the understanding of the early church (not using the earliest of exegetes for information), (*The Hermeneutical Spiral*, 212-16).

59. Robert H. Stein, *Mark*, BEC (Grand Rapids: Baker, 2008), 18-19. Stein also notes that although the Gospel of Mark may read very much like a piece of fictional literature (a drama), he notes that "this is not because it is written in the genre of a Greek tragedy but because it tells the story of the most important person who ever lived—Jesus Christ, the Son of God!" 20.

Reader-response criticism "emphasizes the role of the reader in determining meaning" (Powell, *What Is Narrative Criticism*, 16). It is the reader who becomes the center of authority for interpretation, not the text. See also, Jeffrey A. D. Weima, "Literary Criticism," in *Interpreting the New Testament: Essays on Methods and Issues*, ed. David Alan Black and David S. Dockery (Nashville: Broadman and Holman, 2001), 159-60; Greg Clark, "General Hermeneutics," in *The Face of New Testament Studies: A Survey of Recent Research*, ed. Scot McKnight and Grant R. Osborne (Grand Rapids: Baker, 2004), 114-16; Kevin J. Vanhoozer, *Is There A Meaning in This Text?* (Grand Rapids: Zondervan, 1998), 27-29, 367-68.

secular world."⁶⁰ As a matter of fact, Resseguie notes three strengths to narrative criticism. The first strength focuses on the narrative text as a whole. He writes, "Narrative criticism views the text as a whole. One of the acknowledged strengths of the narrative-critical method is that it avoids the fragmentation of the text associated with forms of historical criticism. . . . Narrative critics are interested in narratives as complete tapestries in which the parts fit together to form an organic whole."⁶¹

The second strength examines the nuances of the narrative as literature. In other words, "the narrative critic attends to the nuances and interrelationships of texts: its structure, rhetorical strategies, character development, arresting imagery, setting, point of view, and symbolism."⁶² The third strength involves the effects of the narrative on the reader. "Since narrative criticism analyzes the narrative point of view, it can describe the text's effects upon a reader. . . . Narrative point of view exists to persuade the reader to see the world in a different way, to adopt a new perspective, or to abandon an old point of view."⁶³

---

60. Powell, *What Is Narrative Criticism*, 19. Stamps also argues that narrative criticism operates "with an underlying assumption that a text in all its parts has an overarching unity, this methodological assumption has been used to counter arguments for compositional incoherence. . . . Narrative criticism has the means for integrating discourse digression and disjunction into the larger discourse purpose," "Rhetorical and Narratological Criticism," 236.

61. Resseguie, *Narrative Criticism of the New Testament*, 38. Jeannine K. Brown sees narrative criticism as a strength for interpreters. She states, "A method for understanding the Gospels that focus on their literary and storied qualities by moving beyond understanding their smaller units (pericopes) to interpreting the entire story at the book level. Narrative criticism interprets a Gospel in its final form rather than in relation to issues of the text's production (e.g., source or form criticism)" (*The Gospels as Stories: A Narrative Approach to Matthew, Mark, Luke, and John* [Grand Rapids: Baker, 2020], 193-93.

62. Ibid., 39.

63. Ibid., 40. Although Resseguie does not speak of a commitment to the historicity of the text as a strength of narrative criticism, the significance behind his strengths is the commitment to the text as a unified whole that avoids fragmenting the text in search of meaning. The strength of narrative criticism is that the meaning of a narrative stems from an understanding of the unity of the elements that constitute the narrative.

Although Stein's critique should not be ignored, one should not lose the emphasis of narrative criticism. It focuses on the final form of the text. The reader analyzes the arrangement of the textual components of narrative, or story, and assesses their effect on the story. It helps to answer *how* the narrative is put together. Narrative criticism also enables the reader to know *what* the authorial intended message is, through an examination of the elements of narrative. Therefore, narrative criticism provides how the interpreter examines what the biblical author says and how he says it. In other words, narrative criticism complements genre criticism. While genre criticism provides the larger framework by which the reader understands the Gospel of Mark, narrative criticism provides particulars (e.g., structure, setting, etc.) that guide the reader through Mark to understand the historical, biographical, and theological components. The methods, genre criticism and narrative criticism, work together within discourse structure because it is the goal of both to seek to understand the text at the level of genre.

Summary of Narrative

Narrative is an arrangement of events (structure) within a given context (setting) that enables the interpreter to treat the text as a whole or unified communicative act. This unified whole (plot), joins together people, animals, and non-human entities (characters) and their perspectives (point-of-view) to tell a story. It is through the study of these elements (narrative criticism) that author, text, and reader come together. Narrative therefore is a literary vehicle that facilitates the reading and hearing of the story itself to interpret and understand the story more fully.

Gospel as a Sub-genre: Theological Narrative Biography

Traditionally scholars have used features or characteristics that are representative of either the structure or content of the text to define the Gospels. The purpose of this section is to propose a definition of a sub-genre category of narrative that may account for the Gospel's unique features. This book proposes that the Gospels are theological narrative biographies.[64]

The preceding discussion clearly states that the Gospel accounts are stories or narratives, communicated through various elements. Robert Fowler states, "The Gospel writers produced neither volumes of learned exegesis nor sermons, rather, they told stories; and if we wish to understand what the Gospels say, we should study how stories are told."[65] Therefore the Gospel accounts ought to be studied as narratives.

The Gospel accounts are narratives. However, they are more than narratives. Though the Gospels share features of the larger category, narrative, they are unique and unlike any other type of narrative, for the unifying focus is the central character, Jesus Christ.[66] Due to this unifying focus they go beyond simply reporting biographical and historical information, they also explain and contain theology.[67] The depiction of Jesus in any one Gospel account is

---

64. The rationale behind classifying the Gospels as a sub-genre; that is, theological narrative biographies, is to capture the different aspects unique to the Gospel accounts. The term *theological* represents the applicational aspect of the narrative for the reader; that is, the Gospels were written and geared to awaken and subsequently strengthen the reader's faith. The term *narrative* represents how the Gospel is structured. The term *biography* represents the life of the central figure of the story, Jesus Christ.

65. Robert M. Fowler, "Using Literary Criticism on the Gospels," *ChrCent* 26 (May 1982): 87-95.

66. Roy B. Zuck writes, "The Gospels are collections of stories, far more packed with action than is customary in narrative. The overriding purpose of the Gospel stories is to explain and praise the person and work of Jesus . . . through his actions, his words, and the responses of other people" (*Basic Bible Interpretation: A Practical Guide to Discovering Biblical Truth* [Colorado Springs, Colo: Victor Books, 1991], 132).

Graham N. Stanton agrees. He writes, "The Gospel writers give both the story [words and works] of Jesus and the significance of his story to their hearers AND readers. . . . Story and theology are intertwined. They tell the 'story' of Jesus in order to address the needs of the Christian communities to which they are writing. . . . The evangelists inform us both about the 'past' story of Jesus of Nazareth and also about the 'present' significance that they attach to Jesus who, they claim, is the Messiah—Christ, the Son of God" (*The Gospels and Jesus*, 2nd ed. [New York: Oxford University Press, 2002], 3-6).

67. There are other types of narrative in the Scripture that do not possess the unique features that the Gospel accounts possess. For example, the book of Acts "nar-

DEATH AND DISCIPLESHIP:
An Analysis of the Predictions of Jesus' Death in the Gospel of Mark

much like that of a portrait. The author, like the artist of a painting, is highly selective in what he includes to communicate his story.[68] The author does this by paraphrasing, explaining, and combining the words and deeds of Jesus in a variety of ways.[69] The Gospels are biographical in that they emphasize Jesus Christ from different evangelists' intended perspectives,[70] all the while communicated as historically accurate.[71]

---

rates the founding events of the church" and does not focus on one unifying character (Carson and Moo, *An Introduction to the New Testament*, 285). Though Acts could be considered as history, it still focuses on communicating events in a given time using characters that formulate a plot.

See also, John B. Polhill, "Interpreting the Book of Acts," in *Interpreting the New Testament: Essays on Methods and Issues* eds. David Alan Black and David S. Dockery [Nashville: Broadman and Holman, 2001], 391-92). Another example of narrative is found in the Old Testament, the Pentateuch. The Pentateuch is narrative communicating historical reporting (Israelite history) and theological interpretation. See, Andrew E. Hill and John H. Walton, *A Survey of the Old Testament*, 3d ed (Grand Rapids: Zondervan, 2009), 59-60. Like that of Acts, the Pentateuch also does not focus on Jesus Christ. Due to the fact that the Scriptures possess other kinds of narrative, the Gospel accounts require a sub-genre.

68. Robert A. Guelich, "The Gospels: Portraits of Jesus and His Ministry," *JETS* 24 (1982): 117-125.

69. Joseph Kudasiewicz states, "From the genesis of the Gospels it follows that they contain in themselves an historical element: the words and deeds of Jesus from Nazareth. But this element was not set forth in the form of naked facts, or as a chronicle or official record but was interpreted theologically. Thus the Gospels are the only synthesis of history and theology of their kind. They contain facts and at the same time interpret their meaning" (*The Synoptic Gospels Today*, trans by Sergius Wroblewski [New York: Alba House, 1996], 52).

70. Ibid, "Not only did the evangelists want to be eyewitnesses of the life of Jesus, but also witnesses to the Good News about salvation. They did not want to write the human history of Jesus but salvation history; they narrated the deeds of Jesus from the viewpoint of salvation" (52-53).

71. Mark L. Strauss offers three ways the Gospel accounts are historical. "They have a history of composition," that is the writers used oral and written sources to assemble their stories. "They are set in a specific historical context. The setting is first-centry Palestine during the period of Roman occupation." The third is that "they are to convey accurate historical information." (*Introducing Jesus: a short guide to the gospels' history and message* [Grand Rapids: Zondervan, 2018], 11-12).

Also typical to the unifying focus of the Gospel accounts, is the arrangement of the Gospel genre; it too is unique. The Gospel accounts do not compare to modern biographies, for each author with varying degree arranges his Gospel topically and chronologically.[72] The Gospel accounts also do not necessarily compare to biographies of the Hellenistic sense known as βίοι.[73] The Gospels however do possess some similar features as those of Greco-Roman biography.[74] Although the Gospels are similar in some respects to ancient biographical writings, they form a distinct group within the broad group of ancient narrative. Due to the content of the Gospels, Arp proposes that the "Gospels may be a unique type of Christian writing, not explainable to any other type of literature in the ancient world."[75] If indeed the Gospels

---

72. Biography is defined as "the histories of individual lives; an account of a person's life; life story" (Victoria Neufeldt, ed., *Webster's New World College Dictionary*, 3d ed. [New York: Macmillan, 1997], 140).

Ryken contends that the Gospels are not typical modern biographies because they are "too episodic and fragmented, too self-contained in their individual parts, and too thoroughly a hybrid form with interspersed nonnarrative elements. The Gospels are an encyclopedic or mixed form" (*How to Read the Bible As Literarture*, 132).

73. Ancient (Greco-Roman) biography is defined as βίοι; that is, simply 'lives.' Cf. Burridge, *What Are the Gospels?*; Charles H. Talbert, *What Is a Gospel? The Genre of the Canonical Gospels* (Philadelphia: Fortress, 1984); David E. Aune, *The New Testament in Its Literary Environment*, 17-76.

74. "Greco-Roman biography was a powerful propaganda tool which often had a teaching or didactic function, presenting the subject as a paradigm of virtue. . . . Greco-Roman biography is prose narration about a person's life, presenting supposedly historical facts which are selected to reveal the character or essence of the person often with the purpose of affecting the behavior of the reader," (William Arp, Course notes for NT8, Seminar in Gospel Studies, Baptist Bible Seminary, Clarks Summit, Pa, fall 2005, 2).

The Gospels possess similar features as those of the Greco-Roman βίοι. There is a high degree of correlation between the generic features of the Greco-Roman βιοι and the opening, external, and internal features of the canonical Gospels demonstrating that they are the work of narratives with a chronological structure that is narrowly focused on the works and words of Jesus Christ. See Burridge, *What Are the Gospels*, 133-53, 160-90, with the connection to the canonical Gospels 193-219.

75. Arp, Course notes for NT8, 3. They possess a form and function that makes them unique. "Formally, a Gospel is a narrative account about the public life and teach-

are unique, is there still a way to classify them using genre? In other words, what are the characteristics of a Gospel that lead to a definition? This book proposes a definition of the Gospels as a sub-genre, a theological narrative biography. Also, what are the contents and the function of the Gospel?

Characteristics of Gospel

There are two characteristics of a Gospel that lead to the proposed definition. These characteristics highlight the Gospel as a sub-genre of narrative. They are biography and theology. These characteristics can lead to difficulty in establishing a definition, for often an emphasis is placed on one characteristic as opposed to the other rather than an incorporation of all or some of the more prominent characteristics. A brief, though not exhaustive, look at the characteristics that pertain to a definition of Gospel is illustrated here. The proposed definition that incorporates the major characteristics from the various definitions surveyed is a theological narrative biography.

Gospels are Biographical

The most common way to characterize a Gospel is biography. The biography typifies the words and deeds of a character. The evangelists arranged the life of Jesus through chronology or topics to address the specific needs of the community to whom they were writing.[76] Therefore, many scholars look at the life of the character to characterize, and thus define, a Gospel because of the dominating presence of a unifying focus through the central figure, Jesus Christ.[77]

---

ing of Jesus which is composed of discrete tradition units which the writer placed in the context of Scriptures." This keeps the Gospels at the biography-level. "Functionally, a Gospel consists of the message that God was at work in Jesus' life, death, and resurrection affecting the promises found in the Scriptures." This makes them unique and unlike any other biography. (Arp, Course notes for NT8, 3).

76. DeSilva, *An Introduction to the New Testament*, 148.

77. Larry W. Hurtado contends that Jesus is one of the formal features of the Gospel accounts. "The Gospels are all narratives about Jesus that include examples of his deeds and sayings in a loose chronological framework that concentrates on the period between the beginning of his ministry and his death/resurrection" ("Gospel

The Gospels also portray continuous narratives of Jesus that represent the biographical nature of the genres of Greco-Roman literature, for they too promoted the life story of a hero. There is, therefore, similarity in this between the Gospel accounts and Greco-Roman biographical genres. The difference lies in the story's emphasis. The Greco-Roman biography was written in such a way to glorify virtues of the main character; whereas the evangelists, though they too focus on the person and character of Jesus, the emphasis is on Jesus' significance in relationship to his divine, appointed purpose, and the relationship of Jesus to those who follow him.

The Gospel, characterized as biography, was attested by scholars throughout the past century. In 1915 Clyde Votaw for example compared the Gospels to ancient biography.[78] Votaw's description of a Gospel promotes Christian movement and can be called the 'biographies of Jesus.' His definition of biography is called a popular biography; that is, a biography that "aims to make one acquainted with a historical person by giving some account of his deeds and words, sketchily chosen and arranged, even when the motive of the writer is practical and hortatory rather than historical."[79] Though Votaw commenced the way for an understanding of the Gospel accounts as popular biography, the early consensus among New Testament scholars followed more closely the form-critical method reflected by Karl L. Schmidt.[80] His view claimed that the Gospels were basically collections of the Jesus traditions. The motivation for the Gospel accounts was not literary, but kerygmatic, the proclamation of the significance of Jesus.

In more recent developments, three scholars have made attempts to determine the genre of the Gospels. They all have come to the consensus that the Gospels are to be characterized as biography. In 1977 Charles Talbert re-examined the genre of the Gospels.[81] He concluded that all the Gospel accounts

---

(Genre)," in *Dictionary of Jesus and the Gospels*, ed. Joel B. Green, Scot McKnight, I. Howard Marshall [Downers Grove, Ill: InterVarsity Press, 1992], 278).

78. Clyde Weber Votaw, *The Gospels and Contemporary Biographies in the Greco-Roman World* (Philadelphia: Fortress, 1970).

79. Ibid., 5.

80. Hurtado, "Gospel (Genre)," 277.

81. Charles H. Talbert, *Literary Patterns, Theological Themes and the Genres of Luke-Acts* (SBLMS, 20; Missoula, Mont: Scholars Press, 1974) and most notably

were written in terms of myth rather than history. He also declared that all Gospels were didactic biographies; that is, practical and hortatory rather than historical. Aune, however argued for a definition of biography that indeed spoke to its historical character. He wrote, "Biography may be defined as a discrete prose narrative devoted exclusively to the portrayal of the whole life of a particular individual perceived as historical."[82]

In 1982 Philip Shuler also attempted to situate the Gospels in the Greco-Roman biography environment.[83] He defined the Gospels by using a subtype of biography called the encomium or laudatory biography. This is described as a biography told for the specific purpose of praising the central character.[84]

The third scholar to define the Gospel genre was Richard Burridge in 1992.[85] He used genre criticism and literary theory as his starting point and agreed that genre ought to be used as an instrument for meaning. He understood genre as a group of literary works that shared family resemblances that ultimately functioned to guide interpretation. The text therefore possesses both external and internal features.[86] It is these generic features that Burridge used to demonstrate the similarities between the Gospel accounts and their counterparts, the Greco-Roman biographies; thus, defining the Gospels as βίοι, or "lives."[87]

It is unlikely that the Gospel writers used a specific Hellenistic or Roman biographical template in constructing the Gospels. However, it is clear that they recount the life of a character, Jesus Christ. They are portraits of which communicate certain words and deeds of Jesus Christ and it is through these

---

What Is a Gospel? The Genre of the Canonical Gospels.

82. Aune, *The New Testament in Its Literary Environment*, 29.

83. Philip L. Shuler, *A Genre for the Gospels: The Biographical Character of Matthew* (Philadelphia: Fortress, 1982).

84. Ibid., 37.

85. Burridge, *What are the Gospels?*

86. Ibid., 42. These genre features include opening features (e.g. title, opening words), subject, external features (e.g. size or length, structure or sequence, use of literary units), and internal features (e.g. the content of the work, style, tone, mood, occasion for writing) 111.

87. Ibid., 63.

portraits that readers see the authors' intention and purpose. The Gospels therefore are biographies.

Gospels are Theological

The Gospels have not always been characterized, nor defined using a connection with literary features. In the early twentieth century, two German scholars, using the form-critical method, characterized the Gospels as a development of kerygma; a totally unique genre in the ancient world.[88] Martin Dibelius and Rudolf Bultmann argued that the final form of the Gospels emerged from a process of oral tradition. It was the oral tradition based on the community of the early Church that served as the means for the evangelists' kerygma and therefore served to characterize the Gospel accounts, not the genre of narrative. This kerygma "always emphasized the death and resurrection of Jesus, included proofs from the Old Testament, and referred to Jesus' exaltation to the right hand of God and imminent return to save and to judge, concluding with a call for repentance and faith. Through evangelistic preaching and catechetical instruction, according to this view, the basic kerygma was expanded, illustrated, and commented upon by the addition of stories and sayings of Jesus."[89] The Gospels therefore were neither historical nor literary; but rather they were dogmatic and cultic. The understanding was that the Gospels were "expanded cult legends in which the Hellenistic mythological interpretation of Christ has been

---

88. Martin Dibelius, *Die Formgeschichte des Evangeliums* (Tübingen: Mohr Siebeck, 1919) and Rudolf Bultmann, *The History of the Synoptic Tradition* (New York: Harper & Row, 1963). Kerygma refers to the gospel proclamation; especially as taught in the Gospels.

89. Aune, *The New Testament in Its Literary Environment*, 24. Robert Guelich reports Dibeius' clarity regarding the composition of the Gospels. He writes, "The Gospels represent simply the final phase in the evolution of the early Christian tradition with the primitive Church's kerygma at its core. The final product, the Gospels, and the process itself were influenced especially for Dibelius by three factors: The primitive communities' eschatology, the Church's mission, and the kerygma of Jesus' death and resurrection" ("The Gospel Genre," in *The Gospel and the Gospels*, ed. Peter Stuhlmacher [Grand Rapids: Eerdmans, 1991], 186).

superimposed on the story of Jesus."[90] The problem with this view, however, is that it placed too much emphasis on the early Church community and not enough emphasis on the biblical writer. The idea of the Gospels as biographies has not been abandoned and the discussion has been re-opened. The kerygmatic hypothesis is no longer dominating the discussion.[91]

The Gospels were constructed using related episodes to not just capture the importance of the life of Jesus Christ, but also with a wider importance, the reader. The authorial intent, in which each of the Gospels selectively portrayed Jesus Christ through his words and deeds, was the means by which the evangelists developed the salvation-history meaning of Christ's messianic mission on behalf of the characters in the story and the reader. This theology that runs throughout the Gospel accounts is centered on the biographical and historical setting of the Son of God, Jesus Christ.[92] The Gospels, therefore, are theological.

Gospels are Theological Narrative Biographies

It is difficult to consider a definition of Gospel through the use or emphasis of one characteristic, either biography or theology, or even history. Since a single characteristic potentially leads to an incomplete picture of a definition of the Gospel as a sub-genre, it is best to incorporate all the characteristics. This book therefore proposes a definition that incorporates biography and theology. The proposed definition also incorporates the genre, of

---

90. Robert H. Gundry, "Literary Genre 'Gospel'," in *New Dimensions in New Testament Study*, ed. Richard N. Longenecker and Merrill C. Tenney (Grand Rapids: Zondervan, 1974), 99.

91. Helmut Koester, "From the Kerygma-Gospel to Written Gospels," *NTS* 35 (1989): 361-81.

92. Kudasiewicz writes, "They did not want to provide a range of information to be remembered but to preach the Good News of salvation to all. The proclamation of the kerygma brought this about, that the evangelists composed works out of authentic history, but their central point of interest was not historical nor biographical but religious and theological. The evangelists did not want to write a life of Jesus but to show that he was the Messiah, the Son of God and the Savior" (*The Synoptic Gospels Today*, 56).

which it is a part; that is, narrative. The sub-genre of the Gospels is theological narrative biography.[93]

The theological narrative biography is defined as a sub-genre of narrative that encompasses the Gospel accounts. The Gospels are theological narrative biographies that are told as stories, or narratives, that catalogue episodes centered around one unifying character, Jesus Christ, and these episodes are written in such a way that they serve to awaken and subsequently strengthen the faith of the reader, Christ's followers.

As demonstrated earlier in this chapter, the Gospel accounts fit into the larger generic category of narrative. They do so based upon the possession of the common elements of narrative, for both the Gospel accounts and narratives have structure, plot, setting, characters, and point-of-view. The Gospel accounts however are a unique sub-genre. They possess more than a biographical characteristic. They also have a theological purpose. A description of the proposed sub-genre of narrative, the theological narrative biography, follows.

First, the Gospels are constructed as stories. The literary medium, by which the Gospels are communicated, is narrative. They are constructed through unified communicative acts known as episodes or events. Theological narrative biography accounts for the literary medium, or *how* the author's intended message is communicated. The author is selective and purposeful in each episode regarding those aspects of Jesus' life that help to communicate his message to his intended audience. The organization of episodes contrib-

---

93. Strauss classifies Gospels as historical narrative motivated by theological concerns. He contends that the biblical author's intention is historical accuracy, biographical information about Jesus, and calling people to follow Jesus (*Introducing Jesus*, 13). There is not much difference to Strauss' position the proposal in this book. See also, Mark L. Strauss, *Four Portraits, One Jesus: A Survey of Jesus and the Gospels*, 2d ed (Grand Rapids: Zondervan, 2020), 33-38.

Jonathan T. Pennington has a similar understanding to Strauss, and therefore this book. He offers a fuller classification of Gospels. He states, "Our canonical Gospels are theological, historical, and aretological (virtue-forming) biographical narratives that retell the story and proclaim the significance of Jesus Christ, who through the power of the Spirit is the Restorer of God's reign" (*Reading the Gospels Wisely: A Narrative and Theological Introduction* [Grand Rapids: Baker, 2012], 35).

utes to the whole and does so through narrative. Therefore, the proposed definition incorporates *narrative* in its sub-genre category.

Second, the Gospels are illustrations of the public life, teachings, miracles, death, and resurrection of a unifying figure; the biography of Jesus Christ as it is set in a historical context. The historical context and the sayings and stories of Jesus are true, though they may not contain all the details of any one episode. Therefore, the proposed definition incorporates *biography* in its sub-genre category.

Third, the Gospels have a theological purpose. The Gospels are not written to simply chronicle biographical information within a historical context. Rather their purpose is for the reader to learn who Jesus is and how-to live-in light of knowing Him.[94] The Gospels are history and theology intertwined. They were written to awaken faith. They were disciplinal; that is, geared to be disciple oriented. Constantine R. Campbell and Jonathan T. Pennington state,

> Simply, the Gospels are not disinterested history but rather have a clear theological goal and a formative purpose. The Gospels are not the mere history that other apostles build on to teach theology in the rest of the New Testament. They *are* historical, and the apostles do reflect on the Jesus traditions for their theological and moral teachings, but the Gospels themselves are also theological documents with the specific goal of inviting people to become disciples of Jesus . . . they are preaching, teaching, and calling people to follow Jesus. . . . This is what the canonical Gospels are: the central stories about Jesus that tell what happened and why it matters, all with a call to become followers of the Jesus whom they are describing, creating a community around devotion and allegiance to him.[95]

---

94. Hans F. Bayer states, "The selections are cast in the genre of an ancient biographical account (bios), all of which is to shape and influence the readers/hearers in a significant way. Their lives are to be profoundly transformed by what they hear and read" (*A Theology of Mark: The Dynamic between Christology and Authentic Discipleship*, Explorations in Biblical Theology series ed. Robert A. Peterson [Phillipsburg, NJ: P&R Publishing, 2012], 18).

95. Constantine R. Campbell and Jonathan T. Pennington, *Reading the New Testament as Christian Scripture: A Literary, Canonical, and Theological Survey*

Therefore, the proposed definition incorporates *theological* in its sub-genre category.[96]

Summary of the Definition of Gospel

A sub-genre that aims to account for all the characteristics common within the Gospels as they are communicated through their literary genre, the narrative, are biography and theology. The proposed sub-genre definition, theological narrative biography, aims to account for the purposeful intention of the biblical author. This purposeful intention is the theology the biblical author seeks to communicate through his story. It is not the intent to complicate matters by introducing new terminology; but rather to propose a sub-genre category that explicates the true nature of the Gospel accounts found within Scripture.

Content of Gospel

The Gospels are centered on one primary, formal feature: Jesus Christ. They are narratives explicating the words and deeds of Jesus as told by the evangelists who wrote about him. The general focus of these accounts is from the beginning of Jesus' ministry to his death and resurrection. These stories include various instruments used by the authors to depict their Gospel accounts.

First, the authors use the interaction between Jesus and various characters, including nature. The disciples are among one of the major characters whom the biblical authors emphasize. It is the communication and reaction of these characters that highlights Jesus' revelatory identity and supernatural power. Second, the authors also use charges that are brought against Jesus to confirm his identity. It is often the goal of the antagonist (e.g., Pharisees and Scribes) to disprove, discredit, or contradict the claims of Jesus' identity.

(Grand Rapids: Baker, 2020), 72. See also Jonathan T. Pennington, *Reading the Gospels Wisely*, 3-35.

96. See also David E. Garland, *A Theology of Mark's Gospel: Good News About the Messiah, the Son of God*, Biblical Theology of the New Testament, gen. ed. Andreas J. Köstenberger (Grand Rapids: Zondervan, 2015), 85-89.

Third, the authors also use literary motifs to delineate Jesus' identity. These literary motifs include miracle stories, sayings, and parables. Although the primary goal of all these motifs is not necessarily to reveal Jesus' character, they "are literary vehicles that legitimate the presentation of Jesus as Messiah, or Son of God."[97] It is through the sayings and parables of Jesus that one finds real-life connections to the disciple-oriented life; a true follower of Jesus. The Gospels are therefore "dominated by attempts to demonstrate and confirm the supreme significance of the identity of Jesus conceptualized in terms of various types of eschatological deliverers."[98]

Function of Gospel

The Gospels are narratives that function to convince the reader/hearer that Jesus Christ is the Son of God.[99] They also function within a historical and cultural milieu in which the biblical authors used situations and circumstances of everyday community life to portray Jesus as the Son of God. The evangelists wrote with historical and theological premises. They function in various ways to portray Jesus' identity. They are biographical (they highlight Jesus as the hero), historical (they are truth, history about the hero), partial (they record who the hero says he is), purposeful (they are to spiritually grow the reader, not just chronicle events), and disciplinal (they are geared to be disciple-oriented). Simply put, the Gospels are Christian literary works to awaken and subsequently strengthen the faith of its readers.

Summary of Gospel

The Gospel accounts are narrative stories with Jesus Christ as the unifying focus. These Gospels report biographical and historical information, while also explaining the theological significance for the reader. They are arranged top-

---

97. Aune, *The New Testament in Its Literary Environment*, 57.

98. Ibid., 55.

99. Ronald F. Thiemann states the purpose for the Gospel accounts; that is, to draw the reader into the story so that he/she may respond to the unfolding of Jesus' identity. ("Radiance and Obscurity in Biblical Narrative," in *Scriptural Authority and Narrative Interpretation*, ed. Garrett Green [Philadelphia: Fortress Press, 1987], 33).

ically and chronologically with similarities to that of ancient Greco-Roman βίοι. The Gospels were written to facilitate the reading and hearing of the life and identity of Jesus Christ with the purposeful intention and responsibility of awakening one's faith as a Christ follower.

Conclusion

The New Testament is a collection of various kinds of writings. These various kinds of writings are called literary genres. Literary genres provide a basic framework for the interpreter, and it is through literary genre that the biblical author shapes his text. In other words, literary genre helps a reader not only grasp the content of the text but also the way in which the author chooses to communicate it. When various kinds of writings are examined, a sub-discipline of New Testament studies, genre criticism, is used. Genre criticism discovers the situational circumstances and unique features of the text; thus, identifying the text as one kind of genre as opposed to another.

Genre criticism is a function of discourse structure. Like discourse structure, genre criticism also examines the text in its final form. Discourse structure is the component of discourse analysis that examines the text (see chapter two). As a result of the examination of the text, the two generic categories that best represent the Gospels emerge. They are: narrative (genre) and theological narrative biography (sub-genre). These two categories assume the interpreter looks at the text holistically.

Narrative is a communicative act written within a given setting, using characters to convey a plot through a point-of-view that the author typically composes in sequential order. Simply put, narrative is a story. The reader examines the narrative. He does so utilizing yet another sub-discipline of New Testament studies; that is, narrative criticism. Narrative criticism assists the reader in the exegetical task by accounting for the elements of narrative and demonstrating their relationship to the whole. Narrative criticism therefore focuses upon the coherence of the text and its final form. In other words, narrative criticism provides the reader with how he can examine what the biblical author says and how he says it.

DEATH AND DISCIPLESHIP:
An Analysis of the Predictions of Jesus' Death in the Gospel of Mark

Although narrative is the generic literary medium by which one examines the Gospel accounts, the Gospels are more than narrative. They are unique and unlike any other type of narrative, for they report biographical, historical, and theological information regarding a central character, Jesus Christ. Due to their unique nature, the Gospels fit into a sub-genre of narrative. The Gospel accounts therefore are theological narrative biographies.

The theological narrative biography accounts for the following: the literary medium in which the Gospels were written (narrative), the life of Jesus Christ as the central unifying character (biography), and the application to the life of the reader (theology). The intended purpose of the Gospel accounts is to identify Jesus Christ as the Son of God and to urge the responsibility as followers of Christ to awaken and subsequently strengthen their faith. The following chapter demonstrates how the Gospel of Mark is a theological narrative biography.

Chapter Four

Studying the Gospel of Mark as Literature

Introduction

The focus of the preceding chapter was the classification of the Gospel accounts as genre (narrative) and sub-genre (theological narrative biography). The sub-genre is necessary since the Gospels are unique and unlike any other narrative. The examination of genre and sub-genre explicates the basic framework or macro-structure of the Gospels. This explication of a macro-structure is discourse structure, a component of discourse analysis.

This chapter likewise incorporates discourse structure. However, whereas the discussion of discourse structure was related to all Gospel accounts in the preceding chapter, this chapter is limited to the Gospel of Mark. A study of the elements of the narrative of Mark's Gospel will demonstrate that it is a story comprised of episodes. These brief episodes are structured through three geographic locations (Galilee, "on the way" to Jerusalem, and Jerusalem) and are communicated through the expressions and responses of various characters or groups treated as characters (religious & governmental authorities, disciples, and crowd) as they interact with Jesus Christ and his teachings, miracles, death, and resurrection.

DEATH AND DISCIPLESHIP:
An Analysis of the Predictions of Jesus' Death in the Gospel of Mark

Mark's story contains a theological emphasis. It is more than biography and history. The theological emphasis is the unique feature of the Gospel accounts that serves as the basis for its sub-genre category, theological narrative biography. Mark's story emphasizes two aspects. He declares, defines, and affirms the identity of Jesus Christ as the Son of God throughout his story. This is the formal aspect. Mark also emphasizes the responsibility of the disciples thus providing the significance and application of Jesus' identity to the reader. This is the functional aspect. In other words, Mark identifies who Jesus is and knowing this, what Jesus' disciples are to do.

LITERARY GENRE: THE GOSPEL OF MARK AS NARRATIVE

Mark developed and composed his story through a narrative comprised of brief episodes structured together, communicated in and around Galilee and Jerusalem during Rome's military control over Israel. Mark is concerned with the life of Jesus and his disciples, Roman and Jewish governments, as well as other followers. Mark's narrative is put forward as a story that essentially conveys an account of the good news about Jesus Christ (cf. Mk 1:1).[1] Stein states that Mark is "the biography of Jesus interwoven in a historical narrative."[2] The Gospel of Mark is a narration of the life of Jesus as the Son of God told as a story through various historical accounts within the life of Jesus. Achtemeier states, "We must look at it [the Gospel of Mark] as a totality and

---

1. Robert A. Guelich, *Mark 1-8:26*, WBC 34a (Nashville: Thomas Nelson, 1989), xxi. He also contends that Mark's use of 'gospel' in the prologue of his story offers a logical designation for similar writings; that is, 'The Gospel according to . . . .'

2. Robert H. Stein, *Mark*, BEC (Grand Rapids: Baker, 2008), 21. Contra Robert H. Gundry. He concludes that the Gospel of Mark is a "loose disposition of materials," or "a collage, not a diptych or a triptych or any other carefully segmented portrayal of Jesus" (*Mark: A Commentary on His Apology for the Cross* [Grand Rapids: Eerdmans, 1993], 1048-49).

allow it to tell its own story.... We must respect the narrative as it stands and follow its invitation to enter into the narrative world it creates."[3]

A broad look at the elements of narrative throughout the Gospel of Mark demonstrates the coherence and unification of the whole text, thus validating the classification of the Gospel accounts as narrative. This analysis will assist with an understanding of the arrangement of the components typical to a narrative (*how* the story is told) and the argument of the narrative (*what* is the content of the story). This facilitates a means to study Mark.

The Gospel of Mark: Structure and Plot

To understand Mark as narrative, one must identify the structure and plot of the Gospel. Tannehill however, remarks that "outlining narratives is not a neat endeavor."[4] This may explain why there are numerous proposals for Mark's narrative structure among commentators who treat Mark as a story. After summarizing and evaluating various proposals, a proposal is offered. It is a synthesis of the various proposals, thus providing an eclectic approach to the analysis of the structure of Mark.[5]

---

3. Paul J. Achtemeier, *Mark*, Proclamation Commentaries 2d ed, rev and exp (Philadelphia: Fortress, 1986), 42.

4. Robert C. Tannehill, "The Disciples in Mark: The Function of a Narrative Role," in *The Interpretation of Mark*, ed. W. Telford (Studies in New Testament Interpretation, Edinburgh: T & T Clark, 1985), 170.

5. The proposals discussed here do not include all possible analyses of Mark. The scholars discussed are those who consistently evaluate the Gospel of Mark based on narrative or story. Although this book discusses Mark as narrative or story, some commentaries have not followed an analysis of Mark as narrative or story and therefore have structured Mark based on a topical outline, or verse-by-verse outline. These commentaries include (though not exhaustive): Karen A. Barta, *The Gospel of Mark* (Wilmington, Del: Glazier, 1988); Edwin K. Broadhead, *Mark* (Sheffield, England: Sheffield Academic Press, 2001); R. Alan Cole, *Mark*, Tyndale New Testament Commentaries, rev ed (Grand Rapids: Eerdmans, 1989); Adela Yarbro Collins, *Mark*, Hermeneia: A Critical and Historical Commentary on the Bible (Minneapolis, Minn: Fortress, 2007); David E. Garland, *Mark*, NIV Application Commentary (Grand Rapids: Zondervan, 1996); Robert H. Gundry, *Mark: A Commentary on His Apology for the Cross*; Douglas R. A. Hare, *Mark* (Louisville, Ky: Westminster John Knox, 1996); Mary Healy, *The*

DEATH AND DISCIPLESHIP:
An Analysis of the Predictions of Jesus' Death in the Gospel of Mark

Various Proposals for the Structure of Mark[6]

Among the various proposals regarding Mark's narrative structure, some of them conclude that Mark's structure is a three-fold division. The means by which the structure of Mark is communicated is through theology, geography, or theme. For example, Robert Tannehill focuses on theology; that is, the commissioning of Jesus Christ and his various roles as the Son of God. He understands the structure of Mark through a three-fold division: the commissioning of Jesus and his ministry (1:1-8:26), the commissioning of Jesus and his teaching of the disciples (8:27-10:52), and the commissioning of Jesus to his death (11:1-16:8).[7] He concludes that Mark's goal was to present Jesus Christ as the Son of God. He concludes that Jesus is the central figure throughout the Gospel by which the Gospel's full effect is felt. Tannehill's proposal illustrates the plot of the story of Mark through a Christological emphasis.[8]

Gospel of Mark (Grand Rapids: Baker, 2008); Morna D. Hooker, *The Gospel According to Saint Mark*, Black's New Testament Commentaries 2 (Peabody, Mass: Hendrickson, 1991); Sherman E. Johnson, *A Commentary on the Gospel According to St. Mark*, Harper's New Testament Commentary 2 (Peabody, Mass: Hendrickson, 1972); Ronald J. Kernaghan, *Mark*, IVP New Testament Commentary 2 (Downers Grove, Ill: InterVarsity Press, 2007); John J. Kilgallen, *A Brief Commentary on the Gospel of Mark* (New York: Paulist, 1989); William L. Lane, *The Gospel of Mark*, NICNT (Grand Rapids: Eerdmans, 1974); and Joel Marcus, *Mark 1-8*, The Anchor Bible Series 27 (New York: Doubleday, 2002); George Martin, *The Gospel According to Mark: Meaning and Message* (Chicago: Loyola Press, 2005); Thomas C. Oden and Christopher A. Hall, *Mark*, Ancient Christian Commentary on Scripture: New Testament 2 (Downers Grove, Ill: InterVarsity Press, 1998); Cyril S. Rodd, *The Gospel of Mark*, Epworth Commentaries (Peterborough, UK: Epworth Press, 2005); Robert H. Stein, *Mark*; Dennis Sweetland, *Mark: From Death to Life* (Hyde Park, N.Y.: New City Press, 2007); Vincent Taylor, *The Gospel According to St. Mark* (London: Macmillan, 1957).

6. For a brief and helpful summary of the current proposals, see Mark L. Strauss, *Mark: An Exegetical Commentary on the New Testament* (Grand Rapids: Zondervan, 2014), 44-45.

7. Robert C. Tannehill, "The Gospel of Mark as Narrative Christology," *Semeia* 16 (1979): 57-95.

8. Ibid., 60. See also Robert L. Humphrey, *Narrative Structure and Message in Mark: A Rhetorical Analysis*, Studies in the Bible and Early Christianity 60 (Lewiston: Edwin Mellen Press, 2003), 4-6. Humphrey illustrates the plot of the story

On the other hand, R. T. France organizes the structure of Mark through three geographical locations.⁹ He discerns Mark's structure, whether it was intentional by Mark or not, as a drama in three acts. The plot then is the culmination of Jesus' ministry in a single climactic act based in and around three locations: Galilee (1:14-8:21), road to Jerusalem (8:22-10:52), and in Jerusalem itself (11:1-16:8).

James Brooks also analyzes Mark's structure through three divisions yet focuses on one theme.¹⁰ This theme is the 'good news about Jesus Christ' in

---

through what he calls three 'key narrative moments.' It is these three narrative moments that punctuate and reiterate the author's plot: the affirmation of Jesus as God's Son. These moments are: the announcement of John the Baptist that Jesus is greater than he (1:2-13); the testimony of Peter that Jesus is the Christ (8:27-9:13); and the witness of Jesus himself as the Messiah (14:1-16:8). Humphrey's proposal illustrates that plot of the story of Mark, as it is told through the theological lens of various characters. These characters depict Jesus' identity.

See also the theological approach by Vernon K. Robbins (*The Composition of Mark's Gospel: Selected Studies from Novum Testamentum*, Brill's Readers in Biblical Studies 3 [Leiden: Brill, 1999], 103-20. Robbins' approach relates to three literary units consisting of three parts. In these parts, Jesus and his disciples travel, Jesus interacts, and then Jesus summons or sends his disciples, 119. His divisions are 1:14-3:6; 3:7-5:43; 6:1-8:26; 8:27-10:45; 10:46-12:44; 13:1-15:47.

9. R. T. France, *The Gospel of Mark*, NIGTC (Grand Rapids: Eerdmans, 2002), 11-20. Benjamin L. Gladd contends that "Mark's narrative progresses geographically from Jesus's baptism in the Jordan to his ministry in Galilee and then on to Jerusalem" (*Handbook on the Gospels: Matthew, Mark, Luke, John* [Grand Rapids: Baker, 2021], 106-09).

See also Bas M. F. Van Iersel, *Reading Mark*, trans. W. H. Bisscheroux (Edinburgh: T. & T. Clark, 1989), 19-26. He sees Mark's structure through a chiastic arrangement of the geographical locations with two hinge passages (1:14-15 & 15:40-41) connecting the outer with the inner parts of the story.

10. James A. Brooks, *Mark*, NAC 23 (Nashville: Broadman and Holman, 1991), 32-35. There are two other examples that conclude theme as the basis for Mark's narrative structure. They are: Ernest Best, *Mark: The Gospel as Story* (Edinburgh: T. & T. Clark, 1983); and David Rhoads, Joanna Dewey, and Donald Michie, *Mark As Story: An Introduction to the Narrative of a Gospel*, 2d ed. (Minneapolis, Minn: Fortress Press, 1999). The theme used by Best and Rhoads, et al. is centered on the opposition toward Jesus and lack of popularity among authorities. Best captures the structure of the plot using a three-fold division; that is, works, teachings and miracles of Jesus

DEATH AND DISCIPLESHIP:
An Analysis of the Predictions of Jesus' Death in the Gospel of Mark

Mark 1:1. Brooks' organization, therefore, is as follows: the good news about Jesus' proclamation of the kingdom of God (1:14-8:21), the good news about Jesus' teaching on discipleship (8:22-10:52), and the good news about Jesus' death (11:1-15:47).

The preceding analyses of Mark's narrative structure capture the story through differing means; that is, theology, geography, or theme. Though each of these analyses has differing chapter and verse divisions within the structure, they each identify a three-fold structure to Mark's narrative.

Others analyze the structure of Mark and conclude it best to divide the Gospel into two major sections. Scholars state that Mark's structure is communicated through an introduction and two parts. They are the Gospel's opening statement (1:1), geography, and Christological emphases. For example, Robert Guelich divides Mark into two halves (1:16-8:26 and 8:27-16:8); with the first fifteen verses serving as a prologue. He notes that "the plot of Mark's Gospel is given to the reader in the heading of 1:1. It revolves around the 'gospel' or 'good news' concerning 'Jesus Messiah,' Son of God."[11] With Jesus as the central figure throughout the story, thus demonstrating that 1:1 serves as a title depicting the contents of the whole narrative; Guelich states that the first half of the Gospel depicts Jesus' public ministry (1:16-8:26); whereas the second half focuses on Jesus' death (8:27-16:8). In other words, Mark's whole story, which is composed of two halves, relate to the fact that Jesus is the Son of God (1:1).

(1:16-8:26), journey 'on the way' to Jerusalem (8:27-10:52), and the death of Jesus (11:1-16:8), (p. 128).

    Rhoads, Dewey, and Michie also capture the narrative in a three-fold fashion, though they do not provide the chapter and verse divisions of Mark. Their plot involves Jesus in conflict with demons, illness, and nature, Jesus in conflict with the authorities, and Jesus in conflict with the disciples, (p. 77). See also Gilbert G. Bilezikian who understands Mark as a well-arranged dramatic narrative that has analogies to that of ancient tragedy (*The Liberated Gospel: A Comparison of the Gospel of Mark and Greek Tragedy* [Grand Rapids: Baker, 1977]).

    11. Robert A. Guelich, *Mark 1-8:26*, xxiv. See also Guelich, "Mark, Gospel of," 515-16. Strauss similarly divides the Mark using both a prologue (1:1-13) and an epilogue (16:1-8) with the rest of Mark divided in two halves: The Authority of the Messiah (1:14-8:21) and The Way of Suffering of the Messiah (8:22-15:47), (*Mark: Exegetical Commentary on the New Testament*, 45).

James Edwards also divides the Gospel of Mark into two sections (1:1-8:26 and 8:27-16:8) but does so based on the two major geographical locations; that is, Jesus' ministry in Galilee (1:1-8:26) and Jesus' 'way to' Jerusalem (8:27-16:8).[12] Eugene Boring also structures the Gospel of Mark based on geography. However, he believes Galilee and Jerusalem has symbolized theological overtones.[13] These two locations correspond to Mark's Christology. In part one (1:1-8:21), the author declares Jesus to be the Son of God and illustrates this through the many words and deeds of Jesus. The problem encountered in this part of the story is that no human character recognizes his identity. In part two (8:22-16:8), Jesus reveals his own identity as the Son of Man who will suffer, die, and be raised the third day.

Craig Blomberg, like that of Boring, also claims the Gospel of Mark falls into two main sections (1:14-8:30 and 8:31-16:8).[14] Though Blomberg's divi-

---

12. James R. Edwards, *The Gospel According to Mark*, The PNTC (Grand Rapids: Eerdmans, 2002), 20-21. See also Mary Ann Tolbert. She argues for a two-part division based on geography: part one consists of the first ten chapters in and around Galilee and part two comprises chapters eleven through sixteen, which take place in and around Jerusalem (*Sowing the Gospel: Marks' World in Literary-Historical Perspective* [Minneapolis, Minn: Fortress, 1989], 113-14).

Yet another example is that of C. S. Mann. He organizes the Gospel of Mark into two sections. But the sections demonstrate a reliance on inverted parallelism, or chiasm rather than a connection with the opening statement or geography (*Mark*, The Anchor Bible Series [New York: Doubleday, 1986]).

13. Eugene M. Boring, *Mark: A Commentary* (Louisville, Ky: Westminster John Knox, 2006). He demonstrates Mark's theological significance by stating "Part one begins with Jesus' call of the disciples to become 'fishermen who fish for people' (1:16-20) and concludes with Jesus' challenge to them, 'Do you not yet understand?' (8:21). Part two begins with Jesus' welcome by the crowds in Jerusalem, who finally join those who crucify Jesus, and concludes with the postresurrection command to return to Galilee to follow Jesus, who 'goes before' them. The two parts are joined by the important transitional section 8:22-10:52, which both separates and joins part one and part two by representing the 'way' of Jesus from Galilee to Jerusalem (and back, 16:7!) and the transition from blindness to sight" (5). Idem, "Mark 1:1-15 and the Beginning of the Gospel," *Semeia* 52 (1990): 43-81.

See also Willi Marxsen, *Mark the Evangelist* (Nashville: Abingdon, 1969), 55. Marxsen claims that the geographical references serve Mark's theological purpose.

14. Craig L. Blomberg, *Jesus and the Gospels: An Introduction and Survey*

DEATH AND DISCIPLESHIP:
An Analysis of the Predictions of Jesus' Death in the Gospel of Mark

sions of Mark's structure are like Boring and communicate a Christological emphasis, Blomberg's means of communicating this structure is not through geography. The first half of the Gospel (1:14-8:30) seems to focus on Jesus' miracles through a series of stories that invite opposition and hostility. The second half of the Gospel (8:31-16:8) emphasizes Jesus' teachings as he moves to Jerusalem and his death on the cross.

The above analyses by Guelich, Edwards, Boring, and Blomberg conclude that Mark's narrative structure is captured through the introduction of the Gospel, the opening verse (1:1), and through the means of geography, or a theological emphasis. Their structure however is illustrated by dividing the Gospel of Mark into two halves.[15] These analyses by Guelich, Edwards, Boring, and Blomberg argue that Mark's narrative structure, thus communicating his plot, is more clearly seen in two parts rather than three.

Through the analyses of Mark's narrative structure, one can see that although the means of capturing the story by Guelich, Edwards, Boring, and Blomberg is similar to the preceding analyses of Tannehill, France, and Brooks, the difference lies in the narrative divisions of Mark; that is, a two-part division (generally, chapters 1-8 and 8-16) as opposed to a three-fold division (generally, chapters 1-8, 8-10, and 11-16). There is some difference as to the allocations of chapter and verse within the divisions; this is evident in the preceding summaries. However, this should not detract from the consensus of many of these scholars and their conclusions. They conclude that the narrative structure of Mark is captured through both the means of geography and an emphasis on Christology.

2d ed (Nashville: Broadman and Holman, 2009), 129-30.

15. Two others to note, Hans F. Bayer (*A Theology of Mark*, 21-22) who closely follows the work of Eduard Schweizer, ("Mark's Theological Achievement," in *The Interpretation of Mark*, ed. W. R. Telford [Edinburgh: T&T Clark, 1995], 63-87) combine literary, theme, and geography to produce an outline of Mark: Demonstration of Jesus' Authority 1:16-8:26 and Testing Jesus' Authority in Suffering 8:27-16:8.

An Eclectic Proposal to Mark's Structure: Three-fold Identity[16]

Mark's narrative structure is captured through a synthesis of the above analyses. This synthesis is an eclectic approach called three-fold identity. The reason for the eclectic approach is to illustrate how Mark weaves together geography *and* theology to communicate his story. Geography and theology are not only common among scholars, but they also best point to Mark's purpose.[17] In other words, the geographical locations (Galilee, on the way to Jerusalem, and Jerusalem) are used as the means to communicate the theology, or Mark's purpose; which is the message of the opening verse of the Gospel 1:1. Mark's purpose for his story is to explicate the identity of Jesus Christ as the Son of God found in the title of Mark's story (formal aspect, "who is he?" 1:1). As Mark explicates the identity of Jesus, he also provides the applicational significance to his story – the responsibility of a follower of Christ (functional aspect, "what are the disciples to do?" 8:22-10:52).[18] Therefore, Mark utilizes geography and theology to write the story of Jesus Christ.

Geography

Mark composes his story through three geographical settings; the region of Galilee (1:1-8:21), the way to Jerusalem (8:22-10:52), and Jerusalem itself (11:1-16:8) to portray Jesus' identity, the formal aspect of Mark's story.[19] He uses geography to capture the essence of the story of Jesus through his travels.

---

16. See also David E. Garland, *A Theology of Mark's Gospel*, 99-101; Russell Small, "Mark," in *Approaching the New Testament: A Guide for Students*, 42-54.

17. Guelich also claims that geography and theology can be the basis for Mark's structure. (*Mark 1-8:26*, xxxvi). See other options reported by Kevin W. Larsen, "The Structure of Mark's Gospel: Current Proposals," *CBR* 3, no.1 (2004): 140-60. Rikki E. Watts proposes that the structure of Mark's story has a dual perspective of salvation and judgment within the context of the Isaianic New Exodus (*Isaiah's New Exodus in Mark*, Biblical Studies Library [Grand Rapids: Baker, 1997], 4).

18. Campbell and Pennington (*Reading the New Testament as Christian Scripture*, 105-06) also claim that identity and responsibility are Mark's emphases.

19. Marcus claims that though several structural outlines exist for the Gospel of Mark, he claims that "there does seem to be an overarching geographical framework to the Gospel, within which literary and theological structures play their roles" (*Mark 1-8*, 63).

DEATH AND DISCIPLESHIP:
An Analysis of the Predictions of Jesus' Death in the Gospel of Mark

Jesus' ministry in and around Galilee is followed by his journey southward toward Jerusalem, which ultimately culminates in the climax of Mark's story; Jesus' death and resurrection in Jerusalem.[20]

Although the geographical section breaks may not be clearly discernible, for example does the middle section begin at 8:22 or 8:27. An understanding that Mark's story is a flowing narrative is apparent and his structure is discerned through a reading of the text. Therefore, as one reads the text, the following conclusions are made. The first section of Mark's story is communicated through various episodes where Jesus' ministry is primarily in and around Galilee (1:14-8:21). Mark's focus is on the declaration of Jesus' identity. Jesus primarily declares his identity through his teachings and miracles. But Mark's story seems to take a turn at 8:22. This shift is demonstrated not only because of a change in geography (Bethsaida), but also a change in focus (disciples); thus, demonstrating the relationship between geography and content.

The middle section of Mark's story demonstrates that Jesus is more narrowly focused on the disciples; that is, teaching them how to respond and live in light of knowing his true identity (8:22-10:52). To teach his disciples, Jesus must focus on his identity; that is, he defines himself as the suffering and self-sacrificing Messiah.

Mark identifies the final section of his story through a geographical shift. It is here that Jesus now approaches Jerusalem (11:1). Jesus' ministry changes once again. His ministry now is focused on affirming his identity. He enters the eventual place of his death and resurrection, Jerusalem (11:1-16:8) proving he is indeed who he said he was. Therefore, not only does Mark use a change in geography as the means to communicate his story, but also relates these geographical settings to the identity of Jesus Christ, the unifying focus of the narrative.

Theology

The three-fold geographical settings serve as the means to communicate the theological message of Mark's story, the identity of Jesus Christ as the Son

---

20. See also Sweetland, *Mark: From Death to Life*, 17. Gundry disagrees. He concludes that "Walking through Mark takes us hither and yon with little or no discernible pattern" (*Mark*, 1046).

of God. In the beginning of Mark's story, an introductory verse sets the stage with the Christological emphasis for the readers.[21] This opening verse, the 'good news about Jesus Christ, the Son of God' grabs the readers' attention. It is placed at the beginning of Mark's story so the reader can answer the question concerning Jesus' identity.[22] Morna Hooker claims that Mark's theological purpose is found in 1:1. She writes,

> "Mark has chosen to present 'the gospel of Jesus Christ' in the form of a narrative.... Mark has provided a guide to his narrative in the form of a prologue that provides the information we need to read the rest of his Gospel, and so gives us a succinct summary of his christology.... The gospel is more than the message that Jesus preached. It is, in fact, Jesus himself – that is, the gospel *about* Jesus Christ. So, from 1:9 onward – with the exceptions of 6:14-29 and 14:66-72 – Jesus is the central figure in the narrative."[23]

---

21. Boring agrees. He claims that Mark is a carefully structured narrative that is composed through the author's Christology provided through his title, 1:1 ("Mark 1:1-15 and the Beginning of the Gospel, 43).

22. Jack D. Kingsbury claims that Mark's focus is on Jesus' identity as the 'Messiah, Son of God' that is ultimately revealed by the Roman Centurion in 15:39 (*The Christology of Mark's Gospel* [Philadelphia: Fortress 1983]). See also Guelich, *Mark 1-8:26*, xl. Joel B. Green states that the answer to the question, 'who is Jesus,' is found in verse one. (*The Way of the Cross: Following Jesus in the Gospel of Mark* [Eugene, Ore: Wipf & Stock], 20).

23. "Who Can This Be?" in *Contours of Christology in the New Testament*, ed. Richard N. Longenecker (Grand Rapids: Eerdmans, 2005), 80-81. See also Edwards who claims that "Jesus is the uncontested subject of the Gospel of Mark, and he is portrayed as a man of action" (*The Gospel According to Mark*, 13).

Achtemeier also claims that Mark's narrative is to be seen through this verse. He writes, "Yet, for the whole of Mark's narrative, as for this verse, the only one through whom we can gain life is Jesus. It would appear, therefore, that the power of Jesus is also present with his power to save. Apparently the narrative of Jesus' deeds and words, accepted as a narrative of deeds done and words spoken with the authority of God's royal Son, is able to save a person's life.... That means that when Mark speaks of the 'beginning of the gospel of Jesus Christ,' he is not referring to where a book or even a public career begins, but rather to the fact that God's saving acts, which make up the 'gospel,' began with the career of Jesus.... Where the gospel is present, there Jesus'

DEATH AND DISCIPLESHIP:
An Analysis of the Predictions of Jesus' Death in the Gospel of Mark

The episodes of the story of Mark help the reader "wrestle with the question 'Who then is this man that even the wind and the sea obey him?' (4:41)."[24] These episodes elucidate Mark's authorial emphasis; that is, Jesus Christ is indeed the Son of God. Mark composes this story through the teachings, miracles, death, and resurrection of Jesus Christ as he travels from Galilee to Jerusalem.

The question of identity for Mark runs throughout his story, for each section of the story explicates his identity. The first section (1:1-8:21) declares Jesus as one who causes astonishment and possesses unprecedented authority (cf. 1:21-22). Various characters try to make sense of his teaching and miracle-work (cf. 4:41), but they are not able to do so. The central section (8:22-10:52) breaks through with Peter's confession that Jesus is the Christ (8:29), but this section also continues to report that the disciples are those men who struggle to follow Jesus due to their lack of understanding. Therefore, Jesus further defines who he is (formal aspect); the suffering and self-sacrificing Messiah, and what the disciples ought to do as a result (functional aspect).

The last section (11:1-16:8) affirms Jesus' identity as the Son of God through Jesus' own words (14:62), as well as the words of the Roman Centurion at Jesus' death (15:39). This section also testifies to Jesus' resurrection (16:6); a testament to Jesus' ability to predict both his death and resurrection (8:31, 9:31, and 10:34). This ability is only demonstrative of God. The following table (table one) shows the cohesive relationship between the three sections of Mark's story; thus, demonstrating that the three-fold identity structure of Mark's story is correct. The three sections are Jesus' Galilean Ministry (1:14-8:21), "on the way" to Jerusalem (8:22-10:52), and Jerusalem (11:1-16:8).

---

power is present and perhaps even Jesus himself!" (*Mark*, 64).

24. Stein, *Mark*, 21.

Table 1. Three-fold Identity of Mark's Story

Aspect of Mark's Story	Jesus' Galilean Ministry (1:14-8:21)	"On the way" to Jerusalem (8:22-10:52)	Jerusalem (11:1-16:8)
Formal Aspect "Who Is Jesus?" (1:1 – Ἰησοῦ Χριστοῦ υἱοῦ θεοῦ)	*Illustrates & Declares Jesus' Identity* 1:1, 11 (Son of God) ⟷ 3:11; 5:7 (Son of God) ⟷ 6:50 ("I am" is here, ἐγώ εἰμι)	*Defines Jesus' Identity & Mission* First passion prediction (8:31) ⟷ Second passion prediction (9:31) ⟷ Third passion prediction (10:33-34)	*Affirms Jesus' Identity* Jesus speaks to his identity (14:61-62) Jesus suffers and is killed (15:16-41) Jesus rises again, after three days (16:1-6)
Functional Aspect "What Are His Disciples to Do?"	*Actions of the Disciples* Follow Jesus (1:16-20; 2:13-17) ⟷ Service on behalf of Jesus (3:13-19) ⟷ Obedience to Jesus (6:7-13)	*Characteristics of the Disciples* Loyally following (8:34-9:1) ⟷ Willingly serving & accepting others (9:35-37) ⟷ Sacrificially serving (10:41-45)	*Failures of the Disciples* Failure of obedience (14:32-42) Failure to follow (14:50-54) Failure of loyalty (14:66-72)

DEATH AND DISCIPLESHIP:
An Analysis of the Predictions of Jesus' Death in the Gospel of Mark

Mark uses cohesion throughout his story.[25] Cohesion is shown by the horizontal arrows that connect the three sections of his story. Due to the repetition of concepts and the explication of details pertaining to both Jesus' identity and the responsibility of the disciples, the emphasis falls on the central section (8:22-10:52).[26] The premise that Mark's central section 'hangs together' within Mark's story, is shown in table one. In other words, Mark's central section offers the reader multiple connections that point both backward and forward as it relates to the formal and functional aspects of Mark's story. Therefore, the cohesion of Mark's story, as seen through the three sections, clearly illustrates a top-down approach to discourse analysis. The following conclusions can be made.

First, Mark shows a relationship between the central section and the rest of the story because he explicates Jesus' identity. He does so by pointing back (1:14-8:21) to the multiple times Mark reports Jesus' identity as the Son of God. Mark's report of Jesus' identity serves as cohesive ties connecting the first section to the central section of Mark's story. In other words, Jesus' three predictions of his death, within the central section, further define what has already been declared by Mark as the author (1:1), confirmed and approved by God himself (1:11), acknowledged by the demons (3:11; 5:7), and stated by Jesus (6:50). Mark declares Jesus' identity as God's Son and as Mark's story continues, Jesus will define his role as Messiah on his own terms through the predictions of his death. Thus, connecting the central section to the first section of the story.

The central section also points forward to Jesus' identity. Mark's story implements cohesive ties to affirm his identity. The ties are Jesus' own words (14:61-62) and the words of the Roman Centurion (15:39). Mark is also able to report the affirmation of Jesus' identity because Jesus' predictions come true. Jesus predicts he will suffer, be killed, and rise again (cf. 8:31, 9:31; 10:33-34), and he indeed suffers, dies, and rises again (15:16-41; 16:1-6). The final cohesive tie that explicates Jesus' identity is geography. Mark reports in Jesus' final prediction that the destination of his suffering is Jerusalem (10:32). The

---

25. Cohesion was discussed in chapter two. See pages 34-36.
26. A discussion of the central section and its cohesive nature is discussed in chapter 5.

reader can make the connection that this is where Jesus will die in the next chapter (11:11ff).

Second, Mark also shows a relationsip between the central section and the rest of Mark's story because he explicates the responsibility of the disciples. Mark demonstrates cohesion regarding the disciples' role that is based on Jesus' identity, not only within each passion prediction (see table two – chapter 5), but also by pointing back to the disciples' various actions within the first section of Mark's story. For example, the disciples followed Jesus (1:16-20; 2:13-17), served others (3:13-19; 6:41-42), and obeyed Jesus (6:7-13). It is clear within the central section that the disciples were not aware of all the implications of following Jesus; thus, leading to their misunderstanding (cf. 8:32b-33; 9:33-34; 10:35-40). As a consequence, Mark reports Jesus' expectations for the disciples (cf. 8:34-9:1; 9:35-37; 10:41-45).

The central section also points forward to the failure of the disciples (11:1-16:8). Although Jesus clearly specifies the characteristics his disciples are to exemplify, they still find it difficult to obey (14:32-42) and loyally follow (14:50-54, 66-72). It seems clear that Mark shows the disciples' obedience in the first part of his story only to report that they struggle later in his story. The central section seems to show Jesus taking an active role to clarify the disciples' responsibility, yet Mark later shows their failure in the last section of his story (11:1-16:8). Therefore, upon knowing Jesus, the disciples do not understand what it means to follow Jesus.

Understanding relationships between the central section and Mark's story confirms the theme of the story. The central section fits into the story to explicate the theme; that is, the details of Jesus' identity (Mark's Christological title, 1:1). The central section also portrays the responsibility of the disciples (8:34-9:1; 9:35-37; 10:41-45), which relates to the theological significance for the reader. Therefore, the three-fold identity of Mark best represents the structure of his story.

Summary: The Gospel of Mark: Structure and Plot

Mark's story is structured as a narrative. It is structured through geography that illustrates the journey of the Son of God. However, there are specific movements within this geography that relate to Jesus' identity, which is Mark's theological emphasis. Geography and theology for Mark are inextricably tied together. Galilee is where Mark *declares* Jesus' identity through his teachings and miracles (1:14-8:21). "On the way" to Jerusalem is where Mark *defines* Jesus' identity through the repetition of Jesus' three predictions of his death (8:22-10:52). The city of Jerusalem itself is where Mark *affirms* Jesus' identity as the Son of God through his suffering, death, and resurrection (11:1-16:8). Therefore, the three-fold identity approach to the structure of Mark's story best captures his message.

The Gospel of Mark: Setting

The setting of a narrative provides the 'world' in which the episodes take place and characters function to tell the story. Setting is more than location and more than time, for it "may illuminate or bring new significance to otherwise obscure features."[27] At this point, it is important to note that the author provides the setting. He determines what the reader is to know through reading and imagination.

Spatial Setting

The Gospel of Mark is told through the means of a combination of travel and geography. It is the journey throughout the Gospel that binds the story together. But it is not just movement across a landscape. Rather it is a journey that moves one to the climax of the story; that is, Jesus' death. Therefore, it is the 'way' to the cross. Mark begins with Jesus' baptism in the Jordan River and then moves throughout Galilee and beyond. During this movement Jesus' identity is declared as the Son of God since he teaches like no other rabbi, heals the sick, saves the poor, feeds thousands of people, and quiets the wind and sea (1:14-8:21). Jesus continues to move "on the way" to Jerusalem where he will eventually suffer death. It is during this movement that Jesus instructs his disciples regarding the cost to follow him, as well as define his role as the

---

27. R. Alan Culpepper, *Mark*, Smyth and Helwys Bible Commentary (Macon, Ga: Smyth and Helwys, 2007), 25.

suffering servant (8:22-10:52). He arrives in Jerusalem where he is welcomed by the acclamation of crowds only to be crucified by Roman and Jewish authorities (11:1-16:8). It is during Jesus' crucifixion that his identity is affirmed as the Son of God (15:39).

Although the movement of Mark's Gospel is primarily geographical, Mark communicates the episodes of Jesus' ministry in specific places. Jesus' ministries and the respective places include: Jesus' teachings (seashore [2:13; 4:1; 10:1]; synagogue [1:21, 39; 6:2]; villages [6:6]; Temple [11:16-17, 29ff; 12:35-40]), miracles (synagogue [1:23, 39; 3:1-5; 6:5]; homes [1:31-34; 2:2-12; 7:25-30]; seaside/on the sea [4:35-41; 5:8, 29, 34, 41-42; 6:47-50; 7:32-35]; along Jesus' ministry journey [1:40; 3:10-12; 6:32-44, 55-56; 8:1-9, 22-25; 9:17-27; 10:46-52]), death (15:1-47), and resurrection (16:5-6). Rhoads, Dewey, and Michie claim that Mark's structural setting "leads readers to join the journey of 'the way of God.' . . . The story draws readers into the journey and the destiny of Jesus."[28] Thus, the spatial setting plays a vital role in understanding Mark's story.[29]

Temporal Setting

The Gospel of Mark is told through several different temporal venues. As Jesus, his disciples, and the crowds of various sizes move across the landscape, episodes that make-up Mark's story occur during a general length of time, as well as the specificity of the length of time.

Mark's story is generally told through the time period of days rather than weeks or months.[30] Mark indicates the passing of days through episodes that are separated by evening and morning (cf. 1:32-35; 11:11-12, 19-20; 14:17-

---

28. Rhoads, Dewey, and Michie, *Mark as Story*, 72.

29. For more detail regarding the setting of Mark see Guelich, "Mark, Gospel of," 516-17.

30. Powell indicates that nothing happens in Mark's story that needs longer than a day to explain. He states, "A crowd remains with him 'for three days' (8:2). He teaches that he will rise from the dead 'after three days' (8:31). He is transfigured on the mountain 'after six days' (9:2). The Passover is reported to be coming 'after two days' (14:1). He is accused of claiming he will rebuild the temple 'in three days' (14:58; 15:29)" (*What Is Narrative Criticism*, 80).

15:1; 15:42-16:2), the moving on to a new day (cf. 2:1; 11:12), and the kind of day (Sabbath day [1:21; 2:24, 3:2; 6:2; 16:1] and Feast of the Passover [14:1-2, 12-25]).

Mark's story also includes the specificity of the day; that is, the period of the day: evening or morning. Typically, the evening is a time of winding down or relaxation. However, in Mark, it can be a time of great activity. These activities include times of new ventures (1:32-34; 4:35-36; 6:47-50), times of preparations (6:35; 11:11; 14:22-24, 25, 32-34; 15:42), and times of trouble/turmoil/danger (4:35-37; 6:48; 14:27, 43, 66-72). The activities in the morning include prayer (1:35), preparation (15:1), and unique perspectives (11:20; 16:2-8). Thus, Mark's story is told in a sequence of episodes that do not just involve geography, but also chronology.

Social, Cultural, and Political Setting

The Gospel of Mark is told through a specific social and cultural climate. This is seen through two venues: the geographical setting and the characters' social class. As Mark writes his story across the landscape, opposition becomes apparent between the two primary geographical settings, Galilee, and Jerusalem. Van Iersel states, "Jerusalem is the centre and capital of the country, the seat also of political power and the temple authorities. Galilee, on the other hand, is on the periphery, a faraway province whose inhabitants are looked upon with suspicion by Jerusalem, partly because of their being mixed with non-Jewish populations."[31] This opposition also demonstrates a distinct classification between people groups and their social standing.[32] For example, the governmental rulers in the Gospel of Mark include the Roman appointed

---

31. Van Iersel, *Reading Mark*, 22.

32. France states, "Mark's geographical symbolism, if such it is, is not a matter of great theological weight; it is rather a vehicle of his dramatic retelling of the story of Jesus, serving to draw out the intensely opposite reactions which he provoked, the contrasting soils into which the good seed had to be sown" (*The Gospel of Mark*, 35).

For a detailed discussion of the Roman social classes of people see Duane F. Watson, "Roman Social Classes," in *Dictionary of New Testament Background* ed. Craig A. Evans and Stanley E. Porter (Downers Grove, Ill: InterVarsity Press, 2000), 999-1004.

king in Galilee, Herod Antipas (6:14-29), the Roman procurator over Judea and Jerusalem, Pilate (15:1-15), and the Judean authorities which include the high priest Caiaphas, high priests, elders and the Sanhedrin (14:53-65). The society depicted in Mark's story seems to illustrate a class society. Other than the rulers, the Pharisees and the scribes top the list (2:24; 3:6; 7; 8:11; 11:27-12:38-40). The Pharisees and scribes were those who interpreted and upheld the Law of Moses. While on the other hand, the rest of the people in Mark are common folk. These people include fishermen (1:16-20), lepers (1:40-45), tax collectors (2:14), publicans and sinners (2:15-17), and beggars (10:46-52).

The political climate of Mark's story is the nation of Israel under the military control of the Roman Empire. This military control is enforced by Herod Antipas and Pilate. This political environment was especially difficult for those living under the dominion of Roman rule within Galilee and Jerusalem and is made evident in Mark's story (10:42; 12:13-17; 13:9). This political regime also served as the appropriate setting for those in opposition to Jesus and his ministry (14:53-15:41).

Summary: The Gospel of Mark: Setting

The setting of the Gospel of Mark is oriented in two major areas: Galilee and Jerusalem. It is in these two locations that Jesus' identity as the Son of God is declared and affirmed. Most of the episodes that comprise Mark's narrative occur during the time of a day rather than a month or year. At times however, Mark is specific both with the kind of day and the location in which the episodes of his story occur. Mark's story also depicts a cultural environment where people of different classes and status function as characters to help facilitate the portrayal and thus the validation of Jesus' identity. In other words, the teachings and miracles of Jesus occur with the common folk near or around Galilee; whereas the death and resurrection events involve the military, political, and religious authorities in and around the city of Jerusalem.[33]

---

33. Van Iersel notes the apparent contrast between locations and people groups within the story of Mark. He writes, "In Galilee Jesus is very active: he makes a new beginning, finds a number of supporters, gets response, helps the sick and handicapped, casts out demons, and resists his adversaries. Jerusalem is the scene of the

DEATH AND DISCIPLESHIP:
AN ANALYSIS OF THE PREDICTIONS OF JESUS' DEATH IN THE GOSPEL OF MARK

The Gospel of Mark: Characters

The characters in the Gospel of Mark serve as agents to carry out the plot. They are not only agents *in* the plot, but their actions are also an expression *of* the plot. In Mark, there are four primary characters: the Son of God, Jesus Christ; the authorities (both governmental and religious); the disciples; and the common folk (typically described as the crowds who follow Jesus).[34]

The Son of God, Jesus Christ

The reader discovers that the plot of the story revolves around the opening verse, "the good news about Jesus Messiah, the Son of God (1:1)." Mark expresses this message throughout the episodes of the story. In other words, from the very beginning the reader sees that Jesus is the central figure through the announcement and anointing by God (1:1-11). Jesus is the Son of God because God has given him this authority to be the Son, his "beloved Son (9:7)."

There are others who acknowledge Jesus is the Son of God. They are: the demons (1:25; 3:11-12; 5:7), the disciple Peter (8:27-29), and the Roman centurion (15:39). Mark reports that Jesus is the Son of God through the clear declarations of characters. Yet apart from this, Jesus' identity still escapes other characters. He illustrates Jesus' identity primarily through his teachings, miracles, death, and resurrection.

The first way Mark declares Jesus' identity is through the responses to his teaching. Mark seldom informs his readers of the content of Jesus' teaching, and yet it is apparent that his emphasis lies more in the person of the teacher – one of authority (1:21-22; 6:1-6; 11:16-18; 12:35).[35] Jesus' teaching caused the hearers

---

passion narrative, in which Jesus plays a passive rather than an active part; here he announces the end of the temple and the world, loses his supporters, fails to get a hearing, cures no one, does not cast out any demons, and is defeated by his adversaries" (*Reading Mark*, 22).

34. The basis of the treatment of these characters will only come from the Gospel of Mark. There will not be a construction of the background or history of these characters from other Gospel accounts.

35. There are however some of his teachings in which Mark provided the content (e.g., Olivet Discourse in chapter 13 and Jesus' parables, namely in chapter 4).

to be amazed or overwhelmed[36] for he was no ordinary teacher. His teaching demonstrated his authority due to his prophetic wisdom and insight. As a matter of fact, his teaching was questioned (11:27-33) because he did not need authority to validate his teaching, just a simple "truly" or "amen" was sufficient.

The second way Mark declares Jesus' identity is through his miracles. His identity assumes the prerogatives that only God possesses (2:7); therefore, he provides the means for the performing of miracles. Jesus' miracles consist of healing the sick, saving the poor, exorcising demons, feeding thousands of people, walking on water, and quieting the stormy sea. These actions of Jesus clearly demonstrate his extraordinary character. In fact, Jesus is so extraordinary that he astounds those who see what he does, causes others to question who he is, and invites opposition from those in authority.

The third way Mark declares Jesus' identity is through his death. The significance of Jesus' death for Mark's theology is his willing obedience toward the heavenly Father and his vulnerability to suffer execution at the hands of the government and religious authorities.[37] Jesus' death must take place (8:31, use of δεῖ); therefore implying his death is a part of the divine plan.[38]

---

36. ἐκπλήσσω "to cause to be filled with amazement to the point of being overwhelmed, amaze, astound, overwhelm" (Walter Bauer, *A Greek-English Lexicon of the New Testament and other Early Christian Literature*, 3d ed. Rev and Ed by Frederick William Danker [Chicago: University of Chicago Press, 2000], 308.

37. Francis J. Moloney claims, "He is the Christ and the Son of God as the crucified one. This is a matter of major importance for Mark: Jesus is the crucified Christ and the crucified Son of God. It is in and through crucifixion that Jesus fulfills God's messianic design and shows that he is the beloved Son of God, in whom the Father is well pleased (1:11; 9:7). However, the tragic end of Jesus' life is not a dreadful fate that simply falls unjustly upon him. Mark associates the categories of Messiah and Son of God with Jesus' death because he wants his readers and hearers to be aware that the crucifixion of God's Son and Messiah are part of God's larger design" (*Mark: Storyteller, Interpreter, Evangelist* [Peabody, Mass: Hendrickson, 2004,] 142).

38. Collins, *Mark*, 80. Stein states, "Jesus' death is part of the divine plan for his life. It is not a tragedy; an example of how things can take an unfortunate turn or how the best laid plans can go awry. On the contrary, in the death of Jesus all things go exactly according to the divine plan" (*Mark*, 34). δεῖ is a divine passive indicating that God ultimately is acting as the agent in Jesus' death; it is necessary that Jesus suffers, dies, and rises again.

DEATH AND DISCIPLESHIP:
An Analysis of the Predictions of Jesus' Death in the Gospel of Mark

Although Jesus knows the inevitability of his death, He continues "on the way" to Jerusalem (10:32) where he accepts his fate, as well as the hostility of authorities awaits his arrival.

Jesus' death demonstrates his identity. The purpose of his death (8:31; 9:31; 10:32-34) is to be a ransom for many (10:45). Jesus has a God-given commission; to serve as the replacement or substitute to assure the release of a slave from his owner. In this case, ransom humanity from sin and death. The reason for his death is the claim that Jesus is the Son of God. It is Jesus' "response to the high priest's question, that he is the Messiah and the Son of the Blessed One (14:61-2)."[39]

The fourth way Mark declares Jesus' identity is through his resurrection. Jesus' death is not the end. Everything in Mark's story has led to this episode. This is the final scene, and it invites the readers to reflect on the fact that God's Son has now risen from the dead. As a result, Jesus' predictions that he will suffer, die, and rise again are true (cf. 8:31; 9:31; 10:34). Jesus' death also vindicates his innocence. The significance of the suffering Son of Man[40] speaks to his obedience[41] and that justification has arrived in the world. His crucifixion and therefore resurrection also brings hope to the world. His resurrection brought "life; not death; salvation, not corruption . . . Mark presented the assurance that something had been done about human mortality: someone had defeated death – and it was a crucified man. And if a *crucified* man can be raised from the dead, then *anyone* can be raised!"[42] Jesus' resurrection is

---

39. Hooker, "Who Can This Be?" 94.

40. Moloney claims Mark associates 'Son of Man' "with suffering and vindication. . . . Jesus of Nazareth, the crucified Christ and Son of God, who is also the suffering, but ultimately vindicated, Son of Man" (*Mark: Storyteller, Interpreter, Evangelist*, 146).

41. Peter Bolt states the significance of Jesus' resurrection. He writes, "The human courts treated Jesus as a sinner, condemned him to death and handed him over to the wrath of God. His resurrection, however, is a concrete event in human history that announces to the world that the human courts were wrong, and that Jesus died as an innocent man. This confirms that he was the obedient Son. His obedience is a crucial factor in the salvation of humanity (cf. 3:31-35; 14:36)" (*The Cross from a Distance: Atonement in Mark's Gospel*, New Studies in Biblical Theology 18 [Downers Grove, Ill: InterVarsity Press, 2004], 149).

42. Ibid., 171.

an event that came into humanity's world; that is, to benefit the whole world. As a result, people now have a future, even amidst the present suffering world.

The Authorities (Governmental and Religious)

Mark's story involves those in opposition to Jesus as the Son of God. Though the groups of authorities are different, government and religious, their opposition is united (3:6).[43] The governmental authorities were concerned that their right to rule was given to them by God; therefore, they protected this right. They also protected the Temple and kept social order. The religious authorities on the other hand confronted Jesus regarding legal issues, purity regulations, and his authority in general (teaching, healing, and permitting on the Sabbath). The importance to their opposition was their cooperative effort to destroy Jesus. Due to this union, they are treated as one character group.

Although governmental and religious groups had substantial social and political authority, they feared the people (11:18; 12:12; 14:1-2; 15:15) and maintained their position through manipulation (15:9-13) and hypocrisy (12:38-40). Their primary goal was to oppose the one who had "true authority" from God (1:22), Jesus Christ. Therefore, the governmental and religious authorities conspired against him (3:6; 15:1) and were deceitful (14:1) and envious (11:18; 15:10). Although God had given them authority to rule, they misused it by placing unbiblical demands upon people (2:27; 7:2-5),[44] by leaving the people as without a shepherd (6:34), and by lording over the people (14:43-49; 15:11, 15).

---

43. See the following works regarding the authorities: Emil Schürer, *The History of the Jewish People in the Age of Christ (175 B.C.-A.D. 135)* rev and ed G. Vermes, and F. Millar, 2.381-403; 2.404-14 (Edinburgh: T&T Clark, 1973-87); Jack D. Kingsbury, *Conflict in Mark: Jesus, Authorities, Disciples* (Minneapolis, Minn: Fortress Press, 1989), 14-21.

44. For example, Rhoads, Dewey, and Michie state, "The authorities [do not] love their neighbors as themselves. They do not interpret the laws and traditions to meet the needs of the people. They think that people were made for laws rather than laws for people. They will fulfill outward rituals and traditions—fasting, washing hands, whole burnt offerings—but they have evil designs in their minds" (*Mark As Story*, 118).

DEATH AND DISCIPLESHIP:
An Analysis of the Predictions of Jesus' Death in the Gospel of Mark

The governmental and religious groups lacked understanding. At times Mark demonstrated that they only had a human understanding of Scripture; therefore, they were often in error. This lack of understanding is seen through a willful blindness and hardening of the heart (2:5-8, 25-26; 3:5; 7:5-6; 10:1-12; 11:27-33; 12:13-40). As a result of this hardening of the heart, they lacked genuine faith. Therefore, the religious group asked Jesus for a sign (8:11-12) and the governmental and religious groups asked for the miraculous to occur (15:30-32); primarily these authorities served themselves. They objected to the rule of God and refused to change. They possessed an inability to see and therefore blasphemed God. They rejected Jesus' power and envied his popularity. In serving themselves and opposing the Son of God, the governmental and religious authorities repudiated God.

The Disciples

The followers are typically viewed in two circles, a narrow circle (the twelve disciples) and a broader circle (others also called).[45] Both of these groups are the beneficiaries of Jesus' ministry (teaching, miracles, death, and resurrection). However, for the most part when Mark references the disciples, he is speaking of the narrower circle of followers. The disciples play an important role throughout Mark's story. Although they may not be the 'central' character, France contends that they often serve as the eyes through which Mark tells the story of Jesus.[46] The disciples also are more than historical figures. They are the early group of followers that exemplify those who carried out the mission of the kingdom of God through their wholehearted commitment (1:18, 20; 2:14; 10:28-30), through their privileged insight (4:11), and through their united effort regarding proclamation (3:14-15; 6:12-13, 30).[47]

---

45. Guelich characterizes the two groups as "both a narrower circle comprised of the Twelve who are called to be 'with him' and specially commissioned to share in his ministry of teaching, healing and exorcism (3:13-14; cf. 5:18; 6:7-13) and a larger circle who also are called (e.g., Levi 2:13), commissioned (e.g., 5:19-20) 'followers' (e.g., 2:15-17)" ("Mark, Gospel of," 522).

46. France, *The Gospel of Mark*, 28. "It is about how twelve ordinary men who met Jesus and entered into a new dimension of living" (28).

47. Ibid., 28.

The disciples are mentioned throughout Mark's story. They are mentioned either in a positive or negative way; thus, illustrating their commitment, their lack of understanding, their fear and faithlessness, their selfish ambition, and their eventual abandonment of Jesus. The positive way Mark illustrates the disciples is through their commitment. They followed Jesus when he called them (1:16-20; 2:14). The importance to the commitment, and therefore an expression of Jesus' authority, lies in the fact that the disciples left their livelihood (1:16-18) and families (1:19-20) to be followers of Jesus (8:34-38).[48]

Mark illustrates the disciples through their lack of understanding; through a hardened heart (6:52; 8:17). It is through two episodes, namely the feeding of the five thousand (6:32-44) and four thousand (8:1-9), that the disciples do not grasp the significance of the identity of the one they follow. Mark also illustrates the disciples through their fear and faithlessness. This fear is due to God's awesome power. They are frightened because Jesus displays the power of God by calming the storm (4:35-41) and walking on water (6:45-50). This fear is due to a lack of trust & understanding in the midst of the rule of God.[49]

Fourth, Mark illustrates the disciples through their selfish ambition. This proves they possess a human mind-set. They waited for Jesus' triumphant march into Jerusalem to overthrow the Roman government and desired a reward because they had followed him (9:33-34; 10:35-40). Not only did the

---

48. Rhoads, Dewey, and Michie argue that the disciples fulfill their calling. They write, "They become fishers for people—leaving work and family to follow, going to him on the mountain, then proclaiming, exorcising, and healing when he authorizes them to do so. They serve Jesus by following his instructions to take him in the boat, to find a donkey for him, and to prepare the Passover meal. They go with him anywhere he permits them, staying with him despite storms, trips to the desert, corrections, warnings, and little or no praise or assurance of reward" (*Mark As Story*, 124).

49. Ibid., 125. "Their fear and lack of understanding are interrelated. Their fear for their well-being prevents them from understanding, and their inability to understand leaves them frightened. Thus, the issue is not a lack of intelligence. Mark is showing something more profound. Fear inhibits understanding, and misunderstanding generates fear."

disciples desire to be honored, but they also did not want to experience a shameful death.

Finally, Mark communicates the disciples' character through their abandonment (14:50). They abandoned Jesus because of their fear and overestimation of the ability to be faithful (14:26-31, 32-42). The disciples misunderstood Jesus' message and ministry. As a result, they followed, feared, denied, and abandoned their leader and teacher Jesus Christ, the Son of God.

The Common Folk (the crowd)

The crowd, ὄχλος or πλῆθος, refers to the common people.[50] The appearances of the common folk however did not always refer to the whole crowd. The common folk appear throughout the story with little or no connection to one another (e.g., Simon's mother-in-law [1:29-31]; the woman with an issue of blood [5:25-29]; the Syrophenician woman [7:24-30]; the deaf and dumb man [7:31-37]; the blind man at Bethsaida [8:22-26]; and blind Bartimeus [10:46-52]). The appearances of the crowd are brief, but important. The crowd demonstrates faith. However, this faith is not a turning to Jesus in repentance and belief. They instead are coming to Jesus for the purpose of changing their poor situation (2:3-5; 5:34; 9:23-25; 10:52). The crowd also often obstructs access to Jesus; therefore, sometimes the crowd stands in opposition to Jesus. Not only do the common folk demonstrate faith and opposition, they also demonstrate humility because they "have a disregard for personal status and power, and a capacity for service."[51] The common folk have a desire to serve others (e.g., 2:4; 6:55-56; 7:32; 9:14-17; 10:13-14; 12:41-44) and to serve Jesus (e.g., 2:15; 3:19-20; 14:3-9; 15:21, 43-46; 16:1-2). As a result, Jesus ministers to the common folk.

---

50. Edwards claims that Jesus' popularity was so significant that Mark refers to the crowds forty times before chapter 10 (*The Gospel According to Mark*, 74). For more information see Kingsbury, *The Christology of Mark's Gospel*, 78-80.

51. Rhoads, Dewey, and Michie, *Mark As Story*, 130.

Summary: The Gospel of Mark: Characters

The story of Mark is told through the various expressions of four characters: Jesus, the authorities, the disciples, and the crowds. Jesus was one who taught with authority. He also possessed an extraordinary identity because he enjoyed the prerogatives of God. But it was mainly in and through his death and resurrection that Mark's story finds its climax. It is therefore through what Jesus does that invites expressions such as: opposition, commitment, amazement, and faith. Mark also makes it clear that these various expressions overlap between characters.

The authorities' primary role was to oppose and seek the destruction of Jesus. Jesus' actions were a challenge and threat to the rulers of the government and religion. The disciples on the other hand, did not oppose Jesus. Rather they were committed and fearful at the same time; following Jesus wherever he went but doing so not really knowing who they were following. The common folk demonstrated faith in the abilities of Jesus; but they came to him only trusting that he would change their situation. It is in the life of these four characters, represented through various and reliable expressions, that the reader is invited to consider Mark's story.

The Gospel of Mark: Point of View

Mark's story is basically written from two different points of view: the narrator and the characters. Mark dominates the telling of the story. It is through his point of view that the reader captures the characters' opinions, thoughts, and emotions.[52] The characters on the other hand, depict a world that provides the reader with first-hand information. In other words, though their actions,

---

52. Norman R. Petersen describes this third-person point of view as the omniscient point of view of a narrator. He writes, "That the narrator knows everything that needs to be known about the agents and events; that he is entirely free to move as he will in time and place, and to shift from character to character, reporting (or concealing) what he chooses of their speech and actions; and also that he has 'privileged' access to a character's thoughts and feelings and motives, as well as to his overt speech and actions" ("Point of View in Mark's Narrative," *Semeia* 12 [1978], 105-06).

words, etc. are written by Mark, the reader directly hears/reads the characters' view of the situation at hand. It is not from the narrator's point of view.

Mark as narrator, captures the historical episodes in the structure that he deems best to communicate the story about Jesus Christ.[53] He then integrates the setting, the characters and their actions and depicts the story through episodes and his point of view. For example,[54] in the stilling of the storm (4:35-41) Mark begins the episode by describing a scene in which he presents information as if he was with Jesus and his disciples. He records Jesus' command, "let us go over to the other side." He continues this close perspective throughout the episode by reporting on the significance and danger of the storm using the result clause, "waves beat into the ship *so that it was now full*" and the informative statement that "Jesus was asleep in the hinder part of the boat." Mark then shifts the perspective to that of the characters in which the reader can imaginatively hear and see the words spoken by the disciples, "Master, do you not care that we are close to dying?" And the words spoken by Jesus, "Peace be still." The scene ends with the disciples' frightening discovery that they do not know the identity of the one in the boat with them who possesses power over nature.

This brief example demonstrates how point of view is understood both from the narrator and the characters. Mark draws the reader into the story through his and the characters' point of view. To accomplish this purpose, Mark selects and arranges historical episodes into the narrative plot.

Summary of The Gospel of Mark as Narrative

Mark is a narrative that essentially declares, defines, and affirms Jesus as the Son of God. Mark reports Jesus' teaching, miracles, death, and resurrection

---

53. An example of an author using the structure to communicate a particular theme/subject matter is Mark's collection of miracle stories in 4:35-6:56. Here he uses several miracles stories (Jesus' power over nature: 4:35-41; 6:45-52; Jesus' power over demons: 5:1-20; Jesus' power over disease: 5:25-34; 6:1-6; 6:53-56; Jesus' power over death: 5:21-24, 35-43) to demonstrate Jesus' power as the Son of God.

54. This is but one example in the story of Mark. This does not indicate that all episodes are written in this way. However, it does demonstrate to the reader the typical way in which the narrator communicates his story.

through historical episodes.⁵⁵ Jesus' words and deeds point to his authority because he possesses divine prerogatives. It is due to Jesus' divine prerogatives that the authorities, disciples, and crowd respond and therefore are revealed as those who are opposed, committed, and amazed respectively.

The elements of the narrative (structure, setting, characters, and point of view) are present as Mark tells his story. Mark organizes his narrative around three geographical locations (Galilee, "on the way" to Jerusalem, and Jerusalem); while maintaining a Christological emphasis – Jesus is the Son of God. Consequently, the reader must not miss Mark's strategy to communicate his purpose as he weaves geography and theology into his narrative. Mark uses the geographical movement of Jesus and the authorities, disciples, and crowd to declare, portray and confirm his identity as the Son of God. Those involved convey various expressions that illustrate their relationship to Jesus as the Son of God, for they either commit to him or oppose him, and sometimes both. Mark tells the narrative from perspectives that are engaging and accommodating to the reader's understanding. The Gospel of Mark is a narrative establishing the identity of Jesus Christ.

LITERARY SUB-GENRE: THE GOSPEL OF MARK AS THEOLOGICAL NARRATIVE BIOGRAPHY

Mark composes a story about a central unifying character: Jesus Christ. The Gospel of Mark is a story (narrative) that chronicles the life of Jesus Christ (biography), within a historical context (history), and has significance for the reader (theology). The preceding genre discussion demonstrates that Mark's

---

55. Achtemeier states that Jesus is the central figure of the narrative. Mark's Christology is influenced by the beginning of the story, 1:1. Mark's narrative thus revolves around "what Jesus says and does, and the significance of what happens to him" (*Mark*, 52-53).

Boring agrees. He too claims that Mark's story is about Jesus, one "who appears in almost every scene and is the subject of most of the verbs in Mark. . . . To tell the story of Jesus is to tell the self-defining story of God" (*Mark: A Commentary*, 3).

DEATH AND DISCIPLESHIP:
An Analysis of the Predictions of Jesus' Death in the Gospel of Mark

narrative structure consisted of weaving together geography and theology. Mark's Christological emphasis originates with the opening verse of the story and is reported throughout the story by the means of three geographical locations. This emphasis is the identity of Jesus Christ as the Son of God.

The discussion here will more carefully develop details of Mark as a theological narrative biography. Mark's theological purpose goes beyond simply identifying Jesus Christ. There is a greater significance for the reader. Mark records how Jesus' disciples, and consequently his readers, ought to live in light of knowing his identity.[56]

Mark formulates a portrait of Jesus through his teachings, miracles, death, and resurrection. Jesus puts forth a message (1:14-15). This message is the gospel; that is, the redemption of God brought to humanity. Mark not only puts forth the gospel message of Jesus Christ, but he also demonstrates how one is to relate to this message.[57] Therefore, if one knows Jesus Christ and his message, how ought he to follow Jesus? The pivotal issue for Mark centers on the identity of Jesus Christ and how one ought to follow him. Sweetland contends that the identity of Jesus is inextricably tied to following Jesus. He states, "Mark is very interested in his readers' understanding of who Jesus is. We will see that misunderstanding the identity of Jesus leads to misunderstanding discipleship."[58] There are two questions Mark answers throughout his story: "who is Jesus?" And in light of this, "what are his disciples to do?"[59] These

---

56. Peter Bolt agrees that all aspects (biography, history, and theology) must be incorporated into an understanding of Mark's Gospel. He writes, "Some later narrative studies make it a trichotomy by adding the category of narrative. But rather than pitting these three against one another, we should see it as eminently more sensible to recognize them as three aspects of the Gospel of Mark. Mark is narrative about theologically significant historical events" ("Mark's Gospel," in *The Face of New Testament Studies: A Survey of Recent Research*, ed. Scot McKnight and Grant R. Osborne [Grand Rapids: Baker, 2004], 409).

57. An example of Mark illustrating how one ought to relate to Jesus' message is the blind man, Bartimeus (10:46-52). Bartimeus placed his faith in Jesus, whether he could see or not. No longer was he a bystander *alongside* of the road unable to follow Jesus; rather after placing faith in Jesus and receiving sight, he was able to follow Jesus *on* the road.

58. *Mark: From Death to Life*, 17.

59. Strauss states that Christology and discipleship dominate Mark's story

two questions speak into the formal and functional aspects of the Gospel of Mark. As a matter of fact, Green states, "Mark is not interested in identifying Jesus for the sake of producing the right answer; he is concerned with much, much more than getting his doctrines correct. Equally transparent is the related Markan concern with appropriate response to Jesus."[60] Thus, as the reader answers these two questions, the sub-genre classification, theological narrative biography, provides the theological significance and therefore the application of Jesus' identity to the reader. To have answered the one question is to have answered the other.

Formal Aspect: "Who is Jesus?"

The Gospel of Mark answers the question "who is Jesus?" in a number of ways. First, Mark answers this question through the Christological title[61] or the opening statement of his story (Ἀρχὴ τοῦ εὐαγγελίου Ἰησοῦ Χρστοῦ [υἱοῦ θεοῦ],[62] "The beginning of the Good News about Jesus Christ, [Son of God]"

(*Mark: Exegetical Commentary on the New Testament*, 41).

60. *The Way of the Cross: Following Jesus in the Gospel of Mark*, 19.

61. Garland states, "The opening line functions as a title or incipit of the gospel (1:2-16:8). The absence of a verb makes it more likely that this opening line serves as a title rather than a verbless sentence" (*A Theology of Mark's Gospel*, 101).

62. Although there is much debate regarding the phrase υἱοῦ θεοῦ, the longer reading is taken as original. Tommy Wasserman states, "The main question is whether the phrase 'Son of God' was accidentally omitted from an original or added by some scribes in order to expand the divine name or the title of the book" ("The 'Son of God' Was in the Beginning (Mark 1:1)," *JTS* 61, pt 1 [April 2011]: 20). The basis for the longer reading as original is both external and internal evidence. The longer reading has strong manuscript support:)¹, A, B, D, L, W, Δ.

The shorter reading however has less external support:)*, Θ. (Patristic and versional support seems to be diverse and favorable for both readings.) Internal evidence also provides support for the longer reading, namely authorial style. Wasserman states, "The argument from Markan style is often appealed to in favour of the longer reading, since the idea of sonship forms a crucial theme in Mark (1:11; 3:11; 5:7; 8:38; 9:7; 12:6; 13:32; 14:36, 61; 15:39) and would be appropriate to indicate in the title or introduction" (42).

Eldon Epp agrees and states, "to rule it [the phrase] out . . . might be to remove

1:1).⁶³ This is the first clear statement that Mark uses for the identification of Jesus. It is these introductory words that alert the reader to the significance that is to follow⁶⁴ for it provides a key to understanding the whole book.

---

from the opening sentence the author's dramatic announcement of a major theme for the entire work that follows" ("Textual Criticism in the Exegesis of the New Testament, with an Excursus on Canon," in *A Handbook to the Exegesis of the New Testament*, ed. Stanley E. Porter (Leiden: Brill, 2002)," 47). See also Lane, *The Gospel According to Mark*, 41, n. 7; Hooker, *The Gospel According to Saint Mark*, 34; Alexander Globe, "The Caesarean Omission of the Phrase 'Son of God' in Mark 1:1," *HTR* 75 no, 2 (April 1982): 217.

Those in favor of the shorter reading are: Jan Slomp, "Are the Words 'Son of God' in Mark 1:1 Original?" *BT* 28 (1977): 143-50; Peter M. Head, "A Text-Critical Study of Mark 1:1 'The Beginning of the Gospel of Jesus Christ," *NTS* 37 (1991): 621-29; Adela Yarbro Collins, "Establishing the Text: Mark 1:1," in *Text and Contexts: The Function of Biblical Texts in their Textual and Situational Contexts*, eds. Tord Fornberg and David Hellholm (Oslo: Scandinavian University Press, 1995), 111-27. The main argument in favor of the shorter reading is the unlikelihood of an accidental omission in the beginning of a Gospel.

63. Ἰησοῦ Χριστοῦ is taken as an objective genitive; that is, "the gospel [about, concerning] Jesus Christ."

64. France states, "Mark's book is intended, therefore, to pass on the good news about Jesus. This news has been hitherto the subject of primarily oral declaration ... but Mark's book is an attempt to communicate it in written form" (*The Gospel of Mark*, 52).

Edwards agrees, "In v. 1 Mark declares the essential content of the *euangelion*, the 'good news.' The Gospel of Mark is thus not a mystery story in which readers must piece together clues here and there to discover its meaning; nor is it a pedestrian chronicle of dates and places without purpose or significance; nor is it reducible to a mere system of thought. Rather, from the outset Mark announces that the content of the gospel is the person of Jesus, who is the Christ and Son of God" (*The Gospel According to Mark*, 26). See also Guelich, *Mark 1-8:26*, 9-10; Gundry, *Mark: A Commentary on His Apology for the Cross*, 32; Hooker, *The Gospel According to Saint Mark*, 34; Lane, *The Gospel of Mark*, 44; and Marcus, *Mark 1-8*, 146-47; Stein, *Mark*, 40-41; Dennis Sweetland, *Mark: From Death to Life*, 17-20.

Robert L. Humphrey claims that the prologue (1:1-13) is one of three key narrative moments in Mark that provide Mark's message, (*Narrative Structure and Message in Mark: A Rhetorical Analysis*, 29ff).

Second, Mark answers the question regarding Jesus' identity through the divine confirmation by God at Jesus' baptism and transfiguration (Σὺ εἶ ὁ υἱός μου ὁ ἀγαπητός, "you yourself, are my son, the beloved one" 1:11 and Οὗτός ἐστιν ὁ υἱός μου ὁ ἀγαπητός, "This one is my son, the beloved one" 9:7). There is little doubt that these passages speak to the declaration & affirmation that Jesus is God's Son; the former, a declaration (1:11) to the reader/hearer and the latter, an affirmation (9:7) to the disciples.[65] God's voice declares who Jesus is, not what he has become. There is no adoptionistic view tenable through the text, rather it can only be contrived based on one's dogmatic considerations elsewhere.[66] Therefore, in both passages Jesus is referred to as God's beloved Son.[67]

Third, Mark answers the question through the confession of Peter. Jesus asks the disciples for the public's view as to his identity (8:27-28); but then also asks the disciples for their understanding ὑμεῖς δὲ τίνα με λέγετε εἶναι, ("but who do you yourselves say that I am?" 8:29). Peter's confession identifies Jesus as the Χριστός, ("Messiah"). This response is representative of the titular statement in 1:1. As Mark reports elsewhere (cf. 1:1, 11; 9:7; 14:61-62; 15:39) Peter's confession was true, for it was his understanding of the significance of his confession that was proved to be erroneous (cf. 8:31-33).[68]

Fourth, Mark also answers the question through the commentary of others. As one reads through the story, he is reminded several times of Jesus' identity. The troubling aspect to this truth is that Jesus' identity is not clear-

---

65. France states, "Jesus is here explicitly identified in the terms used in Mark's heading, υιος θεου. In the narrative that follows there will be secrecy and paradox, but here in the prologue there is open declaration. The reader need be in no doubt, whatever the reactions of the actors in the story" (*The Gospel of Mark*, 79).

66. For a view that Ps 2:7 implies adoption see Mitchell Dahood, *Psalms: Introduction, Translation, and Notes,* vol. 1:1-50, Anchor Bible (Garden City, N.Y.: Doubleday, 1966), 11-12.

67. The word ἀγαπητός functions as a filial term denoting a special relationship between Son and Father. It could mean the same as John's term μονογενής ("one and only") in John 1:14, 18. See France, *The Gospel of Mark*, 82; Guelich, *Mark 1-8:26*, 34; Stein, *Mark*, 59.

68. Ralph P. Martin, *Mark: Evangelist and Theologian* (Exeter: Paternoster Press, 1972), 129.

ly known by his own followers, but outsiders instead. For example, demons clearly know that Jesus is the Son of God (1:24). Although Mark communicates the demons' acknowledgment of Jesus as ὁ ἅγιος τοῦ θεοῦ ("the Holy One of God"), this is probably synonymous with Jesus' identity as υἱός θεοῦ ("Son of God," 3:11; 5:7). They recognized the special relationship that existed between Jesus and God. Another example is the Roman Centurion at the scene of the cross (15:39). He claims that Jesus was the Son of God, (ἀληθῶς οὗτος ὁ ἄνθρωπος υἱὸς θεοῦ ἦν ["surely, this man was the Son of God"]). France argues that this is the climax of the crucifixion scene; that is, "what is new is the source from which the declaration comes, the first human witness to describe Jesus as υἱὸς θεοῦ, and mean it, and that witness not a disciple or even a Jew at all, but a Gentile army officer with no previous connections with Jesus."[69] Mark communicates what the Centurion saw; a dying man; but more than that, the Son of God.[70]

Last, Mark reports Jesus' identity through the words and deeds of Jesus Christ himself. Jesus declares that he is indeed the Messiah, Son of God before the Sanhedrin (14:61-62). Due to the accusation of blasphemy and therefore the necessity to confirm this; Jesus is asked by the Sanhedrin if he was the Messiah-Son of God Σὺ εἶ ὁ Χριστὸς ὁ υἱὸς τοῦ εὐλογητοῦ ("are you the Christ, the Son of the blessed?") and he answers with a strong affirmative answer ἐγώ εἰμι ("I am"). But Jesus not only affirms his identity, but he also states his role as the exalted Son of Man (Ps 110:1) – who possesses the highest honor at the right hand of God, and the coming Son of Man (Dan 7:13) – who will be the Anointed of God with power and majesty as the eschatological judge. Jesus therefore is more than a suffering Messiah; he is an exalted and vindicated Messiah that fulfills the eschatological mission of God.

---

69. France, *The Gospel of Mark*, 659.

70. Hooker writes, "For Mark, it is this Gentile soldier who gives to Jesus the title which hitherto has been spoken only by the heavenly voice or by unclean spirits acknowledging their master. . . . Whether Mark thinks that the centurion is aware of the true significance of his words is not clear. . . . Nevertheless, the centurion stands at this point as the representative of those who acknowledge Jesus as God's son. His words form the climax of Mark's gospel, for they are the words used in the confession of Christian faith, and they are found in the mouth of a Gentile at the moment of Jesus' death" (*The Gospel According to Saint Mark*, 379).

Jesus also affirms that he is the Son of God through his deeds. Through various episodes involving Jesus as teacher and miracle-worker, Mark reports that Jesus' actions identify him as having prerogatives of God. They are Jesus as authoritative teacher (1:21-22; 6:1-6; 11:16-18; 12:35) and Jesus as miracle-worker (1:25-26, 31, 34, 39, 41-42; 2:5, 12; 3:5, 10-11; 4:39; 5:19-20, 28-29, 34, 41-42; 6:5, 32-44, 49-51, 56; 7:25-30, 31-35; 8:1-9, 22-26; 9:17-27; 10:46-52; 11:12-21). There are two other events Mark uses to report Jesus' identity; they are his death (15:16-41) and his resurrection (16:1-6).

It is clear through this brief examination that Mark intends to declare and therefore, affirm Jesus' identity as the Son of God through episodes into a holistic narrative story. The events that answer the identity question, report the biographical and historical aspects of the life of Jesus Christ. These aspects also make a connection to the theological significance for the reader.

Functional Aspect: "What Are His Disciples to Do?"

Mark's intent is not to stop simply at cataloging information or doctrine and thus give the reader a Christology. Rather his intent is to move the reader to the applicational significance based on an understanding of Jesus' identity. Therefore, there is a close connection between "who Jesus is" and "what disciples are to do." Mark's intent is to transform his audience on the nature of discipleship based on a thorough understanding of the identity of Jesus Christ as the Son of God.

The Gospel of Mark answers the question regarding discipleship in a number of ways. First, it illustrates the actions of a disciple. Mark structures the first section of his Gospel account, where Jesus' ministry is in and through Galilee (1:14-8:21), into three major parts (1:14-3:12; 3:13-6:6; 6:7-8:21).[71] This first section of Mark declares and illustrates Jesus' identity as the Son of God while carrying with it the actions of discipleship; that is, the call, the commission, and the work of the ministry. Each of these are tied to the identity of Jesus in the following ways: the call highlights both the abruptness of the encounter and immediacy of the disciples' response (1:16-20; 2:13-17),[72]

---

71. Green, *The Way of the Cross*, 50.

72. Both 1:17 and 2:14 offer clausal complements to Jesus' call (verbs of

thus indicating the force and power of Jesus' presence. The commission or appointment of the Twelve highlights the priority of presence with Jesus and the purpose to evangelize (3:13-19), thus demonstrating the importance of Jesus' teaching. The third characteristic highlights the empowering and engaging ministry given to the disciples (6:7-13), thus signifying Jesus' ability to deal with evil forces. It is the connection therefore, between identity and discipleship that is Mark's intent for his readers.

Second, Mark illustrates the characteristics of a disciple. Mark structures the central section of the story (8:22-10:52) into a three-fold pattern where the disciples find themselves traveling with Jesus "on the way" to Jerusalem. This central section illustrates the connection between Jesus' identity, and the follower's responsibility because of the identity of Jesus. This, therefore, requires a proper definition of Jesus' role and function as Messiah. This central section consists of three things. First, it contains Jesus' three predictions of his death (8:31; 9:31; 10:33-34), providing within each one *his* definition and role as Messiah. Second, it contains the disciples' misunderstanding when confronted with Jesus' meaning of Messiah (8:32b-33; 9:33-34; 10:35-40). And third, it contains instruction from Jesus to explain the disciples' responsibility as follower based on his identity (8:34-9:1; 9:35-37; 10:41-45).[73] Therefore, this central section in the story of Mark also connects the declaration and definition of Jesus' identity (biography and history) with significance for the reader (theology).

---

saying – εἶπεν λέγει) that function as commands (δεῦτε ὀπίσω μου and Ἀκολούθει μοι respectively, "Come, follow me.") See Rodney J. Decker, *Mark 1-8: A Handbook on the Greek Text* (Waco, TX: Baylor U. Press, 2014), 20-21, 56.

73. Robert H. Stein states, "The threefold pattern found in Mark 8:31-10:45 reveals that, for the Evangelist, Jesus' passion was neither accidental nor tragic but was clearly foreknown by Jesus. . . . Furthermore, the errors of the disciples are used as a foil by which Jesus' teachings on discipleship can be presented. Discipleship, for Mark, means following Jesus and taking up a cross (8:34). It means a willingness even to lose one's life Christ's sake or, to word it differently, to lose one's life for 'the gospel's' sake (8:35). Discipleship, for Mark, means becoming servant of all (9:35), even as Jesus was servant of all (10:45)" (*Studying the Synoptic Gospels: Origin and Interpretation*, 2d ed [Grand Rapids: Baker, 2001], 271).

Based on this central section of Mark, what are the characteristics of a disciple? Following each of Jesus' predictions of his death, Mark emphasizes three main characteristics of a disciple. The first characteristic is loyally following Jesus (8:34-9:1); a single-minded identification with Jesus' message and mission by both "denying oneself" and "following Jesus." In other words, the whole person is to stand under Christ's claim.[74] This truth follows Peter's misunderstanding of what Jesus will do (8:32b-33). Peter's wrong view of messiahship gives him a wrong view of discipleship. Jesus clearly understood his own fate; however, he chose loyalty to the Father's plan even though this plan included his death on the cross (cf. Phil 2:7-8). Therefore, Craig Evans states, "To be a true disciple, one must accept the fate of the Master; and the Master's fate is inextricably bound up with his identity, purpose, and mission. True discipleship cannot emerge in isolation from true Christology."[75]

The second characteristic is willingly serving while accepting others. A disciple is not to be preoccupied with being the greatest (9:35-37); service is to be directed to all, especially the insignificant ones. This truth follows the disciples' discussion as to who will be the greatest; that is, who will be the greatest among themselves. But clearly Jesus' death revolutionizes the thinking of a follower. Because being a follower does not entail greatness, but service. Therefore, Green states, "The primary issue is not who receives honor from the rest, but who gives honor to the least. 'Welcoming' has to do with showing respectful service . . . Jesus asks his disciples to understand that the

---

74. Each of Jesus' predictions of his death indicates that Jesus foreknew his own destiny; a predictive power in knowing both the fact and manner of his death reserved for one with divine prerogatives. Each of these predictions demonstrate Mark's connection with identity, 'who is Jesus?' and function, 'what is a disciple to be?' This central section of Mark is exemplary of sections that both precede and follow it.

75. Craig A. Evans, *Mark 8:27-16:20*, WBC 34b (Dallas, Tex: Thomas Nelson, 2001), 30. Graham Twelftree states, "The idea of taking up one's cross would have been a graphic metaphor not only for Mark's readers but for all who lived in the Roman world. . . . Thus, in being called to take up his cross the follower of Jesus was being asked to forfeit his life. His life was to be given over into the hands of another" ("Discipleship in Mark's Gospel," *StMRev* 141 (1990): 9).

greatest honor is extending respectful service to those with no status at all, to the powerless, to those whom society-at-large largely overlooks."[76]

The third characteristic is sacrificially serving with humility. A disciple is not to pursue power and prestige (10:35-40); rather one is to insist on being a servant and doing so with humility.[77] This truth follows the request of James and John to sit at the right and left of Jesus, the positions of honor. However as do all of Jesus' predictions of his death, he turns this request upside down and contrasts the world's value system with his teaching and ultimate example of service. Jesus speaks of greatness with service, not power and prestige, for power and prestige focus on the love for self instead of others. Jesus' example of humility and love for others is demonstrated in his purpose of his death (10:45). Stein states, "Jesus does not die the death of a martyr. He dies rather a vicarious and substitutionary death for 'many.' Thus his death is not only the supreme example of what it means to be 'great' in the kingdom of God, that is, being a servant and slave of all; it is also the once-for-all sacrifice."[78] Therefore, Evans states, "Jesus' followers must seek to serve and not vie for positions of authority; they must be willing to suffer and not flee from persecution; they must be willing to be last and not insist on being first."[79]

Last, the Gospel of Mark illustrates the failures of the disciple. Mark writes his final section of his story in Jerusalem (11:1-16:8). It is here that Mark speaks of the coming Messiah who is to be "the ransom for many." Although this section of the story does not provide specific instructions related

---

76. Green, *The Way of the Cross*, 74. Dennis Sweetland states, "The result is that Jesus turns things upside down; he teaches that true greatness means giving yourself in personal service to the one from whom you can receive no benefit in return" (*Our Journey with Jesus: Discipleship According to Mark* [Wilmington, Del: Michael Glazier, 1987], 64).

77. The text states 'whoever wants to be first must be a slave of all.' Edwards states, "The pronouncement is, of course, an oxymoron, for a slave (Gk. *doulos*), who was inferior even to a servant (Gk. *diakonos*), was in ancient society the last and least of all. The idea of a slave being first is as absurdly paradoxical as a camel going through the eye of a needle (v. 25) – and it probably likewise induced smiles and shaking heads from Jesus' audience" (*The Gospel According to Mark*, 326).

78. Stein, *Mark*, 490.

79. Evans, *Mark 8:27-16:20*, 115.

to discipleship, it does speak to the failure of obedience (14:32-42), the failure of following (14:50-54) and the failure of loyalty (14:66-72) on the part of Jesus' disciples. As Jesus faithfully prepares for his death through prayer to the Father (14:32-42), the disciples exemplify faithlessness in their lack of watchfulness. As Jesus is betrayed into the hands of men (14:43-49), the disciples demonstrate a cowardice and panic. As Jesus identifies himself as Messiah, the Son of God (14:61-62) Peter denies his identification with Jesus three times. Mark communicates Jesus' resolve to follow the will of God, even to the death of the cross. Surely the Son of God is worthy of continuing devotion and allegiance.

Summary of The Gospel of Mark as Theological Narrative Biography

The Gospel of Mark narrates the story of Jesus; thus expressing, through the episodes of Jesus' life, the identity of Jesus Christ as the Son of God. But the Gospel of Mark is not just about knowing Jesus; it is also about following Jesus. This is the purpose of the theological narrative biography, to awaken and subsequently strengthen the faith of the reader. This enables the reader to connect the 'what' and 'why' of Mark's intent. In other words, Mark not only writes his story with a Christological emphasis but also an applicational significance to the readers' life.

Mark answers 'who is Jesus' through the opening Christological statement, the confirmation of God, the confession of Peter, the commentary of others, and the words of Jesus himself. All of this supports the declaration and confirmation that Jesus' identity is indeed the Son of God. Mark also answers 'what are his disciples to do' by recording the actions of a disciple, the characteristics of a disciple, and the failures of a disciple.

The connection between form (Jesus' identity) and function (disciples' responsibility) enables the reader to see how Mark ties together the 'what' of his story with the 'why'. In other words, it seems clear that Mark utilizes the narrative structure (genre) of the story and more specifically the theological narrative biography (sub-genre) to communicate and therefore connect the doctrinal emphasis of knowing (identity) Jesus with the practical emphasis of following (responsibility) him. Mark makes this connection throughout the whole story and namely, through the central section of the book. The reader can comprehend the intention of the author through understanding how Mark writes the Gospel as genre and sub-genre, or form and function.

Conclusion

The Gospel of Mark is a story about Jesus Christ. It is best analyzed using two literary categories; that is, genre (narrative) and sub-genre (theological narrative biography). These two genre categories capture the uniqueness of the Gospel accounts because they include the biographical, historical, and theological components of narrative. These two categories therefore best explain Mark's story. His purpose is also biographical, historical, and theological.

Mark organizes his narrative around three geographical locations (Galilee, "on the way" to Jerusalem, and Jerusalem); while maintaining a Christological emphasis of Jesus' identity. Consequently, the reader must not miss Mark's strategy to communicate his purpose as he weaves geography and theology into his narrative. Mark uses the geographical movement of Jesus along with the authorities, disciples, and crowd to declare, define and affirm his identity as the Son of God. Those involved convey various expressions that illustrate their relationship to Jesus as the Son of God, for they either commit to him or oppose him, and sometimes both. Mark tells the narrative from perspectives that are engaging and accommodating to the reader's understanding. The Gospel of Mark is a narrative establishing the identity of Jesus Christ.

Mark's story is not just about the identity of Jesus Christ, it is also about following Jesus Christ. Mark involves the reader in his story. He demonstrates the significance of his story to the reader by demonstrating the importance of knowing and following Jesus; thus, providing the application of his story.

Chapter Five

Discourse Analysis of the Passion Predictions

Introduction

Two key components of discourse analysis are necessary complements of the hermeneutical process leading to a proper interpretation of the passion predictions and their function within the Gospel of Mark. These key components are discourse structure and discourse texture. Chapters three and four focused on discourse structure. The focus of this chapter is discourse texture.

Discourse texture involves an examination at the level of the text and its features, or micro-structure. Therefore, this examination of the central secton of Mark's story, clearly illustrates a bottom-up approach to discourse analysis. The textual features that are examined include: metafunctions of language (use of language), cohesion (relationship of language), prominence (emphasis of language), and discourse boundaries (limitations of language). Mark's use of language, as it is demonstrated through his intentional choices of words, communicates meaning. In other words, what is Mark's intended meaning and therefore significance of each passion prediction within the central section?

DEATH AND DISCIPLESHIP:
An Analysis of the Predictions of Jesus' Death in the Gospel of Mark

This chapter utilizes three analyses to discover the function of Jesus' three predictions of his death within the central section and their relationship to Mark's story. The first analysis is called the Greek text analysis. This analysis reflects the grammatical, lexical, and semantic meanings, and functions of Mark's choice of words, phrases, and sentences. It is through the translation of Mark's text that the reader can identify some, or all, the textual features within each passion prediction (e.g., cohesion, prominence, etc). The second analysis is called the verb analysis. This analysis explains Mark's choice of verbs and their conjugation. The intent is to analyze the verbs through verbal aspect.[1] Verbal aspect, therefore points to levels of prominence that Mark implements to communicate the background, foreground, and frontground of the story to the reader.[2] In other words, the verb analysis helps to portray the role and prominence each event within the narrative possesses for each of Jesus' predictions of his death.

The last analysis is called the role analysis. This analysis shows the relationship of the various events to one another. It is a graphic representation of Mark's choice of words, phrases, and sentences he brings together to communicate the whole intended meaning. It further represents the significance of each of the predictions of Jesus' death, the disciples' misunderstanding of his prediction, and Jesus' instructions based upon their misunderstanding that ultimately shows how each one relates to Mark's story.

The purpose of this chapter is to examine each of Jesus' predictions (8:31-9:1; 9:31-37; 10:32-45) as they occur in the central section of the Gospel of Mark. The examination however is not without purpose. Utilizing discourse analysis, the examination will explicate the role and therefore the theological

---

1. Verbs in all moods are examined. Verbs in all tenses, except for the future tense, are examined. The future tense is not considered for the following reasons. Decker states, "Although there is diversity regarding the explanation, most scholars working in this area have concluded that the future form is not a parallel category with present, aorist, and perfect forms. . . . Porter has argued that the future is aspectually vague (i.e., does not convey an aspectual value such as perfective, imperfective, or stative) and that it is not a tense per se" (Rodney Decker, *Temporal Deixis of the Greek Verb with Reference to Verbal Aspect*, Studies in Biblical Greek 10 [New York: Peter Lang, 2001], 112).

2. Verbal aspect was discussed earlier in chapter 2.

significance of Jesus' predictions and their cohesive relationship within the central section of the Gospel of Mark and the story as a whole. In other words, how does Mark's central section delineate the relationship between the formal aspect, or the identity of Jesus Christ ('who is Jesus'), and the functional aspect of the story, or the responsibility of the disciples, ('what they ought to do)?

THE CENTRAL SECTION OF MARK: 8:22–10:52

Before an examination of Jesus' passion predictions occurs, validation of the central section is in order.[3] In other words, why is 8:22-10:52 a discourse? The central section of the Gospel of Mark? Utilizing two discourse features of the text (discourse boundaries and cohesion), there are three reasons why Mark's central section is 8:22-10:52. They are: the healing of the blind stories that border the section (discourse boundaries), the repetition of the phrase ἐν τῇ ὁδῷ ("on the way") throughout the section (cohesion), and the repetition of the three-fold pattern within the section (Jesus' predictions of his death, the disciples' misunderstanding and Jesus' teachings on discipleship) also demonstrating cohesion. These three reasons not only validate the limitations of Mark's central section, but also of greater significance, they serve to validate that the structure of Mark's story is to be understood through three geographical locations, not two.[4]

---

3. It is important to note Kevin Larsen's comment. He writes, "While a principle for determining Markan structure is under debate, near unanimous consent exists for a distinct section in the middle of the gospel, beginning at either 8.22 or 8.27 and ending at 10.45 or 10.52" ("The Structure of Mark's Gospel: Current Proposals, *CurBR* 3, no. 1 [2004]: 141). As Larsen claims, many do see a middle section. However, some scholars conclude that Mark's story is structured into two-parts rather than three and therefore combine this middle section with Mark's final section of his story (8:22 or 8:27 – 16:8). These scholars typically divide Mark's story in this way (1:14-8:22/27 and 8:22/27-16:8).

4. One of the implications of this discourse analysis is not only to provide the reader with the significance of the central section within Mark's story; but to also offer an objective explanation as to why Mark's story is structured into three distinct geo-

DEATH AND DISCIPLESHIP:
An Analysis of the Predictions of Jesus' Death in the Gospel of Mark

Discourse Boundaries

Discourse boundaries are features in the text that designate where paragraphs and/or discourses begin and end. These features can include, but are not limited to, inclusio, geography, shifts in grammatical person (e.g., first to third person), and shifts in verb-tense forms.[5] Mark utilizes three features as discourse boundaries. They are: inclusio (2 healing of the blind episodes), geography (journey from north to south), and shifts in verb-tense forms (historical present). These three features establish the boundaries of the central section, beginning at 8:22 and ending at 10:52.

Inclusio As A Discourse Boundary: Healing of Blind Miracles

Mark declares Jesus' identity in the first section (1:14-8:21) of his story as he travels in and around Galilee. This is seen in individual paragraphs or episodes illustrating Jesus' ministry as it is focused on the crowds through teachings and miracles. However, in the central section (8:22-10:52), Mark uses only three healing miracles (8:22-26; 9:14-29; 10:46-52), of which, only the two healing of the blind miracles are discussed here. The focus of Mark's story has clearly changed as the reader moves from the first section to the central section. In other words, the declaration of Jesus' identity has moved away from the publicity and notoriety among the crowd to the definition of Jesus' role as the Messiah within the privacy of the disciples.[6]

---

graphical sections (Galilee 1:14-8:21; 'on the way' to Jerusalem 8:22-10:52; Jerusalem 11:1-16:8) rather than two. As the analysis will demonstrate, Mark did not arrange his story through two locations, for Mark did not combine the middle section with the final section illustrating that his story is told through two locations, Galilee and Jerusalem.

5. Inclusio is a common structuring device where "an author would reintroduce at the end of a section the words, themes or stories that opened that section of discourse. This would be received as a signal of that section's close" (David A. DeSilva, *An Introduction to the New Testament: Contexts, Methods and Ministry Formation* [Downers Grove, Ill: InterVarsity Press, 2004], 199).

6. R. T. France states, "Nor does Jesus spend time any longer teaching the crowds: ὁ ὄχλος is strangely present during what appears to be a private retreat at 8:34, and certain incidents involve a crowd as spectators (9:14; 10:1, 13, 46), but the focus

The two healing of the blind miracles frame the central section or form an inclusio. They serve as discourse boundaries.[7] The two healing of the blind episodes are the only two in Mark's story and significantly serve to portray the disciples' spiritual blindness.[8] The first healing of the blind episode, 8:22-26, serves to introduce the central section. Although Mark seems to conclude the blindness theme that occurs with the disciples (cf. 8:18), blindness may still be lingering. As a result, Mark uses the story of the healing of the blind man of Bethsaida to illustrate gradual healing through Jesus' repeated touch (8:23-25). The healing of the blind man's physical sight will set the stage for Mark's emphasis of the central section; that is, the healing of the disciples' spiritual sight. Mark desires that the disciples clearly see who Jesus is and therefore understand their role because of knowing his identity. Jesus' repeated touch upon the blind man of Bethsaida provided clear sight. Therefore, Mark's re-

---

throughout is now on Jesus' private instruction of his disciples" (*The Gospel of Mark*, NIGTC [Grand Rapids: Eerdmans, 2002], 320).

7. There is some debate as to how the healing of the blind man at Bethsaida serves as a boundary. There are those who see the blind man at Bethsaida as the conclusion of 6:6b-8:21; thus the central section begins at 8:27. See D. E. Nineham, *The Gospel of Saint Mark*, Pelican Gospel Commentaries (Baltimore, Md: Penguin, 1963) 223; Morna Hooker, *The Gospel According to Saint Mark*, Black's New Testament Commentaries 2 (Peabody, Mass: Hendrickson, 1991), 28; Robert Guelich, *Mark 1-8:26*, WBC, 34a (Nashville: Thomas Nelson, 1989), 316).

There are those who see the healing of the blind man at Bethsaida as the beginning of the central section (8:22-10:52). See Ernest Best, "Discipleship in Mark: Mark 8:22-10:52," *SJT* 23 (1970): 323-37; Joel Marcus, *Mark 1-8*, The Anchor Bible 27 (New York: Doubleday, 1986), 381; John R. Donahue and Daniel J. Harrington, *The Gospel of Mark*, The Sacra Pagina Series (Collegeville, Minn: Liturgical Press, 2002), 49; and Norman Perrin and Dennis Duling, *The New Testament: An Introduction*, 2d ed. (New York: Harcourt, Brace, Jovanovich, 1982), 239.

8. Joel Marcus states, "Throughout the section, the Markan disciples show themselves to be 'blind' –terribly imperceptive and in need of the illumination of Jesus' teaching. They ask inane questions (9:10-11; 10:10), make stupid remarks (9:5-6), grasp for personal power (9:33-34; 10:35-40), mistake the merciful nature of Jesus' mission (9:38), and otherwise show themselves deficient in appreciating the unique way in which God's dominion is manifesting itself through Jesus" (*Mark 8-16: A New Translation with Introduction and Commentary*, The Anchor Yale Bible 27a [New Haven, Conn: Yale University Press, 2009], 589).

port of both Jesus' repeated predictions of his death and teachings regarding discipleship are representative of the disciples to also see clearly.

The second healing of the blind episode, 10:46-52, serves to conclude the central section. It forms an inclusio with the first healing of the blind episode (8:22-26). The themes of faith and follower demonstrate Mark's intent in the story of the healing of the blind man, Bartimaeus. Although Mark is wrapping-up the central section, the disciples' lack of faith or unwillingness to follow may still be lingering (cf. 10:32, 52). Thus, Mark uses the healing of Bartimaeus to illustrate the faith of a follower ἐν τῇ ὁδῷ ("on the road," 10:52), rather than an innocent bystander παρὰ τὴν ὁδόν ("alongside of the road," 10:46). Bartimaeus was able to see because of what he heard, not what he had seen (10:49-52). He asked for normalcy, not glory or power (cf. 10:35-37) and thus, because of Bartimaeus' faith, he was able to follow Jesus (10:52). Therefore, this healing episode represents the importance for the disciples to possess faith and a willingness to follow ἐν τῇ ὁδῷ ("on the road"). This will be challenged as they enter Jerusalem where Jesus will die.

Mark utilizes two healing of the blind episodes to grab the readers' attention. The two episodes serve to introduce and conclude Mark's emphasis of the central section; that is, to see clearly who Jesus is, his mission as the Messiah, and willingly and faithfully follow him as a result. Based on Jesus' identity and his teaching, the disciples are to follow him. Later in the story (cf. 11:1ff), it is clear that Jesus' repeated attempts to define who he is and by implication teach how to follow him, were not clearly seen nor heard by his disciples. Dennis Sweetland captures Mark's intent for the central section well. He states,

> Mark wants his readers to understand that what Jesus did at the beginning and the end of his journey (i.e., open the eyes of the blind), he also attempted to do while he was traveling along the way from Caesarea Philippi to Jerusalem. The miracle worker, who is able to cure physical blindness, sets out to cure the spiritual blindness of the disciples in between these two stories. In fact, throughout the central section of the Gospel, Jesus is pictured as opening the eyes of his disciples to a new dimension of his messiahship. These intimate companions of Jesus must

'see' (i.e., understand) the necessity of his suffering and death, and what significance these have for a correct understanding of discipleship.[9]

Geography As A Discourse Boundary: From North to South

Jesus' ministry began in and around Galilee (1:14) and continued throughout the surrounding areas (1:14-8:21). It was not until Jesus came to Bethsaida[10] (8:22) that the movement of his ministry began to progress from the north (Bethsaida) to the south (Jerusalem, 11:1); thus, illustrating Jesus' movement "on the way" to Jerusalem. When one comes to the first blind man healing episode in 8:22, a shift in geography occurs from the preceding episode (8:14-21); that is, Jesus has journeyed from the western side of the Sea of Galilee, Dalmanutha, to the northeast.[11] The first blind man healing episode occurred in a region northeast of Galilee, an area outside of the typical Galilean area where Jesus ministered in the first section of Mark's story (1:14-8:21); thus indicating that Mark uses geography to note shifts in episodes.

Jesus' ministry continued through the central section (8:22-10:52) traveling toward Jerusalem. As Jesus journeys south toward Jerusalem, it is in the second blind man healing episode (10:46-52) that Mark locates Jesus in Jericho.[12] When Mark concludes the second blind man healing episode in 10:52, a shift in geography occurs with the following episode (11:1-11). It is in this following episode that Jesus is nearer to Jerusalem, in the towns of

---

9. Dennis Sweetland, *Mark: From Death to Life*, (Hyde Park, N.Y.: New City Press, 2007), 105.

10. George Martin notes that Bethsaida was about four miles from Capernaum and was located in the territory ruled by Philip, a son of Herod the Great. (*The Gospel According to Mark: Meaning and Message* [Chicago: Loyola Press, 2005], 197).

11. France, *The Gospel of Mark*, 309-10. James A. Brooks states that Dalmanutha is unknown and more than likely is representative of Matthew's location in 15:39 known as Magadala (*Mark*, NAC 23 [Nashville: Broadman and Holman, 1991], 126). See also Marcus, *Mark 1-8*, 498; Robert H. Stein, *Mark*, BEC (Grand Rapids: Baker, 2008), 374-75.

12. Stein indicates that Jericho is about seventeen miles northeast of Jerusalem. (*Mark*, 493). This indicates that Jesus' journey is a movement from north to south toward his destination of Jerusalem.

Bethphage and Bethany (11:1). This also indicates that Mark uses geography to note shifts in discourses.

Mark utilizes geography to indicate the beginning and ending of episodes, thus arranging the central section as a discourse. Mark's movement within his story takes Jesus from the surrounding area of Galilee in the first section (1:14-8:21) and places him in the northeast region of Galilee (8:22) at the beginning of the central section. As Mark reports Jesus' journey south (8:22-10:52) toward his final destination at Jerusalem; his final episode (10:46-52) of the central section locates Jesus just outside of Jerusalem prior to entering Jerusalem (11:1-16:8). Mark's story, and more specifically the central section, is therefore captured through Jesus' geographical movement, or "on the way" to Jerusalem.

Shifts in Verb-Tense Forms As A Discourse Boundary: The Historical Present

A shift in verb-tense forms can also serve as one of the factors indicating boundaries of a discourse. Typical to narrative genre, the backbone of the story is carried through the aorist verb-tense form. Therefore, there are some occurrences where the narrative shifts tense-forms to the historical present, and this signals a new paragraph.[13] In fact, Porter indicates that "Mark frequently uses καί and a verb, often of speaking or location, occasionally in the historic present to mark a new pericope."[14] This is the case in 8:22a and 11:1a; both of which are found in the beginning of the paragraphs that border the central section. This is typical throughout Mark's story.[15]

---

13. This shift in tenses does not include λέγω-historical presents.

14. Stanley E. Porter, *Idioms of the Greek New Testament*, 2d ed, Biblical Languages: Greek 2 (Sheffield: Sheffield Academic Press, 1999), 301-02. See also Constantine R. Campbell, *Verbal Aspect, the Indicative Mood, and Narrative: Soundings in the Greek of the New Testament*, Studies in Biblical Greek 13 (New York: Peter Lang, 2007), 61-64. Campbell states that the historical present in Mark is common to begin discourses. In fact, he concludes of Mark's 151 uses of historical present, 90 of them introduce discourses (68-69). See also Randall Buth, "Mark's Use of the Historical Present," *Notes on Translation* 65 (1977): 7-13.

15. See Decker, *Temporal Deixis of the Greek Verb*, 103-04. The beginning

In 8:22a Mark uses the historical present construction (καί + verb form), καί ἔρχεται εἰς Βηθσαϊδάν ("and he came to Bethsaida"), to begin a new paragraph. Although this shift in verb-tense form does not provide adequate evidence alone for the beginning of the central section, is does indicate that 8:22 begins a new paragraph, of which when both the geography and inclusio features are included, the necessary verification is evident to begin the central section at 8:22 instead of 8:27.[16]

In 11:1a, Mark also uses the historical present, καί ὅτε ἐγγίζουσιν εἰς Ἱερουσαλήμ ("and when they were drawing near to Jerusalem") to begin a new paragraph. Porter demonstrates the conclusion of the central section (10:52) and the beginning of the final section in Mark's story (11:1-16:8) through a shift in verb-tense forms. He states that the shift from the imperfect (ἠκολούθει) in 10:52b to the historical present (ἐγγίζουσιν) in 11:1 opens a new paragraph. The grammatical delineation of the new paragraph is con-

---

of these paragraphs often involves new participants or new locations. Decker also provides explanation regarding the function of the historical present, specifically in Mark. He states, "The aorist is the typical form used in an historical narrative. When the writer wishes to make a narrative transition (e.g., to begin a new paragraph), one of the linguistic means he has at his disposal is the use of a form that is semantically more heavily marked: the imperfective aspect of the present form. This draws attention to the statement and its discourse function" (104).

16. Campbell notes that the historical present and geography can indicate a new paragraph has begun. He writes, "For example, the reason it may be found at the beginning of certain pericopae within Mark is because Mark wishes to highlight that Jesus has moved to a new location, thus a new section has begun. It is not just the fact that an historical present appears that marks a new pericope, but it is because a geographical transition has taken place, and this transition is heightened by use of an historical present of propulsion" (*Verbal Aspect, the Indicative Mood, and Narrative*, 75).

Stephen Levinsohn explains the importance of the historical present and the location of arrival. "When a verb of arrival such as 'come, bring, call together' [i.e., a verb of propulsion] is presented in the present tense in narrative, this indicates that the participant involved either has arrived at or has been brought to the place where a significant interaction of participants is to take place. In other words, the historic present establishes the location in which an important interaction will occur" ("Preliminary Observations on the Use of the Historic Present in Mark," *Notes on Translation* 65 [1977]: 13).

sistent with the details concerning new events related to Jesus' entrance into Jerusalem.

Mark utilizes a shift in verb-tense forms to signify the boundaries of the central section. Mark's story is structured in three sections, though the emphasis is the central section. Mark develops his central section through a shift in verb-tense forms, namely through the historical present.[17] As one moves from within and out of the central section, there is a change in topics; that is, the healing of the blind man at Bethsaida (8:22-26) is different than Jesus' discussion with the disciples (8:14-21), and the healing of the blind Bartimeus (10:46-52) is different than Jesus' entrance into Jerusalem (11:1-11). In other words, the shift in verb-tense forms at both 8:22 and 11:1 appears to serve as discourse boundaries that signify when the central section begins (8:22) and ends (10:52).

Cohesion

Cohesion is what ties a text or discourse together. Cohesion can occur at the word, phrase, sentence, and paragraph level and is established through various features (e.g., chiasm, conjunctions, grammatical persons, prepositions, and repetition). One textual feature that Mark utilizes to tie the central section together is repetition: both at the phrase and paragraph level. The use of repetition within the central section (8:22-10:52) enables the discourse to "hang together" as a section in and of itself.

Repetition As Cohesion: ἐν τῇ ὁδῷ ("On the Way")

The first cohesion feature that Mark uses to structure, and therefore hold together the central section (8:22-10:52) of his story, is through the repetition of the phrase ἐν τῇ ὁδῷ ("on the way," 8:27; 9:33, 34; 10:32, 52).[18] Mark's repeated

---

17. Levinsohn argues that the historical present can serve to highlight certain episodes and themes. He calls this a narrative presentation ("Preliminary Observations on the Use of the Historic Present in Mark," 13). Thus, according to Levinsohn, it seems reasonable to indicate that Mark's use of the historic present provides the reader with the narrative presentation of the central section of his story.

18. There are two other occurrences of a similar phrase. Each one is in the

use of the phrase explicates a movement. As Jesus moves ἐν τῇ ὁδῷ, Mark weaves geography, theology, and discipleship into the story. The repeated use of the phrase references both the disciples' and Jesus' journey. This geographical movement within the central section, namely from north to south, captures part of Mark's "on the way" emphasis that culminates in Jesus' death in Jerusalem.[19]

It is not just a geographical journey from north to south, but also a theological journey indicating that "Jesus is not traveling on 'any' way; as 10:32 finally makes clear, he is on a particular road, the way to Jerusalem. This we know is the way that leads to betrayal, condemnation, and death (10:32-34). More important, it is the way set before Jesus by God."[20] This is not a side trip for the disciples; but for them it is a journey of instruction and submission.

Four of the occurrences (8:27; 9:33, 34; 10:32) of the phrase ἐν τῇ ὁδῷ are tied to each of the three passion predictions.[21] The emphasis of the predictions, and thus the emphasis of the central section, is to identify Jesus as

---

accusative case, εἰς ὁδόν ("into the way," 10:17) and παρὰ τὴν ὁδόν ("alongside of the way," 10:46). Mark uses the preposition εἰς in 10:17 ("into. . .") and παρὰ in 10:46 ("alongside of. . .") but not the preposition ἐν.

19. Graham Twelftree also sees the significance of Jesus' geographical journey 'on the way.' He writes, "The implication is that the whole of Jesus' ministry is to be understood as a journey. In the middle section of Mark, the story moves from Bethsaida to Caesarea Philippi, to Capernaum, to Judea, across the Jordan, back to Capernaum (10.10?) and on towards Jerusalem via Jericho. This movement is encapsulated in the phrase '*on the way*'" ("Discipleship in Mark's Gospel," *StMRev* 141 (1990): 8).

20. Joel B. Green, *The Way of the Cross: Following Jesus in the Gospel of Mark* (Eugene, Ore: Wipf & Stock, 1991), 36.

21. Marcus notes the structural significance of the phrase ἐν τῇ ὁδῷ and its relationship to each passion prediction. He states, "These juxtapositions are again, probably no accident: the 'way' of Jesus and the disciples, which ultimately leads to death in Jerusalem, is the journey on which human blindness is healed" (*Mark 8-16*, 590). Decker proposes an alternative interpretation of the phrase ἐν τῇ ὁδῷ. He states that ἐν + dative can be a prepositional indicator with temporal reference rather than a locative sense. He claims the phrase ἐν τῇ ὁδῷ in 8:27; 9:33, 34; 10:32 ought to be translated ("while on the road") indicating the time of the travel not the location of the travel. (*Temporal Deixis of the Greek Verb*, 79, 211).

the suffering Messiah and therefore delineate the subsequent responsibilities of those who follow Jesus 'on the way.' Mark uses the phrase ἐν τῇ ὁδῷ to establish the call of the disciples; that is, the way Jesus goes is the way he calls his disciples to go.

The final occurrence of the phrase ἐν τῇ ὁδῷ in 10:52 is not related to one of Jesus' passion predictions directly but does establish the importance of faithfully following Jesus "on the way" to Jerusalem. Mark carefully places the episode of the healing of Bartimaeus and the willing obedient response of Bartimaeus to Jesus' call prior to Jesus' entrance into Jerusalem (11:1ff), for the disciples will be asked to faithfully follow Jesus all the way to the cross. Mark may provide the reader with insight regarding the participation of blind Bartimaeus. For example, Mark shifts his use of "on the way" language in 10:46 (παρὰ τὴν ὁδόν) to indicate that Bartimaeus is not a follower of Jesus, for he is *alongside* of the way and not *in* Jesus' way. This is a natural consequence of his blindness. Mark uses the phrase (ἐν τῇ ὁδῷ) to demonstrate that blind Bartimaeus, after receiving sight, now willingly and faithfully follows Jesus 'on the way;' no longer is he an innocent bystander but a committed follower.

Mark utilizes the repetition of the phrase ἐν τῇ ὁδῷ to tie his central section together.[22] The phrase not only provides direction for the reader as to Jesus' geographical journey, but also points to the theological journey. Jesus is traveling to Jerusalem where it is necessary (δεῖ, 8:31) that he suffer and die and rise again; for this points to the identity of Jesus and his mission. Mark may also use the phrase ἐν τῇ ὁδῷ to place the disciples "on the way" as a committed follower of Jesus in the same way as Bartimaeus.

---

22. Bas M. F. Van Iersal claims that the central section to Mark's story could be the center of the story's structure. He validates this by using Mark's text signals, namely the phrase ἐν τῇ ὁδῷ. He writes, "The series contains the text signal that the reader is looking for in 10:32: Jesus is 'on the way . . . to Jerusalem.' The syntagm also contains the text signal itself, the word combination 'on the way' or 'on the road' (ἐν τῇ ὁδῷ), which occurs at the beginning and the end, namely in 8:27 and 10:52, as well as between these two places in 9:33, 34; 10:17 (in the form εἰς ὁδόν). Outside of this part of the text the combination occurs only in 8.3 . . . and 11.8" (*Mark: A Reader-Response Commentary*, trans. W. H. Bisscheroux [Edinburgh: T. & T. Clark, 1998], 77-78).

Repetition As Cohesion: Three-fold Pattern

Another feature of cohesion that Mark uses to hold together the central section (8:22-10:52) of his story, is through the repetition of a three-fold pattern. The three-fold pattern is found in each of the three episodes: Jesus' prediction of his death, the disciples' misunderstanding, and Jesus' teaching to his disciples. Mark's repeated use of this pattern serves to explicate the following truths: the identity of Jesus and definition of his mission (8:31; 9:31; 10:33-34); the disciples' misunderstanding of Jesus' mission (8:32b-33; 9:33-34; 10:35-41); thus, resulting in the teachings of Jesus (8:34-9:1; 9:33-37; 10:35-45). Stein captures Mark's intent of his repeated pattern. He states, "Interwoven throughout this section of Mark is Jesus' explanation of his mission as the Christ, the Son of God, centering on three passion predictions and the example they provide for discipleship."[23] Mark's emphasis is clear. The one who knows Jesus is responsible to follow him. However, one is to follow Jesus based on his teachings not one's own understanding.

The central section clearly evidences a careful arrangement of episodes that delineate an attention to Jesus' identity and the resultant role of the disciples. The passion predictions provide the reader and the disciples with knowledge concerning the identity of the suffering Messiah, with the climax as the final prediction (10:33-34) prior to Jesus entering Jerusalem. The disciples' behavior runs contrary to Jesus' predictions and therefore demonstrates that they are both afraid and without understanding. Thus, Jesus' corrective teaching offers a model for his followers.

Summary

The intent of this section of the chapter was to validate 8:22-10:52 as the central section of Mark's story. Two features of discourse texture point to this conclusion. They are discourse boundaries and cohesion. The discourse boundaries provided the means to indicate where the central section begins

---

23. Stein, *Mark*, 387.

and ends. The healing of the blind men episodes serve as an inclusio or book-ends to the central section. These episodes also provided the reader with a glimpse of the disciples' lack of spiritual sight or understanding; a theme Mark deals with throughout the central section. Mark captured Jesus' movement into (8:22) and out of the central section (10:52) via the healing of the blind episodes. This geographical movement pictures Jesus' movement from north to south, of which his final destination is Jerusalem. His movement in the first part of Mark's story (1:14-8:21) is primarily in and around Galilee and his journey ceases once he arrives in Jerusalem (11:1ff). The geographical markers in 8:22 – 10:52 validate this central section as a separate section.

The shifts in verb-tense forms also validate the boundaries of the central section. The historical present in both 8:22a and 11:1a, which is typical throughout Mark's story as paragraph markers, designate the boundaries of the central section. Therefore, the shift to the historical present in two places indicates a new paragraph; in 8:22a (the healing of the blind man) and in 11:1 (where Jesus enters Jerusalem). This is consistent with the inclusio and in turn is another feature of discourse texture pointing to the conclusion of the central section at 10:52.

The use of repetition throughout the central section provides cohesion that holds the central section together as a cohesive whole. Mark's repeated use of the phrase ἐν τῇ ὁδῷ and the three-fold pattern introduced each time by Jesus' prediction of his death indicates the central section "hangs together." A further examination as to how each of these three predictions function and therefore cohere together within the central section and the story as a whole is the subject of the next section of this chapter.

Jesus' Three Passion Predictions

The central section of Mark's story focuses on two main emphases. Those emphases are the identity and purpose of Jesus Christ (formal aspect) and the responsibility for discipleship (functional aspect). Mark carefully arranges the central section around a three-fold pattern. This pattern is the three passion predictions (8:31; 9:31; 10:32-34), serving as the backbone of the central section. Each of the predictions is then followed by the disciples' misunderstanding and Jesus' instruction on discipleship.

Mark's three-fold pattern is purposeful. It prepares the reader for the significance of the role of two main characters, Jesus, and his disciples.[24] Mark's central section therefore carefully weaves together Jesus' role as the suffering Messiah and the disciples' role as faithful follower. Further examination of the three-fold pattern will demonstrate how the central section coheres, or "hangs together," as a section within Mark's story as a whole.

Jesus' three passion predictions are examined in the following pages using three analyses. The analyses will examine the Greek text (e.g., conjunctions, particles, prepositional phrases, etc.),[25] verbal forms, and the relationship and role of the events within each passion prediction. The analyses show Mark's use of various textual features (e.g., cohesion, prominence); thus, demonstrating to the reader Mark's intended emphasis and relationship of each passion with the whole story.

---

24. Robert H. Stein, *Studying the Synoptic Gospels: Origin and Interpretation*, 2d ed (Grand Rapids: Baker, 2001), 271-72.

25. Jesus' passion predictions are analyzed from the NA27 Greek text. Erwin Nestle, Barbara et Kurt Aland, Johannes Karavidopoulos, Carlo M. Martini, and Bruce M. Metzger, *Novum Testamentum Graece* (Deutsche Bibelgesellschaft: Stuttgart, 1993).

DEATH AND DISCIPLESHIP:
AN ANALYSIS OF THE PREDICTIONS OF JESUS' DEATH IN THE GOSPEL OF MARK

Jesus' First Passion Prediction (8:31-9:1)

Greek Text Analysis

Jesus' First Prediction of His Death

31.   Καὶ   ἤρξατο διδάσκειν[26] αὐτοὺς ὅτι[27] δεῖ[28] τὸν υἱὸν

26. Mark's use of ἄρχομαι signals the reader's attention on development throughout the story (cf. 4:1; 6:2, 34). However, the use of ἤρξατο with the infinitive διδάσκειν, and the pronouncement that follows, could signal a new theme. France states, "The fact that its theme will be repeated prominently from now on, suggests that we should read it as signaling a new and central theme in Jesus' teaching to his disciples" (*The Gospel of Mark*, 333). See also James R. Edwards, *The Gospel According to Mark*, PNTC (Grand Rapids: Eerdmans, 2002), 252; Hooker, *The Gospel According to Saint Mark*, 205; William L. Lane, *The Gospel of Mark*, NICNT (Grand Rapids: Eerdmans, 1974), 294.

Mark's use of this introduction (καί ἤρξατο) signals new teaching that Jesus intends to give his disciples three times throughout the central section; thus, providing cohesion to the section. See Decker, *Temporal Deixis of the Greek Verb*, 84, 216n156. *Contra* Robert H. Gundry notes the importance of the introduction to this first prediction, but views καί ἤρξατο as pleonastic. He notes the introduction typifying Mark's way of demonstrating Jesus' authority. He writes, "The new introduction sports a characteristically Marcan pleonastic καί ἤρξατο, 'and he began.' In view of the authority which Jesus' teaching connotes in Mark . . . and in view of the following prediction of his passion and resurrection . . . 'to teach them' shows that Mark is emphasizing the predictive power of Jesus" (*Mark: A Commentary on His Apology for the Cross* [Grand Rapids: Eerdmans, 1993], 428).

27. This is a recitative ὅτι. "It is a specialized use of the direct object clause after a verb of perception. It is a very common use of the ὅτι clause in the Hellenistic era. In direct discourse, the ὅτι is not to be translated; in its place you should put quotation marks" (Daniel B. Wallace, *Greek Grammar Beyond the Basics: An Exegetical Syntax of the New Testament* [Grand Rapids: Zondervan, 1996], 454-55). Gundry also notes the probability as recitative. He states, "But an undoubtedly recitative ὅτι in another passion-and-resurrection prediction at 10:33 and a probably recitative ὅτι in yet another one at 9:31 favor the same kind here" (*Mark*, 446.

28. The use of δεῖ for Mark is purposeful, for it connects to 1:1, the theme of the story. Presumably it is a divine passive; that is, "the impersonal δεῖ can be a subtle way of speaking of God's agency" (Marcus, *Mark 8-16*, 605). Stein agrees. He writes, "the

> τοῦ ἀνθρώπου πολλὰ παθεῖν καὶ
> ἀποδοκιμασθῆναι ὑπὸ²⁹ τῶν πρεσβυτέρων
>
> καὶ τῶν ἀρχιερέων καὶ τῶν γραμματέων³⁰
> καὶ ἀποκτανθῆναι καὶ μετὰ τρεῖς ἡμέρας
> ἀναστῆναι.

32. καὶ   παρρησίᾳ τὸν λόγον ἐλάλει.³¹

---

necessity of Jesus' death is emphasized. It is necessary because (1) Scripture teaches this (9:12; 14:21, 27), and (2) it is a divinely preordained necessity (δεῖ, *dei*; cf. 8:31; 9:11; 13:7, 10). (The expression 'it is written' [9:12; 14:21, 49] and δεῖ share the same connotation—God's word and will must take place). The divine purpose of Jesus' ministry as the Christ is to fulfill the divine plan and to offer himself as a ransom for many (10:45)" (*Mark*, 401). See also Gundry who claims that Mark uses the construction (δεῖ + the infinitive) even though there is not a corresponding construction in Aramaic or Hebrew, "for its apologetic value in stressing the necessity of Jesus' passion and resurrection: they will happen on good purpose" (*Mark*, 428).

29. The grammatical construction ὑπὸ + genitive indicates agency. In other words, the elders, chief priests, and the scribes are the ones primarily responsible for the actions done unto Jesus (Richard A. Young, *Intermediate New Testament Greek: A Linguistic and Exegetical Approach* (Nashville: Broadman and Holman, 1994), 102).

30. Mark includes the entire list of those that will impose suffering on Jesus; that is, the three main groups that make up the Sanhedrin, the most influential political and religious party in Israel. "Their listing together here makes it clear that this is a comprehensive rejection of Jesus by all the leading representatives of God's people Israel, and thus raises as acutely as possible the paradox of the unrecognized Messiah. By repeating this impressive list later in his gospel, Mark will ensure that at the crucial points of the subsequent confrontation and condemnation in Jerusalem the reader is reminded that the authorities of Israel are united in their rejection of their Messiah" (France, *The Gospel of Mark*, 335). See also Gundry, *Mark*, 431-32.

31. Mark's use of the phrase παρρησίᾳ τὸν λόγον ἐλάλει is not found in Matthew or Luke. In Mark, the adverbial use of παρρησίᾳ represents the 'plain or clear' teaching of the pronouncement in 8:31; that is, gospel message concerning his death and resurrection. Mark's use of τὸν λόγον here and ἤρξατο διδάσκειν in 8:31 combine to indicate not only a new teaching within the story, but also clarify the earlier subtle allusions to his death (cf. 2:20). France notes this use of the phrase in 4:33, "The phrase ἐλάλει αὐτοῖς τὸν λόγον could be understood as a typically Marcan pleonasm, meaning no more than 'he spoke to them' (it could be construed also in 2:2; 8:32, though in the latter case the λόγος is surely

DEATH AND DISCIPLESHIP:
AN ANALYSIS OF THE PREDICTIONS OF JESUS' DEATH IN THE GOSPEL OF MARK

Disciples' Misunderstanding

καὶ   προσλαβόμενος[32] ὁ Πέτρος ἤρξατο ἐπιτιμᾶν αὐτῷ.

33. δὲ[33]   ὁ ἐπιστραφεὶς καὶ ἰδὼν τοὺς μαθητὰς αὐτοῦ
ἐπετίμησεν Πέτρῳ καὶ λέγει ὕπαγε ὀπίσω μου,[34]

σατανᾶ, ὅτι οὐ φρονεῖς[35] τὰ τοῦ θεοῦ
ἀλλὰ τὰ τῶν ἀνθρώπων.[36]

---

the striking pronouncement of 8:31)" (*The Gospel of Mark*, 217).

32. Mark's use of the aorist participle προσλαβόμενος is to communicate Peter's intent to pull Jesus aside in order to teach him undisturbed (Walter Bauer, *A Greek-English Lexicon of the New Testament and Other Early Christian Literature*, 3d ed rev and ed by William Danker [Chicago: University of Chicago Press, 2000], 883). In pulling Jesus aside, Peter indicates that he does not willingly accept Jesus' teaching. Through Peter's action, it is almost as if he is indicating that he is qualified to instruct Jesus.

33. Mark's use of the adversative δὲ indicates the contrastive response to Peter's rebuke; that is, Jesus' rebuke of Peter. See Wallace, *Greek Grammar Beyond the Basics*, 671; Young, *Intermediate New Testament Greek*, 183.

34. Jesus' commanding rebuke, ὕπαγε ὀπίσω μου, is best understood as "get behind me," rather than "get away from me so that I no longer see you," and "get behind me because you are a hindrance to me." Therefore, Jesus is saying correctly follow me as a disciple. In other words, Jesus is asking that Peter assume the position of following him as the other disciples have; not walking ahead of him or beside him. This interpretation is clearly connected with the following paragraph in which Jesus explains what it means to ὀπίσω ("follow") him (8:34). See Gundry, *Mark*, 433; Marcus, *Mark 8-16*, 607-08.

35. Mark's use of φρονεῖς refers to Peter's lack of devotion toward God's plan; he did not "take someone's side, espouse someone's cause," or "give careful consideration to something, set one's mind on, be intent on" (BDAG, 1065-66).

36. In the context, the phrase τὰ τοῦ θεοῦ ("things of God") refers to the δεῖ 'divine necessity' of the suffering, rejecting, killing, and resurrection of Jesus. Peter struggles to follow this gospel message; thus Peter assumes a position that is contrary, or adversarial, to Jesus. It is due to his lack of understanding of Jesus' divine purpose that he instead follows τὰ τῶν ἀνθρώπων ("the things of man"). Wallace classifies the semantic role of the article here as a substantiver; that is, τὰ in this case categorizes the 'things' mentioned earlier in the context (*Greek Grammar Beyond the Basics*, 233-35)

Jesus' Instruction on Discipleship

34 Καὶ προσκαλεσάμενος τὸν ὄχλον[37] σὺν τοῖς μαθηταῖς αὐτοῦ εἶπεν αὐτοῖς. εἴ τις[38] θέλει ὀπίσω μου ἀκολουθεῖν, ἀπαρνησάσθω[39] ἑαυτὸν καὶ ἀράτω τὸν σταυρὸν αὐτοῦ καὶ ἀκολουθείτω μοι.[40]

---

37. Mark's inclusion of the crowd (a group of followers) indicates that Jesus' teaching regarding the following of him is not just for the disciples, but anyone εἴ τις. France states that the phrase εἴ τις "further generalizes the scope of the paragraph; this is not a special formula for the elite, but an essential element in discipleship" (*The Gospel of Mark*, 339); see also Gundry, *Mark*, 433-34.

38. Mark uses a first-class conditional statement (εἰ + indicative) to "assume the reality of the premise for the sake of argument" (Young, *Intermediate New Testament Greek*, 226). In other words, for anyone to follow Jesus Christ then he must fulfill the next three requirements in the apodosis; that is, deny himself, take up his cross, and continually follow.

39. The three third-person imperatives, ἀπαρνησάαθω, ἀράτω, and ἀκολουθείτω in this verse, though often translated as 'let him . . .;' here they are translated as 'he must' to best capture the requirement on the individual (see Wallace, *Greek Grammar*, 485-86).

40. Hooker notes the emphasis of Mark's repetitive use of ἀκολουθεῖν and ἀκολουθείτω. She writes, "The repetition emphasizes the fact that discipleship means following in the same path, and being ready to share in the same fate, as the one who leads: those who want to follow Jesus must follow him even when he is carrying a cross. The apparently clumsy wording thus points to the irony in Mark's story: when the climax comes, those who have opted to follow Jesus will *not*, in fact, be prepared to follow him to the scaffold but will take to their heels and run" (*The Gospel According to Saint Mark*, 209). It is important to note here that ἀκολουθεω is not a technical term for being a disciple; though throughout Mark's central section (8:22-10:52) he seems to take on this role (see BDAG, 36).

DEATH AND DISCIPLESHIP:
An Analysis of the Predictions of Jesus' Death in the Gospel of Mark

35 [41]γὰρ[42]   ὃς ἐὰν θέλῃ τὴν ψυχὴν αὐτοῦ σῶσαι
ἀπολέσει αὐτήν. ὃς δ ἂν ἀπολέσει τὴν
ψυχὴν αὐτοῦ ἕνεκεν ἐμοῦ καὶ τοῦ εὐαγγελίου
σώσει αὐτήν.

36 γὰρ   τί ὠφελεῖ ἄνθρωπον κερδῆσαι τὸν κόσμον
ὅλον καὶ ζημιωθῆναι τὴν ψυχὴν αὐτοῦ;

37 γὰρ   τί δοῖ ἄνθρωπος[43] ἀντάλλαγμα τῆς ψυχῆς αὐτοῦ;

38 γὰρ   ὃς ἐὰν ἐπαισχυνθῇ με καὶ τοὺς ἐμοὺς λόγους
ἐν τῇ γενεᾷ ταύτῃ τῇ μοιχαλίδι καὶ ἁμαρτωλῷ,
καὶ ὁ υἱὸς τοῦ ἀνθρώπου ἐπαισχυνθήσεται αὐτόν,
ὅταν ἔλθῃ ἐν τῇ δόξῃ τοῦ πατρὸς αὐτοῦ μετὰ
τῶν ἀγγέλων τῶν ἁγίων.

---

41. Some authors conclude that Mark structures verses 35-38 in a chiasmus in which the middle two reasons (B and B') take an interrogative form and the outside reasons (A and A') take a subjunctive form (see Gundry, *Mark*, 434; Marcus, *Mark 8-16*, 623; Stein, *Mark*, 405).

    A. ὃς γὰρ ἐαν ("for whoever")
        B. τί γάρ ("for what . . .?")
        B.' τί γάρ ("for what . . .?")
    A.' ὃς γὰρ ἐαν ("for whoever")

42. The γὰρ in verses 35-38 "serve to upack Jesus' statement regarding discipleship in verse 34," Decker, *Mark 1-8: A Handbook on the Greek Text*, 226.

43. Mark's use of the aorist subjunctive of δίδωμι, δοῖ, is a deliberative rhetorical subjunctive. It is a question that "expects no *verbal* response, but is in fact a thinly disguised statement, though couched in such a way as to draw the listener into the text. In the speaker's presentation, there is uncertainty about whether the listener will heed the implicit command." Wallace further qualifies his definition by using Mark's question in 8:37. He writes, "The implication is that 'there is nothing that would compensate for such a loss.' Although the question appears to be asking whether such an exchange is possible, it is really an indictment against gaining the world and losing one's life in the process" (*Greek Grammar Beyond the Basics*, 467). BDAG notes this use of δίδωμι refers to a financial transaction; that is, "of payment, pay (up), give something" (242).

9:1 Καὶ ἔλεγεν αὐτοῖς⁴⁴ ἀμὴν λέγω ὑμῖν⁴⁵ ὅτι εἰσίν τινες ὧδε τῶν ἑστηκότων οἵτινες οὐ μὴ γεύσωνται⁴⁶ θανάτου ἕως ἂν ἴδωσιν τὴν βασιλείαν τοῦ θεοῦ ἐληλυθυῖαν ἐν δυνάμει.

The summary of Greek text analysis

This analysis shows how Mark arranges his words, phrases, and sentences. The analysis of the grammatical, lexical, and semantic structures demonstrates where prominence and cohesion occur within the text; two features of discourse texture. Jesus' first passion prediction explicates these features.

Use of Prominence (theme)

Jesus' first passion prediction (8:31-9:1) defines his mission, purpose and the responsibility of the disciples who desire to follow Jesus. Thus, the arrangement of this first passion prediction not only complements the intent of Mark's story as a whole; that is, it helps state who Jesus is (question of identity, 1:1) and what his disciples ought to do in light of knowing him (question of applicational significance), but it also illustrates how this first prediction "hangs together," or coheres with Mark's story. In other words, Mark's story,

---

44. Mark's use of ἔλεγεν αὐτοῖς serves as a link to the preceding verses, esp. 8:34 and the presence of αὐτοῖς. The content of 9:1; the fate of the disciples, also provides a connection to 8:34-38; therefore, giving rationale for including 9:1 as part of Jesus' teaching.

45. The phrase ἀμὴν λέγω ὑμῖν ("truly I say to you") typifies a pronouncement of authority; especially with the emphatic placement of ἀμὴν.

46. Mark's use of οὐ μὴ γεύσωνται is an emphatic negation subjunctive. This is the strongest negation in the Greek New Testament (οὐ μὴ + aor subj or οὐ μὴ + fut indicative). "The subjunctive denies a *potentiality*. The negative is not weaker; rather, the affirmation that is being negatived is less firm with the subjunctive. οὐ μὴ rules out even the idea as being a possibility" (Wallace, *Greek Grammar Beyond the Basics*, 468). Marcus captures the negative form of Mark's subjunctive. He states, "the people referred to will not have even the slightest experience, the tiniest 'taste,' of death" (*Mark 8-16*, 621). In other words, Mark's use of the double negative here serves as an encouragement to follow Jesus (v. 34).

DEATH AND DISCIPLESHIP:
An Analysis of the Predictions of Jesus' Death in the Gospel of Mark

as it is told through the Christological emphasis of the opening verse (1:1), is explicated in detail through Jesus' first prediction within the central section of Mark's story.[47]

Mark begins Jesus' first prediction of his death (8:31, καί ἤρξατο διδάσκειν) with the details of Jesus' teaching regarding his mission and purpose. It is necessary (δεῖ) that he suffers, is rejected, is killed, and is resurrected. This first prediction of Jesus' death sets the stage for Mark's central section. The first prediction not only identifies the sort of Messiah the reader can expect, but also what God expects. Mark's choice of δεῖ (8:31) demonstrates theme. Theme is a level of prominence that serves to emphasize the message of Mark's story (1:1). Because Mark's message communicates the identity of Jesus, he uses δεῖ in the first passion prediction to specify the divine importance of Jesus' suffering. It is unique that Mark uses δεῖ in Jesus' first prediction only, thus stating God's divine will (δεῖ), Jesus must suffer.[48] Marcus notes the specificity and prominence to Mark's use of δεῖ. He writes, "At the beginning of the present prediction, in contrast to the other two, stands the weighty word *dei*, 'it was necessary;' it is vital for the Markan Jesus to stress, in this first open prophecy of his death and resurrection, that those unexpected occurrences reflect the divine will." Thus, the use of δεῖ (prominence), a discourse feature, further defines Jesus' role and identity (formal aspect of Mark's story); that is, he is the one who must suffer.

Jesus' instruction to the crowd and the disciples (8:34-9:1) may also signal prominence. Mark's unexpected inclusion of the crowd may serve as a possible focal point for the reader by grabbing his attention; and therefore, may indicate the instruction is not just for the disciples, but for any follower.[49] In other words, Mark's story becomes personal for the reader.

---

47. Refer to table one and explanation in chapter four.

48. Marcus, *Mark 8-16*, 613.

49. France argues in favor of Mark's emphasis to the reader. He writes, "From the narrator's point of view, however, the introduction of the ὄχλος serves here, rather like οἱ περὶ αὐτὸν σὺν τοῖς δώδεκα in 4:10, to widen the audience for a key pronouncement; their inclusion in the audience asserts that the harsh demands of the following verses apply not only to the Twelve but to anyone else who may wish to join the movement" (*The Gospel of Mark*, 339).

Use of cohesion (componential tie)

This first prediction also sets the stage for what the disciples are about to encounter as they follow their teacher ἐν τῇ ὁδῷ throughout the central section of the story. Peter, however, unwillingly accepts Jesus' teaching and rebukes him; therefore, no longer closely following (ὀπίσω, 8:33) his master. Rather Peter incorrectly positions himself alongside of (προσλαβόμενος) Jesus and begins teaching him.

Mark uses Peter's misunderstanding of Jesus' prediction as well as his unwillingness to follow appropriately behind Jesus as an opportunity to arrange his story to communicate the first of three main characteristics required to follow (ὀπίσω, 8:34) Jesus. A disciple is to *loyally follow* Jesus with the denial of oneself. Mark's use of ὀπίσω may then be a componential tie in 8:33 and 8:34 to demonstrate cohesion, a discourse feature, between episodes. Thus, signaling to the reader that the two episodes (8:32b-33 and 8:34-9:1) are closely related. Jesus' instruction (8:34-9:1) emphasizes loyalty, the first characteristic required to follow Jesus. This requirement is the denying of oneself (ἀπαρνησάσθω ἑαυτόν) and the taking of one's cross (ἀράτω τὸν σταυρὸν αὐτοῦ).[50] Mark's point is that whoever chooses to follow Jesus Christ (v. 34b) must willingly accept the fate (*contra* Peter, v. 32) that is bound up in Jesus' identity, mission, and purpose (v. 31) and therefore continually follow him (ἀκολουθείτω, v. 34). Therefore, through the emphasis of language (prominence) and the relationship of language (cohesion), part of discourse texture and examined through the grammatical, semantic, and lexical choices, Mark sets the stage for the central section of his story.

---

50. Craig A. Evans states the value and worth of fulfilling these commands. He writes, "Is it worth denying oneself, taking up a cross, and following Jesus? Yes, it is asserted; for to shrink from Jesus' cross (and so suppose that one has saved one's life) is in fact to perish, while to take up Jesus' cross (and so to lose one's life) is in fact to live" (*Mark 8:27-16:20*, WBC, 34b [Dallas, Tex: Thomas Nelson, 2001], 30).

DEATH AND DISCIPLESHIP:
An Analysis of the Predictions of Jesus' Death in the Gospel of Mark

Verb Analysis

Jesus' First Prediction of His Death

31. Καὶ	ἤρξατο	Aor mid ind
	διδάσκειν αὐτοὺς ὅτι	Pres act inf
	δεῖ τὸν υἱὸν τοῦ ἀνθρώπου	Pres act ind
	πολλὰ παθεῖν καὶ	Aor pass inf
	ἀποδοκιμασθῆναι ὑπὸ τῶν πρεσβυτέρων καὶ τῶν ἀρχιερέων καὶ τῶν γραμματέων	Aor pass inf
	καὶ ἀποκτανθῆναι καὶ μετὰ τρεῖς ἡμέρας	Aor pass inf
	ἀναστῆναι	Aor act inf
32. καὶ	παρρησίᾳ τὸν λόγον ἐλάλει.[51]	Impf act ind

Disciples' Misunderstanding

καὶ	προσλαβόμενος	Aor mid ptc
	ὁ Πέτρος ἤρξατο	Aor mid ind
	ἐπιτιμᾶν αὐτῷ	Pres act inf
33. δὲ	ὁ ἐπιστραφεὶς	Aor pass ptc
	καὶ ἰδὼν τοὺς μαθητὰς αὐτοῦ	Aor pass ptc
	ἐπετίμησεν Πέτρῳ	Aor act ind

---

51. Rodney Decker notes that the imperfect may be used for offline information. The statement, in which the imperfect ἐλάλει is used, may simply provide a summary or explanation of the preceding event; therefore, requiring the simple translation "he spoke" rather than the progressive "he was speaking." Rodney Decker states, "These statements do not tell the reader what happens next; they do not advance the storyline in the narrative. They serve rather to summarize or explain what has just been recorded" ("The Function(s) of the Imperfect Tense in Mark's Gospel," Society of Biblical Literature Annual Meeting, Biblical Greek Language and Linguistics Section, New Orleans, La, Nov 2009, 10).

	λέγει⁵²	Pres act ind
	ὕπαγε ὀπίσω μου, σατανᾶ,	Pres act impv
	ὅτι οὐ φρονεῖς τὰ τοῦ θεοῦ ἀλλὰ τὰ τῶν ἀνθρώπων	Pres act ind

Jesus' Instruction on Discipleship

34. Καὶ	προσκαλεσάμενος τὸν ὄχλον σὺν τοῖς μαθηταῖς αὐτοῦ	Aor mid ptc
	εἶπεν αὐτοῖς	Aor act ind
	εἴ τις θέλει⁵³	Pres act ind
	ὀπίσω μου ἀκολουθεῖν,	Pres act inf
	ἀπαρνησάσθω ἑαυτὸν καὶ	Aor mid impv
	ἀράτω τὸν σταυρὸν αὐτοῦ καὶ	Aor mid impv
	ἀκολουθείτω μοι.⁵⁴	Pres act impv

---

52. The use of the historical present λέγει (imperfective aspect) indicates the introduction to the direct discourse between Jesus and Peter and the present tense imperative ὕπαγε and indicative φρονεῖς here simply denotes Mark's intent to draw his readers into the story as it happens before them. Peter's current on-going thoughts φρονεῖς are not representative of a follower of Jesus; therefore, stressing the importance of Jesus' command ὕπαγε ("to follow") and its on-going requirement.

53. Mark's use of the present tense (θέλει) pulls the reader into the story and demonstrates Jesus' intent; that is, to offer an opportunity for others to follow. The choice 'to follow' or 'not to follow' is in the hands of those listening. The same tense is used in verse 36 (ὠφελεῖ), indicating the profitability of the reader 'to possess' or 'not to possess' the whole world.

54. The three imperatives, ἀπαρνησάσθω, ἀράτω, and ἀκολουθείτω represent the heart of what is required to follow Jesus. Though the shift from the aorist tense in the first two commands (ἀπαρνησάσθω, ἀράτω) to the present tense with the last command (ἀκολουθείτω) cannot be pushed too far, there is some significance as to their relationship. With the first two aorist commands, Jesus focuses on the act of becoming a disciple, or the beginning of the journey (cf. 1:16-20) his disciples already willingly accepted; whereas the final command is in the present tense to focus on the on-going nature of being a disciple. See notes 62 and 64 below for further information regarding the aorist and present imperatives as they relate to verbal aspect.

35. γὰρ	ὃς ἐὰν θέλῃ[55]	Pres act subj
	τὴν ψυχὴν αὐτοῦ σῶσαι	Aor act inf
	ἀπολέσει αὐτήν	Fut act ind
	ὃς δ ἂν ἀπολέσει τὴν ψυχὴν αὐτοῦ ἕνεκεν ἐμου	Fut act ind
	καὶ τοῦ εὐαγγελίου σώσει αὐτήν	Fut act ind
36. γὰρ	τί ὠφελεῖ ἄνθρωπον	Pres act ind
	κερδῆσαι τὸν κόσμον ὅλον καὶ	Aor act inf
	ζημιωθῆναι τὴν ψυχὴν αὐτοῦ;	Aor pass inf
37. γὰρ	τί δοῖ ἄνθρωπος ἀντάλλαγμα τῆς ψυχῆς αὐτοῦ;	Aor act subj
38. γὰρ	ὃς ἐὰν ἐπαισχυνθῇ με καὶ τοὺς ἐμοὺς λόγους	Aor pass subj
	ἐν τῇ γενεᾷ ταύτῃ τῇ μοιχαλίδι καὶ ἁμαρτωλῷ,	
	καὶ ὁ υἱὸς τοῦ ἀνθρώπου ἐπαισχυνθήσεται αὐτόν,	Fut pass ind
	ὅταν ἔλθῃ[56] ἐν τῇ δόξῃ τοῦ πατρὸς αὐτοῦ	Aor act subj
	μετὰ τῶν ἀγγέλων τῶν ἁγίων	
9:1 Καὶ	ἔλεγεν[57] αὐτοῖς	Impf act ind

---

55. The use of the subjunctive, ἐὰν + subj (θέλῃ) represents a third-class conditional clause indicating a future condition that is yet to be determined. Young states the subjunctive "conveys the idea that the speaker regards what is expressed by the verb as a possibility, supposition, or desire rather than as a fact" (*Intermediate New Testament Greek*, 137).

56. The use of the subjunctive here, ὅταν + subj (ἔλθῃ), denotes a temporal subordinate clause; therefore, taking on the translation of "when he comes." Decker states, "The predominant pattern in Mark is the use of ὅταν with an aorist subjunctive to describe singular (not repeated) events that precede the event described in the main clause. . . . In this instance ὅταν with the aorist subjunctive (ἔλθῃ) refers to a single, unrepeated event that is prior to the time of the main verb (ἐπαισχυνθήσεται)" (*Temporal Deixis of the Greek Verb*, 87-88). Danker states ὅταν is a particle "pertaining to an action that is conditional, possible, and, in many instances, repeated" (BDAG, 730).

57. The use of the imperfect (ἔλεγεν) indicates direct discourse. Decker states that such a use of the imperfect "may also refer to a general teaching session to a large group in which a general summary of Jesus' teaching is recorded (e.g., 7:14, προσκαλεσάμενος πάλιν τὸν ὄχλον ἔλεγεν αὐτοῖς)" ("The Function(s) of the Imperfect

ἀμὴν λέγω⁵⁸ ὑμῖν ὅτι	Pres act ind
εἰσίν τινες	Pres act ind
ὧδε τῶν ἑστηκότων οἵτινες	Perf act ptc
οὐ μὴ γεύσωνται θανάτου ἕως	Aor mid subj
ἂν ἴδωσιν τὴν βασιλείαν τοῦ θεοῦ	Aor act subj
ἐληλυθυῖαν ἐν δυνάμει.	Perf act ptc

The summary of verb analysis

The verb analysis shows Mark's intentional choices of verbs and their tense-forms. The intent of the verb analysis is to examine and explain Mark's deliberate choices of verbs as they are communicated through verbal aspect; thus, indicating levels of prominence. Prominence is a feature of discourse texture.

According to the verb analysis, Mark uses the aorist tense twenty-two times. The aorist tense (perfective aspect) is the most frequent tense used and catalogues the events within Jesus' first passion prediction (8:31-9:1) from an external, summary viewpoint. The aorist tense is the principal tense for structuring the narrative and sketching the background events which carry the storyline. For example, Mark uses the aorist infinitive when describing Jesus' suffering (8:31),⁵⁹ the aorist participle when transitioning between the actions of two different characters (Peter, 8:32b and Jesus, 8:33-34),⁶⁰ the aor-

Tense in Mark's Gospel," 9).

58. The present tense (λέγω) is used here to indicate direct discourse.

59. Mark's use of the aorist infinitives (παθεῖν, ἀποδοκιμασθῆναι, ἀποκτανθῆναι, and ἀναστῆναι, 8:31; and κερδῆσαι, and ζημιωθῆναι, 8:36) illustrates Campbell's understanding of the aorist infinitive. He states that the aorist infinitive functions as an irrealis infinitive; that is, "the event denoted by the infinitive is necessarily unrealized or uncompleted at the time of the matrix event. . . . Statements about the future, questions, negative statements, and unfulfilled desires all regularly employ the aorist infinitive" (Constantine R. Campbell, *Verbal Aspect and Non-Indicative Verbs: Further Soundings in the Greek of the New Testament*, Studies in Biblical Greek 15 [New York: Peter Lang, 2008], 112). The aorist infinitives in these verses portray the perfective aspect, background, or backbone of the story.

60. Mark's use of the aorist participle (προσλαβόμενος, 8:32b; ἐπιστραφεὶς and ἰδών, 8:33; and προσκαλεσάμενος, 8:34) refers to antecedent temporal reference;

DEATH AND DISCIPLESHIP:
An Analysis of the Predictions of Jesus' Death in the Gospel of Mark

ist imperative (8:34)[61] and aorist subjunctive (8:37-38; 9:1)[62] in portions of Jesus' instruction to his disciples. Mark's purpose is not to highlight all the details within this first passion prediction to indicate prominence. Rather Mark uses the aorist to set the stage for the reader. The present tense on the other hand, is used to highlight events for the reader's attention.

The prominent events of Jesus' first passion prediction lie primarily in the use of the present tense. Mark uses the present tense thirteen times. The present is used to draw added attention to the action to which it refers. In other words, Mark's use of the present tense serves as an internal viewpoint for the reader. For example, Mark uses the present infinitive to highlight the intentional and confrontational actions of Peter (8:32b)[63] and the continu-

---

that is, the action occurs before the time of the main verb. The perfective aspect provides the external, summary viewpoint that one would expect from the author; thus, indicating these actions as background information.

61. (ἀπαρνησάσθω and ἀράτω, 8:34). Campbell classifies the aorist imperative as either specific ("an instruction that is required in light of the specific situation") or general ("an instruction that is required of any, or multiple, situation/s"), (*Verbal Aspect and Non-Indicative Verbs: Further Soundings*, 85).

In other words, how do these imperatives relate to aspect and then moving forward, onto current application? Although Campbell's illustration is from Luke 9:23, the parallel passage to Mark, his insight is important. He states, "Though these two actions are to occur 'daily', the contrast with the present imperative indicates that they are viewed as *prerequisite* to the general instruction of following Jesus; one is to deny himself, and take up his cross, before being able to follow Jesus. As such, the depiction of these commands as aorists is determined by their relation to the present imperative; they are prerequisite and anterior to the latter action, and the perfective aspect of the aorist is well suited to such a function" (89).

62. Mark's use of the aorist subjunctive (δοῖ, 8:37; ἐπαισχυνθῇ and ἔλθῃ, 8:38; γεύσωνται, and ἴδωσιν, 9:1) portrays an external viewpoint that is typical of the perfective aspect. He is viewing the audience's response to Jesus' instructions as particular, concrete, or in summary form; without adding detail (Campbell, *Verbal Aspect and Non-Indicative Verbs: Further Soundings*, 57).

63. The present infinitive expresses ingression (the beginning of an action) within the imperfective aspect (ἤρξατο + ἐπιτιμᾶν, 8:32b) without reference to the length of time it takes to complete the action (Campbell, *Verbal Aspect and Non-Indicative Verbs: Further Soundings*, 104).

al, necessary action required of the crowd and disciples (8:34),[64] the present imperative to highlight Jesus' commands (8:33, 34),[65] the historic present to highlight Jesus' conversation with Peter (8:33),[66] the present subjunctive to highlight the willingness of the hearers (8:35),[67] and the present indicative to highlight the unfolding nature of Jesus' dialogue (8:33, 34, 36; 9:1).[68] There-

---

64. Mark's use of ἀκολουθεῖν in 8:34 portrays an action that is open-ended, expressed from an internal viewpoint (Campbell, *Verbal Aspect and Non-Indicative Verbs: Further Soundings*, 110).

65. The present imperatives (ὕπαγε, 8:33; and ἀκολουθείτω, 8:34) are commands of general instruction. The imperfective aspect is conducive for contexts of general exhortations. Campbell states the reason for the imperfective aspect. He argues, "The present imperative conveys general instruction for the simple reason that its imperfective aspect views an action internally, and thus in an open-ended fashion. The open-ended nature of imperfective aspect is well suited to generality since its viewpoint does not take into account the beginning or end of an action, but rather it as unfolding" (*Verbal Aspect and Non-Indicative Verbs: Further Soundings*, 93). The nature of Jesus' commands in verses 33, 34 are to be customary and normal practice.

66. The historic present (λέγει, 8:33) portrays the beginning of "a specific unit after a sentence introducing the general section in which it falls" (Buist Fanning, *Verbal Aspect in New Testament Greek*, Oxford Theological Monographs, [Oxford: Clarendon, 1990], 232). After Mark's introductory report of Jesus viewing the position of his disciples along with Peter's erroneous position, he highlights Jesus' conversation with Peter using the historic present. This is for the purpose of drawing the reader into the conversation. Wallace states, "The *reason* for the use of the historical present is normally to portray an event *vividly*, as though the reader were in the midst of the scene as it unfolds" (*Greek Grammar Beyond the Basics*, 526). He continues and states, "Such vividness might be *rhetorical* (to focus on some aspect of the narrative) or *literary* (to indicate a change in topic)," 526.

67. The present subjunctive (θέλῃ, 8:35) portrays a state of willingness. This is Jesus' intent by asking 'who will follow?' Campbell states that the present subjunctive typically represents activities that are "unfolding, temporally ongoing, stative, personally characteristic, or distributive" (*Verbal Aspect and Non-Indicative Verbs: Further Soundings*, 54).

68. The five uses of the present indicative (φρονεῖς, 8:33; ὠφελεῖ, 8:36; λέγω, and εἰσίν, 9:1) are not categorized in detail. Campbell notes that an author's use of the present tense in dialogue is not unusual. He states, "In much the same way that the aorist dominates narrative proper, the present dominates discourse. This pattern makes sense given the nature of the narrative proper and discourse; narrative proper creates an inherently remote-perfective context, while discourse creates a proximate-imperfective

fore Mark uses the present tense (imperfective aspect) to portray thematic or foreground prominence.

Mark uses the imperfect (ἐλάλει, 8:32; and ἔλεγεν, 9:1) to explain the preceding event (Jesus' prediction of his death) and to introduce direct discourse (Jesus' warning) respectively. The first use of the imperfect (ἐλάλει) provides offline information; that is, Jesus spoke his words plainly. The second use of the imperfect (ἔλεγεν) introduces Jesus' teaching (9:1).

Mark uses various verb tenses to portray levels of prominence within Jesus' first passion prediction. This verb analysis suggests that Mark is likely emphasizing three events (8:31, 33, and 34). The transition between the three events is marked by two aorist adverbial participles. The three events are all introduced using the present tense-form. These events are: (1) Jesus' teaching (δεῖ, 8:31), which results in Peter's rebuke of Jesus (8:32b), (2) Jesus' command to Peter (ὕπαγε, 8:33), which sets up Jesus' instruction to the disciples, and (3) Jesus' command to the crowd and his disciples to continually follow him (ἀκολουθείτω, 8:34), which is the first responsibility for a discple to follow Jesus.

First, Mark writes that Jesus teaches his disciples the necessity (δεῖ, present, imperfective aspect) of his role; especially given Peter's correct identification of Jesus as the Messiah (cf. 8:29). Jesus' teaching defines his role as the suffering Messiah ("to be rejected," "to be killed," and "to be resurrected"). This is contrary to the definition that Peter had in mind for his conquering Messiah. As a result of this teaching, Mark pauses to highlight Peter's response to Jesus' teaching (8:32b). Mark captures the conversation between Peter and Jesus, though not in detail. It is Peter's rebuke, and therefore his unwillingness to follow loyally his master that necessitates a response from Jesus (8:33); the second event. The second event, following the use of the historical present (λέγει) is when Jesus responds by commanding (ὕπαγε, present, imperfective aspect) Peter to assume the proper position of a disciple; that is, behind and following (ὀπίσω μου) his master regardless of the cost (8:33).

Third, Mark states that Jesus summons the crowd and his disciples and provides them with opportunity to follow loyally (8:34). In fact, Jesus dictates that if one chooses to follow (ἀκολουθεῖν, imperfective aspect) it *must* become customary or normal practice (ἀκολουθείτω, imperfective aspect).

---

context" (*Verbal Aspect, the Indicative Mood, and Narrative*, 124).

The third and final event therefore culminates in Jesus' direct discourse to the crowd as he prepares for his transfiguration.

It is therefore through these three events (8:31, 33, and 34), highlighted through the present tense-form (imperfective aspect) that Mark emphasizes the necessity of Jesus' prediction, Jesus' command for Peter to follow as a loyal disciple, and the summons to others that they also ought to follow Jesus loyally. Mark states who Jesus is, the suffering Messiah (8:31), and what the disciples ought to do because of knowing him (8:34-9:1). The disciples are to be loyal followers, even if this may mean suffering to the point of death on a cross. The following role analysis is a graphic demonstration of Mark's intent for the first passion prediction (8:34-9:1).

Role Analysis

Jesus' First Prediction of His Death

31. καί	Episode Connector/New pericope[69]
he began to teach them	Activity
"It is necessary for the Son of Man to suffer many things and to be rejected by the elders and the chief priests and the scribes and to be killed and after three days to be resurrected"	EVENT-1 [SAYING/TEACHING]
32. καί	Additive Conjunction[70]
he spoke the word plainly	Summary of the teaching

Disciples' Misunderstanding

καί	Additive Conjunction

---

69. See Porter, *Idioms of the Greek New Testament*, 302.
70. The discourse function of καί as an additive marker usually associates material that it introduces with adjacent material. See BDAG, 495; Young, *Intermediate New Testament Greek*, 188.

DEATH AND DISCIPLESHIP:
An Analysis of the Predictions of Jesus' Death in the Gospel of Mark

when he took him aside	Transition (Response to EVENT-1)
Peter began to rebuke him	Activity

33. δέ	Shift Conjunction[71]
when he had turned around	Transition (Jesus' response)
καί	Additive Conjunction
saw his disciples	Activity
he rebuked Peter saying,	Event-2 Introduction
"Get behind me, Satan,	EVENT-2 [COMMAND]
because you are not mindful	
of the things of God,	
ἀλλά	Adversative Conjunction[72]
of the things of men."	

Jesus' Instruction on Discipleship

34. Καί	Episode Connector
when he called the crowd	Transition (Jesus' teaching)
with his disciples	
he said to them,	Saying Activity
"If anyone desires to follow behind me,	Condition to follow
he must deny himself and	
he must take up his cross and	
he must continually follow me	EVENT-3 [COMMAND]

---

71. The discourse function of δέ denotes "a shift or change in thought: either a new development, the introduction of a new character, a change in temporal setting" (Young, *Intermediate New Testament Greek*, 183). Young also states that the use of δέ, "when used with a nominative case article (without a noun), it functions as a switch-reference device, showing a shift in subject from the previous sentence" (184). This is probably more likely the case here, (ὁ δὲ . . .).

72. The discourse function of ἀλλά is adversative; that is, contrasting two elements. The statement following ἀλλά is typically more prominent. See Young, *Intermediate New Testament Greek*, 180. Jesus' point here is Peter's greater concern is with the things of men, not God; hence the use of ἀλλά to show this.

35. γάρ   Supporting Conjunction[73]
    whoever desires to save his life,   Condition (3d class)
    will lose it
    δέ   Shift Conjunction
    whosoever will lose his life on account
    of me and the gospel, will save it

36. γάρ   Supporting Conjunction
    what does it profit a man to gain   Question
    the whole world
    and to forfeit his life?

37. γάρ   Supporting Conjunction
    what can a man give as   Question
    an exchange for his life?

38. γάρ   Supporting Conjunction
    whoever is ashamed of me   Condition (3d class)
    and my words in this adulterous
    and sinful generation,
    καί   Emphasis Conjunction[74]
    the Son of Man will be ashamed of
    him when he comes in the glory

---

73. The discourse function of γάρ typically provides explanations or expositions of what was previously stated (Stephen Levinsohn, *Discourse Features of New Testament Greek: A Coursebook on the Information Structure of New Testament Greek*, 2d ed [Dallas, Tex: SIL International, 2000], 91). Steven Runge states, "The information introduced does not advance the discourse but adds background information that strengthens or supports what precedes" (*Discourse Grammar of the Greek New Testament: A Practical Introduction for Teaching and Exegesis* [Peabody, Mass: Hendrickson, 2010], 52).

74. The discourse function of καί here may be indicating focal prominence; thus, it could be translated as 'even.' Here Mark may be focusing the reader's attention on the fact that the disciple who is ashamed of Jesus, he too [Jesus] will also be ashamed of him. Young states this use of καί is "ascensive and elaborates on the same thought, bringing it to a climax" (*Intermediate New Testament Greek*, 188).

of his Father with the holy angels"

9:1 Καί	Additive Conjunction
he was saying to them,	Saying Activity
"Truly, I say to you that there are some of the ones standing here who by no means taste death until they see the kingdom of God having come in power."	

The summary of role analysis

The role analysis illustrates three events Mark desires to emphasize (8:31, 33, 34). Mark uses the tense-form of verbs and conjunctions to establish prominence and cohesion. As one reads Jesus' first passion prediction, Mark provides the reader with both an internal and external perspective. When Mark desires to pull his audience into the story (internal perspective), to grab their attention, he utilizes the present tense verb. As the reader transitions between events, and reads the background of the story, Mark utilizes the aorist tense verb (external, summary perspective). The verb tense therefore establishes for the reader what may serve as prominent events throughout the passion prediction.

The conjunctions provide cohesion and demonstrate the logical relationships between the three events throughout the passion prediction. Mark uses καί both to begin and connect the various events within the passion prediction. He also uses δέ to introduce movement, or a shift in the pericope. Mark then uses γάρ to support Jesus' preceding teaching regarding loyally following him. These conjunctions provide the reader with ties throughout the passion prediction to understand the significant turning points and events within the passion prediction. The three events, and their logical relationships, are explained.

Jesus' teaching (event 1, the necessity of his identity and mission, 8:31) prompts Peter's rebuke of Jesus (8:32b). Jesus responds not only to Peter (event 2, loyally follow, 8:33) but also to the crowd and the rest of the disciples (event 3, loyalty to follow, 8:34). Here Jesus takes the initiative to appropriately correct Peter and teach others the significance of the relationship between his identity and mission (8:31) and the choice "to follow" or "not to follow" (8:34-9:1). Therefore, the two analyses (Greek text and verb) are represented in the final role analysis. The role analysis represents Mark's emphasis of his story by reporting Jesus' first of three passion predictions.

Mark brings together the formal and functional aspects of his story; that is, the identity of Jesus and his mission, and the responsibility of the disciples that ought to result because they know his identity and mission. Mark therefore weaves throughout the central section of his story three of Jesus' passion predictions to explicate both aspects of his story for the reader. Although Mark tells the reader of Jesus' first prediction and what is required to follow him, the disciples' desire to follow is waning. As a matter of fact, Jesus' second passion prediction further demonstrates the disciples' failures, for they are preoccupied with their status, resulting in Jesus' instruction regarding their service to others.

Jesus' Second Passion Prediction (9:30-37)

Greek Text Analysis

Jesus' Second Prediction of His Death

30.	Κἀκεῖθεν ἐξελθόντες παρεπορεύοντο διὰ τῆς Γαλιλαίας,[75] καὶ οὐκ ἤθελεν ἵνα[76] τις γνοῖ
31. γὰρ[77]	ἐδίδασκεν τοὺς μαθητὰς αὐτοῦ

---

75. Danker claims the use of παραπορεύομαι, here παρεπορεύοντο, with the genitive construction διὰ τῆς Γαλιλαίας indicates a "perspective of the narrator [that] the travelers would have Galilee on either side of them as they went" (BDAG, 770). Contra France who claims that παραπορεύομαι can carry the sense of 'pass by;' that is, "the construction with διὰ would underline the idea of going through incognito" (*The Gospel of Mark*, 371). See also Gundry, *Mark*, 502. The use of διὰ + the genitive is locative (Porter, *Idioms of the Greek New Testament*, 148).

76 The use of the ἵνα here indicates the content of the wish. See *Greek Grammar Beyond the Basics*, 678; *Idioms of the Greek New Testament*, 237-39.

77 The use of γάρ here is probably explanatory; that is, Mark provides the

DEATH AND DISCIPLESHIP:
An Analysis of the Predictions of Jesus' Death in the Gospel of Mark

καὶ ἔλεγεν αὐτοῖς ὅτι[78] ὁ υἱὸς τοῦ
ἀνθρώπου παραδίδοται[79] εἰς χεῖρας
ἀνθρώπων,[80] καὶ ἀποκτενοῦσιν αὐτόν,
καὶ ἀποκτανθεὶς μετὰ τρεῖς ἡμέρας
ἀναστήσεται.

32. δὲ[81]   οἱ ἠγνόουν[82] τὸ ῥῆμα,[83]
καὶ ἐφοβοῦντο[84] αὐτὸν ἐπερωτῆσαι.

---

support for Jesus' preceding proposition (no one is to know where they are; 9:30).

78. See also Marcus, *Mark 8-16*, 666.

79 More than likely the passive voice indicates a divine passive, thus conveying a similar nuance as δεῖ in 8:31; that is, God will hand over his Son to humanity. This indicates the certainty of the event; much like δεῖ in 8:31. This portion of Jesus' teaching may be what the disciples did not understand and were afraid to ask. Perhaps there may have been wider hopes of a popular Messiah to bring about a change that demonstrated a leadership that lorded over others, not submitted to others.

80. Edwards sees a unique sense to "hands of men." He states, "In the first prediction the responsibility for Jesus' suffering is attributed to Jewish leaders, 'the elders, chief priests and teachers of the law' (8:31). But in the second prediction the enemies of the Son of Man are not Jewish leaders but all humanity" (*The Gospel According to Mark*, 283).

81. The adversative use of δέ indicates a contrast to the preceding verse. Although Jesus spoke clearly (cf. 8:32), the disciples did not understand the implications of what he was saying (9:31).

82. Danker states ἀγνοέω, here ἠγνόουν, is a failure to understand "with the implication of lack of capacity or ability, *not to understand*" (BDAG, 13). As Stein states, the important thing is that the disciples understood the words of Jesus well enough to provide the content of Jesus' teaching. However, their failure arises when they could not have responded with "the truth and divine necessity of what he [Jesus] said" (*Mark*, 440).

83. Mark's use of τὸ ῥῆμα ("the saying") is like a preceding phrase that too captures the essence of what Jesus is saying (cf. Mark's use of τὸν λόγον, 8:32); for it probably concentrates its attention on Jesus' prediction.

84. At this point, it is only speculative to deduce what the disciples were fearful of; especially since Mark does not provide the reader any hints. Are the disciples fearful of what is expected of them (e.g., martyrdom)? Are they fearful of remaining ignorant? Are they fearful of the awesomeness of Jesus' prediction? Potentially France captures it best, maybe "they understand enough to be afraid to ask to understand more" (*The Gospel of Mark*, 372).

Disciples' Misunderstanding

33. Καὶ   ἦλθον εἰς Καφαρναούμ.
Καὶ ἐν τῇ οἰκίᾳ[85] γενόμενος ἐπηρώτα
αὐτούς[86] τί ἐν τῇ ὁδῷ διελογίζεσθε;

34. δὲ[87]   οἱ ἐσιώπων πρὸς ἀλλήλους
γὰρ[88] διελέχθησαν ἐν τῇ ὁδῷ τίς[89] μείζων.[90]

Jesus' Instruction on Discipleship

35. καὶ   καθίσας[91] ἐφώνησεν τοὺς[92] δώδεκα

85. The phrase ἐν τῇ οἰκίᾳ ("in the house") indicates Jesus' ministry has now shifted from a public to a private dialogue between him and the disciples.

86. The fact that Jesus is asking the disciples a question does not imply that he is seeking to gain new information. Rather, Jesus is taking the opportunity to teach them about their apparent shame and guilt (why they remain silent) of what it is they were discussing; that is, who is the greatest.

87. The adversative δέ introduces the contrasting silence of the disciples when asked a question that requires a response.

88. Mark's use of γάρ is explanatory denoting the content of what the disciples were discussing.

89. Wallace contends the function of τίς in the construction τίς μείζων is "an example of an interrogative pronoun used in an indirect question" (*Greek Grammar Beyond the Basics*, 355).

90. According to Wallace, the use of μείζων is a comparative for superlative; thus, indicating the disciples' conversation was about 'who is the greatest,' rather than who is great (*Greek Grammar Beyond the Basics*, 300). France contends that this argument between the disciples about 'who is the greatest' is typical of their own culture. In other words, "questions of precedence and rank were constantly arising" (*The Gospel of Mark*, 339). See also Edwards (*The Gospel According to Mark*, 286).

91. France contends Mark's use of καθίσας is unusual, but more than likely appropriate given the informal setting inside of a house. Although unusual for Mark, it indicates "a deliberate, even formal, piece of instruction" when followed by ἐφώνησεν τοὺς δώδεκα (*The Gospel of Mark*, 373). "This is an issue which must be addressed, and the teacher sits and summons his disciples to gather round and listen" (373).

92. The use of the article τοὺς in the construction τοὺς δώδεκα functions as a

DEATH AND DISCIPLESHIP:
An Analysis of the Predictions of Jesus' Death in the Gospel of Mark

      καὶ λέγει αὐτοῖς εἴ τις[93] θέλει
      πρῶτος εἶναι, ἔσται πάντων ἔσχατος
      καὶ πάντων διάκονος.

36. καὶ   λαβὼν παιδίον[94] ἔστησεν αὐτὸ ἐν μέσῳ αὐτῶν
          καὶ ἐναγκαλισάμενος[95] αὐτὸ εἶπεν αὐτοῖς

37.   ὃς ἂν ἓν τῶν τοιούτων παιδίων δέξηται[96]
         ἐπὶ τῷ ὀνόματί μου,[97] ἐμὲ δέχεται
         καὶ ὃς ἂν ἐμὲ δέχηται, οὐκ ἐμὲ δέχεται
         ἀλλὰ τὸν ἀποστείλαντά με.

---

substantiver with the adjective (δώδεκα); therefore, stressing the quality of a particular group. Wallace states, "the twelve' takes on a technical nuance in the Gospels by virtue of how well known the disciples were. The article thus belongs to the 'well-known' category as well" (*Greek Grammar Beyond the Basics*, 233).

    93. Mark uses the first-class conditional statement (εἴ + indicative) – (see 148n38). In other words, for anyone to be first (πρῶτος, "first, most important"), he must assume the position of ἔσχατος ("least, most insignificant") and διάκονος ("assistant under someone").

    94. Decker contends the use of παιδίων is a lexical indicator of a unit of time ('words related to age') that refers to a 'little child' as opposed to 'child' or 'adult.' (*Temporal Deixis of the Greek Verb*, 86). France states the importance of Jesus' use of a child in his teaching. He claims, "The use of a child as a teaching aid . . . has explicitly to do with status, not with any character traits supposedly typical of children. The child represents the lowest order in the social scale, the one who is under the authority and care of others . . . In this pericope there is no call to become like a child, but rather the injunction to 'receive' the child, to reverse the conventional value-scale by according to importance to the unimportant" (*The Gospel of Mark*, 374). See also Stein, *Mark*, 444.

    95. ἐναγκαλίζομαι, here aor. ptc, ἐναγκαλισάμενος 'take in one's arms, hug someone,' (BDAG, 330).

    96. Mark's use of δέχεται denotes the welcoming so as to treat something or someone as significant rather than ignoring. Gundry notes, "Thus Jesus turns the question of greatness inside out: he shifts attention from greatness among the Twelve to their reception of children, which shows humility in contrast with the self-exalting pride that caused them to argue with one another which of them was the greatest" (*Mark*, 510).

    97. Mark's use of ἐπὶ in the prepositional phrase ἐπὶ τῷ ὀνόματί μου refers to the receiving of insignificant ones, little children, in the name of Jesus; in his authority, in his representation (BDAG, 366).

The summary of Greek text analysis

The Greek text analysis shows how Mark arranges his words, phrases, and sentences. The above examination of Jesus' second passion prediction (9:30-37) demonstrates prominence and cohesion. Like Jesus' first passion prediction (8:31-9:1), the second passion prediction also complements the intent of Mark's story as a whole; that is, informing the reader of Jesus' identity and the disciples' responsibility in responding to this identity.

Use of prominence (focus)

Mark begins Jesus' second prediction of his death like the first prediction. He states the content of Jesus' teaching ("will be handed over to men," "will be killed," and "will rise again"). Similar to the use of δεῖ (8:31), Jesus once again explains the certainty of his mission and purpose through the present divine passive (9:31, παραδίδοται, "will be handed over"). Mark's use of the passive in both predictions thus far, 8:31 and 9:31, not only indicates the certainty of Jesus' mission, but Jesus' second prediction also emphasizes how and by whom Jesus will die. The second prediction indicates not only how Jesus will die; that is, "he will be handed over;" but it also indicates a different group of people responsible. Although the divine passive ultimately places God as the responsible agent, it is clear in Jesus' second prediction that his suffering will be at the hands of men (εἰς χεῖρας ἀνθρώπων). Thus, where the first prediction attributes Jesus' suffering to the Jewish leaders (ὑπὸ τῶν πρεσβυτέρων καί τῶν ἀρχιερέων καί τῶν γραμματέων), it is in the second prediction that Jesus indicates that it is all of humanity. Therefore, Mark's shift in people groups who are responsible for Jesus' death demonstrates focus, a level of prominence that grabs the attention of the reader.

Although this shift is intended to grab the attention of the reader, Jesus' teaching however did not grab the attention of his disciples (cf. 8:32). As a matter of fact, his disciples were unable to comprehend the significance (ἠγνόουν) of his teaching and were fearful to ask for more details (9:32).

Mark uses the disciples' ignorance and fear of speaking to illustrate the irony of the next event (9:33-34). Although the disciples were fearful to speak following Jesus' teaching (9:32), they did find time to argue with one another

(9:34). In other words, the disciples did find time to discuss what was important and meaningful to them; that is, "who was the greatest" (τίς μείζων). The disciples missed the implications of Jesus' teaching. The "implication is that Jesus' greatness lies in the humility of his impending death;"[98] the death by humanity. In other words, when given the opportunity to learn and ask questions in the privacy of their teacher (9:30), the disciples lacked discernment and chose to be preoccupied with the issue of status, not humble service toward others.

Jesus' instruction to the disciples (9:35-37) may also signal prominence. Mark's report of Jesus' unexpected taking (λαβών) of a child and embracing (ἐναγκαλισάμενος) it, serves as a possible focal point for the reader. This grabs the attention of the audience, for this is an action not typically done by a man. Rather, this action is more appropriately connected to a woman or servant. Sweetland adds,

> The radical nature of Jesus' teaching in these verses becomes clearer when we realize that the verb translated here as 'to serve' is often used to refer to male servants who wait on tables or to those performing so-called women's work. Whether this refers to waiting on tables, to daily housework or to the raising of children, it is seen as activity unbecoming for a free man to perform. One of the requirements for following Jesus, therefore, is to engage in a type of activity that by the secular society is considered acceptable only for women and servants.[99]

Use of cohesion (compenential tie)

Mark reports that Jesus uses the preoccupation of the disciples (τίς μείζων) to teach them the importance of serving others (9:35), the second of three main responsibilities required of those who desire to follow Jesus. Mark uses two related concepts about status; that is, superior in importance (τίς μείζων, "who was the greatest," 9:34), and prominence/staus (εἴ τις θέλει πρῶτος εἶναι, "if anyone desires to be first," 9:35). These two concepts serve as a componential tie that demonstrates cohesion between events, thus signaling

---

98. Sweetland, *Mark: From Death to Life*, 116.
99. Ibid., 117-18.

the two events (9:33-34 and 9:35-37) are closely related. Although Mark does not use the same word in both verses, the concept within each phrase denotes superior in importance, most important, or prominent respectively.[100]

It is through Jesus' use of an object lesson, a little child that he pointedly expresses the disciples' role. They must be willingly serving others, even the insignificant of society, not concerning themselves with being the greatest. Jesus' instruction (9:35-37) therefore, emphasizes service to others. This requirement involves being last of all and servant of all (ἔσται πάντων ἔσχατος καί πάντων διάκονος), as well as the willingness to receive even the insignificant of society (τοιούτων παιδίων δέξηται), for this demonstrates humility, the subject of Jesus' teaching (9:31). Jesus exemplifies humility by the handing over of himself to the hands of men; thus, demonstrating that he is not concerned with greatness. Mark's point is that whoever desires to follow Jesus and obtain "true greatness" (*contra* disciples, v. 34), must willingly give of himself in service to those whom one cannot receive a benefit in return. Therefore, through prominence and cohesion, Mark's use of language points to both Jesus' identity (παραδίδοται εἰς χεῖρας ἀνθρώπων) and the significance of this identity that points to the disciples' responsibility (ἔσται πάντων ἔσχατος καί πάντων διάκονος) as they follow Jesus.

Verb Analysis

Jesus' Second Prediction of His Death

30.	Κἀκεῖθεν ἐξελθόντες	Aor act ptc
	παρεπορεύοντο διὰ τῆς Γαλιλαίας,	Impf mid ind
	καὶ οὐκ ἤθελεν	Impf act ind
	ἵνα τις γνοῖ	Aor act subj
31. γὰρ	ἐδίδασκεν τοὺς μαθητὰς αὐτοῦ	Impf act ind
	καὶ ἔλεγεν αὐτοῖς	Impf act ind
	ὅτι ὁ υἱὸς τοῦ ἀνθρώπου **παραδίδοται**	Pres pass ind
	εἰς χεῖρας ἀνθρώπων, καὶ ἀποκτενοῦσιν αὐτόν,	Fut act ind

---

100. μείζων see μέγας, BDAG, 624 and on πρῶτος, BDAG, 893.

DEATH AND DISCIPLESHIP:
An Analysis of the Predictions of Jesus' Death in the Gospel of Mark

		καὶ ἀποκτανθεὶς μετὰ τρεῖς ἡμέρας	Aor pass ptc
		ἀναστήσεται.	Fut mid ind
32.	δὲ	οἱ ἠγνόουν τὸ ῥῆμα,	Impf act ind
		καὶ ἐφοβοῦντο	Impf mid ind
		αὐτὸν ἐπερωτῆσαι.	Aor act inf

Disciples' Misunderstanding

33.	Καὶ	ἦλθον εἰς Καφαρναούμ.	Aor act ind
		Καὶ ἐν τῇ οἰκίᾳ γενόμενος	Aor mid ptc
		ἐπηρώτα αὐτούς	Impf act ind
		τί ἐν τῇ ὁδῷ διελογίζεσθε;	Impf mid ind
34.	δὲ	οἱ ἐσιώπων πρὸς ἀλλήλους	Impf act ind
		γὰρ διελέχθησαν ἐν τῇ ὁδῷ τίς μείζων.	Aor pass ind

Jesus' Instruction on Discipleship

35.	καὶ	καθίσας	Aor act ptc
		ἐφώνησεν τοὺς δώδεκα	Aor act ind
		καὶ λέγει αὐτοῖς	Pres act ind
		εἴ τις **θέλει**	Pres act ind
		πρῶτος εἶναι,	Pres act inf
		ἔσται πάντων ἔσχατος καὶ πάντων διάκονος	Fut mid ind
36.	καὶ	λαβὼν παιδίον	Aor act ptc
		ἔστησεν αὐτὸ ἐν μέσῳ αὐτῶν	Aor act ind
		καὶ ἐναγκαλισάμενος αὐτὸ	Aor mid ptc
		εἶπεν αὐτοῖς	Aor act ind
37.		ὃς ἂν ἓν τῶν τοιούτων παιδίων δέξηται	Aor mid subj
		ἐπὶ τῷ ὀνόματί μου, ἐμὲ δέχεται	Pres mid ind
		καὶ ὃς ἂν ἐμὲ δέχηται,	Pres mid subj

| οὐκ ἐμὲ δέχεται | Pres mid ind |
| ἀλλὰ τὸν ἀποστείλαντά με. | Aor act ptc |

The summary of verb analysis

The verb analysis examines and explains the verb choices as they are portrayed through verbal aspect; thus, indicating various levels of prominence. As stated earlier, prominence is a feature of discourse texture. The verb analysis points to the following conclusions.

Mark uses the aorist tense fifteen times, the tense most frequently used. Like the conclusions regarding the aorist tense (perfective aspect) found in the first passion prediction, Mark also uses the aorist within Jesus' second passion prediction (9:30-37) to catalogue the events from an external summary viewpoint. The aorist carries the story forward. It provides the reader with the major events within the story. For example, Mark uses the aorist participle when he transitions from scene to scene (9:30, 31, 33, 35, 36 (2x)),[101] the aorist subjunctive in two dependent clauses (purpose clause, 9:30 and relative clause, 9:37),[102] the aorist infinitive (9:32) to note the disciples' fear of asking Jesus about his teaching,[103] the aorist substantive participle (9:37)

---

101. The uses of the aorist participle include: ἐξελθόντες, 9:30; ἀποκτανθείς, 9:31; γενόμενος, 9:33; καθίσας, 9:35; λαβὼν and ἐναγκαλισάμενος, 9:36. Each of these participles denotes a transition in scenes and serves to carry the narrative along for the reader. Each of these participles are temporal.

102. Mark uses the aorist subjunctive in 9:30 (γνοῖ) with the complementary ἵνα to denote the purpose for Jesus' desire that no one know where they are. There are no unfolding details as to the purpose for Jesus' desire, only that he wanted privacy; a concrete event (See Campbell, *Verbal Aspect and Non-Indicative Verbs: Further Soundings*, 57). Mark's other use of the aorist subjunctive (δέξηται, 9:37) serves as a relative clause to the main verb (εἶπεν, 9:36). The choice 'to receive' or 'not to receive' is a, concrete situation; without the details of the event as it unfolds.

103. Mark's use of the aorist infinitive (ἐπερωτῆσαι) may be an infinitive that is "predisposed to the aorist infinitive" (Campbell, *Verbal Aspect and Non-Indicative Verbs: Further Soundings*, 116). This usage here may fit into the category of an achievement verb that simply denotes an event or an act. The preference for the aorist (perfective aspect) here may be Mark's way of communicating the disciples' fear; that is, their fear to question Jesus without providing the details as to why (external, summary viewpoint).

DEATH AND DISCIPLESHIP:
An Analysis of the Predictions of Jesus' Death in the Gospel of Mark

to indicate the one who sent Jesus [God, the Father],[104] and the aorist tense in general noting the actions of various characters in order to provide background information as he tells the story (9:33, 34, 35, 36 (2x)).[105] Therefore, Mark's use of the aorist tense-form (perfective aspect) provides the mainline of the narrative. The imperfective aspect on the other hand, utilizes the imperfect tense-form nine times and the present tense-form seven times. The imperfective aspect differs from the perfective aspect, for it portrays the foreground of the narrative illustrating prominence through the author's choice of verbs, an internal viewpoint.

Mark uses the imperfect tense for offline information; that is, those statements that do not necessarily advance the storyline. For example, Mark uses the imperfect tense to set the scene for the second passion prediction (9:30 (2x)),[106] to set the stage for Jesus' opportunity to teach his disciples (9:33), and to explain the responses to events (9:32 (2x), 34).[107] The other three uses of the imperfect however, are used to introduce direct discourse (9:31 (2x), 33).[108]

---

104. The substantival aorist participle (τὸν ἀποστείλαντά, "the one who sent," 9:37) expresses antecedence; that is, the actions of God, sent Jesus [με], occur before those, who choose to do so, receive Jesus.

105. Each of the aorist verbs (ἦλθον, "they came," 9:33; ἐσιώπων, "[they] argued," 9:34; ἐφώνησεν, "he called," 9:35; ἔστησεν, "he stood," 9:36; εἶπεν, "he said," 9:36) portray the actions of various characters without involving any detail. Mark uses the aorist tense (perfective aspect) to carry along the narrative.

106. Mark uses the imperfect tense two times (παρεπορεύοντο, "they passed through," and ἤθελεν, "he desired," 9:30) to set the scene. In other words, "these statements are not the point of the pericope, but they are helpful in understanding the context in which events take place" (Decker, "The Function(s) of the Imperfect Tense in Mark's Gospel," 11). Mark therefore sets the scene in the Galilean territory with the privacy of his disciples.

107. Mark uses the imperfect tense three times to explain events (ἠγνόουν, "they did not understand," 9:32; ἐφοβοῦντο, "they were afraid," 9:32; ἐσιώπων, "they were silent," 9:34). Each of these imperfects, two of which are positioned at the beginning of verses 32 & 34, are verbs noting/explaining the contrasting responses (use of δὲ) of the disciples to Jesus' teaching and question respectively. The second imperfect (ἐφοβοῦντο) carries with it the same function as the first (ἠγνόουν) due to the καί.

108. The first use of the imperfect tense (ἐδίδασκεν γάρ, "for he was teaching," 9:31) may serve "as an imperfect in an explanatory statement using γάρ" (Decker, "The Function(s) of the Imperfect Tense in Mark's Gospel," 9). Here Mark explains the pre-

Discourse Analysis of the Passion Predictions

Mark's other use of the imperfective aspect, the present tense, is used to draw added attention to that which it refers.

Similar to the first passion prediction, Mark also uses the present tense to highlight various events within the second passion prediction. For example, Mark uses the futuristic present to highlight the certainty of Jesus' death (9:31), the historic present to indicate when a new unit, or paragraph begins (9:35), the historic present to highlight Jesus' conversation with his disciples (9:35),[109] the present infinitive to highlight the state of being for those who follow Jesus (9:35),[110] the present subjunctive to highlight the willingness of the hearers (9:37),[111] and the present indicative to highlight the unfolding nature of Jesus' dialogue with his disciples (9:35, 37 (2x)).[112]

---

ceding desire (ἤθελεν) of Jesus; that is, he wants to teach his disciples. The second use of the imperfect introduces a general teaching session (ἔλεγεν αὐτοῖς, "he said to them," 9:31). It is here that Mark records the general content of Jesus' teaching. The third use of the imperfect (ἐπηρώτα αὐτούς, "he was asking them," 9:33) introduces Jesus' question to the disciples regarding their arguing with one another.

109. The historic present (λέγει, 9:35) highlights the beginning of a specific unit of teaching. After Mark's description of the disciples' actions (9:33b, 34), he uses the historic present for the purpose of drawing the reader into the conversation. The conversation Jesus is about to have with his disciples will revolutionize their thinking regarding service toward others. Gundry notes, "λέγει, 'he says,' emphasizes the following words, whose appropriateness to the Twelve's unconfessed topic of argument and whose accuracy of prediction in that none of the Twelve will take precedence over the others during their lifetimes will display Jesus' supernatural knowledge: 'if anyone wishes to be first, he will be last of all'" (*Mark*, 509).

110. The present infinitive (εἶναι, 9:35) expresses imperfective aspect. This complementary infinitive is portrayed through an internal viewpoint indicating an open-ended activity; that is, the disciples desire to follow Jesus must be in a state of humility and serving others.

111. The present subjunctive (δέχηται, 9:37) portrays the state of willingness of his disciples. Jesus' intent is to present the disciples with an opportunity to act on his teaching; that is, to represent him and do as he [Jesus] would do.

112. The three present indicatives serve to pull the reader into the story. Mark's use of the present (θέλει, 9:35) demonstrates Jesus' intent to offer an opportunity for others to follow him; but to do so by welcoming his understanding of what it means to be great. The other two uses of the present tense, both of which are in 9:37 (δέχεται), stress the importance of not pursuing greatness.

DEATH AND DISCIPLESHIP:
An Analysis of the Predictions of Jesus' Death in the Gospel of Mark

The verb analysis suggests that Mark is emphasizing two events (9:31, and 35). The transition between the two events is marked by aorist adverbial participles (γενόμενος, v. 33 and καθίσας, v. 35). These events are: (1) Jesus' teaching (παραδίδοται, 9:31), which Mark then interrupts the story using δὲ to change characters and portray the disciples' contrastive response (9:32); and (2) Jesus' teaching regarding service (9:35) following the use of λέγει, which is a result of the disciples' discussion ἐν τῇ ὁδῷ (9:33-34).

First, Mark writes that Jesus teaches his disciples the necessity (παραδίδοται, pres pass) of his role as the suffering Messiah through the futuristic present (παραδίδοται, "will be handed over,") and future (ἀποκτενοῦσιν, "will be killed," and ἀναστήσεται, "will rise") verbs. This "handing over" seems to be a play on words. In other words, it is the Son of Man that will be handed over to the "hands of men" and he will be killed. This act of humility is not what the disciples had in mind; in fact, they are expecting greatness. As a result of Jesus' teaching, the disciples respond with ignorance and fear.

Mark transitions to Capernaum, where he captures Jesus' question to the disciples regarding their conversation with one another on the way. However, the disciples' response is one of silence, for they were ashamed of their interest in the status of greatness. Mark then continues the story. He portrays Jesus as the authoritative teacher, for he sits and calls the Twelve to teach them.

The second event involves Jesus' response to the disciples' misunderstanding regarding status. He informs them (λέγει) that those who desire (θέλει) to be prominent, or most important, must first be lowly and full of service. Therefore, Jesus calls the disciples and provides them with opportunity to experience "true greatness." It is the one who willingly receives even the insignificant in society (e.g., παιδίον) is truly great. In fact, Jesus directly addresses his disciples with their responsibility (9:37). Mark portrays the priority of service through a shift from the aorist subjunctive (δέξηται) to the present subjunctive (δέχηται). This demonstrates that the one, who willingly accepts his rightful position as servant (ἔσται πάντων ἔσχατος καὶ πάντων διάκονος, v. 35), serves others on the ground of Jesus' name (ἐπὶ τῷ ὀνόματί). In other words, just as the disciple has received this child, he also has received Jesus and ultimately God himself.

Discourse Analysis of the Passion Predictions

It is therefore through these two events (9:31 and 35) that Mark emphasizes the necessity of Jesus' prediction, and Jesus' projected realm for his disciples; to be servants of all. Mark's intent continues to be the communication of Jesus' identity; that is, the Messiah that necessitates suffering (9:31), and what the disciples ought to do as a result of knowing him (9:35-37). The disciples should not be concerned with being the greatest, but servants, even if this means serving the insignificant ones. The following role analysis is a graphic demonstration of Mark's intent for the second passion prediction (9:30-9:37).

Role Analysis

Jesus' Second Prediction of His Death

30. when they came out from there,	Transition (New Setting)
they passed through Galilee	Setting
and	Additive Conjunction
he did not wish that anyone should know	
31. γάρ	Supporting Conjunction
he was teaching his disciples	Setting Scene
καί	Additive Conjunction
he said to them,	Event-1 Introduction
"The Son of Man will be handed over	EVENT-1 [SAYING]
into the hands of men and they will kill him	
and after being killed,	
on the third day he will rise."	
32. δέ	Shift Conjunction
they did not understand the saying	Response to EVENT-1
καί	Additive Conjunction
were afraid to ask.	Response to EVENT-1

DEATH AND DISCIPLESHIP:
An Analysis of the Predictions of Jesus' Death in the Gospel of Mark

Disciples' Misunderstanding

33.	Καί	Additive Conjunction[113]
	they came to Capernaum	Setting
	καί	Additive Conjunction
	when he was in the house	Setting
	he asked them,	
	"What were you arguing about with one another on the way?"	Saying activity
34.	δέ	Shift Conjunction
	they were silent,	Response to Jesus' question
	γάρ	Supporting Conjunction
	they had argued with one another on the way who was the greatest.	Activity

Jesus' Instruction on Discipleship

35.	καί	Episode Connector
	when Jesus sat down,	Transition (Jesus' Teaching)
	he called the Twelve	Activity
	καί	Additive Conjunction
	said to them,	Event-2 Introduction
	"If anyone desires to be first he will be last of all and servant of all."	EVENT-2 [CONDITION]
36.	καί	Additive Conjunction
	when Jesus took a child,	Transition (Jesus' Teaching)
	he stood [the child] in their midst	Activity
	καί	Additive Conjunction

---

113. The discourse function of καί here is joining elements together to continue the main line of the plot. Although there is a change in setting (Capernaum), Mark is still using the same characters as the preceding verses (cf. 9:30-32).

Discourse Analysis of the Passion Predictions

when he hugged [the child] in his arms he said to them,	Transition (Jesus' Example) Saying Activity
37. "Whoever receives one of such little children as these in my name, receives me.	Condition to service
καί	Additive Conjunction
whoever receives me [Jesus] receives not me, ἀλλά	Condition to service Adversative Conjunction[114]
the one who sent me [God]."	

The summary of role analysis

The role analysis shows the two events Mark wishes to emphasize (9:31 and 35). Mark uses verb tense and conjunctions to establish prominence and cohesion. As one reads Jesus' second passion prediction, Mark provides the reader with both an internal and external perspective. When Mark desires to pull his audience into the story (internal perspective), to grab their attention, he utilizes the present tense. As the reader transitions between events, and therefore reads the background of the story, Mark utilizes the aorist tense (external, summary perspective). The verb tense therefore establishes for the reader what may serve as prominent events throughout the passion prediction.

The conjunctions provide cohesion and demonstrate the logical relationships between the two events throughout the second passion prediction. Mark uses καί to connect the various events within the passion prediction. He also uses δέ to introduce movement, or a shift in the pericope. The use of δέ interrupts the narrative to provide the disciples' two reponses to Jesus. Mark also uses γάρ as supporting background information. These conjunctions provide the reader with ties throughout the passion prediction to understand

---

114. The discourse function of ἀλλά is adversative; that is, contrasting two elements. Propositions that are introduced with ἀλλά are more prominent than the propositions with which they are contrasted. See Young, *Intermediate New Testament Greek*, 180.

Jesus' point here is the service of the disciples in the community toward insignificant ones will mean they are serving not just Jesus, but even one greater than him; that is, God himself.

the significant turning points and events within the passion prediction. The two events, and their logical relationships, are explained.

Jesus' teaching (event 1, the necessity of his identity and mission) prompts the disciples' response. Their response is one of ignorance and fear (9:32) and an obvious preoccupation with the status of greatness (9:34). It is here that Jesus questions their issue of status (concerning greatness). Then, due to the disciples' response, Mark reports the final event; that is, Jesus' teaching to the disciples (event-2, insistence for service). Jesus takes the initiative to appropriately teach the disciples the significance of the relationship between his identity and mission (9:31) and their choice "to serve" or "not to serve" (9:35-37). In other words, if the disciples so choose to follow Jesus by serving even the insignificant in society, then this culminates in not only the disciples representing Jesus' name, but also God. Therefore, the two analyses (Greek text and verb) are represented in the final role analysis. The role analysis represents Mark's emphasis of his story by reporting the second of Jesus' three passion predictions.

Mark once again brings together the formal aspect of his story, the identity of Jesus and his mission (9:30-31), with the functional aspect, the responsibility of the disciples (9:35-37) that ought to be displayed because of knowing Jesus. The disciples' concern however, was their status among men. Ironically, Jesus as the Son of Man, stated that he "will be handed over" to men, something the disciples misunderstood. Jesus teaches his disciples to be more concerned with serving others, not greatness among men.

Mark therefore weaves throughout the central section of his story three of Jesus' passion predictions to explicate both aspects for the reader. Although Mark tells the reader of Jesus' second prediction and what is required to follow him, the disciples still are plagued with a selfish desire illustrated in their love for self. As a matter of fact, Jesus' third and final passion prediction further demonstrates the disciples' failures, for they are preoccupied with power and prestige, resulting in Jesus' instruction regarding their service toward others.

Jesus' Third Passion Prediction (10:32-45)

Greek Text Analysis

Jesus' Third Prediction of His Death

32.δὲ[115]   Ἦσαν ἐν τῷ ὁδῷ ἀναβαίνοντες εἰς Ἱεροσόλυμα,[116]
καὶ ἦν προάγων αὐτοὺς ὁ Ἰησοῦς, καὶ ἐθαμβοῦντο,
οἱ δὲ ἀκολουθοῦντες[117] ἐφοβοῦντο.

---

115. Mark's use of δὲ ("now") can link narrative events together rather than interrupt the narrative as an adversative supporting a contrast. See BDAG, 213; "a marker linking narrative segments." *Contra* Gundry. He claims the δὲ is adversative denoting a contrast between Jesus and the disciples as a group (10:17) and Jesus, the disciples, and a smaller crowd as a group (10:32) (*Mark*, 570).

Gundry claims (*Mark*, 569-70, 573) that Mark's opening use of an adversative δὲ supports two different groups of people involved in Jesus' journey to Jerusalem; that is 'they ... going up to Jerusalem' (ἦσαν ... ἀναβαίνοντες Ἱεροςόλυμα) refers to the larger crowd that 'was also afraid' (οἱ δὲ ἀκολουθοῦντες ἐφοβοῦντο). And the Twelve refers to 'them' that are behind Jesus (προάγων αὐτοὺς) and 'were amazed' (καί ἐθαμβοῦντο).

The opening δέ links the preceding paragraph (10:23-31) with the Twelve, whom Jesus just had a dialogue. The Twelve is also the subject of the verb ἦσαν (10:32). It would also seem likely then that the Twelve are also the subject of ἐθαμβοῦντο; for the conjunction καί joins these two actions. The second δὲ is adversative; that is, it contrasts the Twelve with a larger crowd (οἱ δὲ ἀκολουθοῦντες ἐφοβοῦντο); for the second δὲ introduces another subject. Verse 32 therefore, concludes with Jesus taking aside (παραλαβὼν) the Twelve to teach them privately. See also France, *The Gospel of Mark*, 411-12; Stein, *Mark*, 478-79. *Contra* Marcus who sees "three concentric circles of adherents in 10:32: the Twelve, 'those following,' and a more loosely defined set of sympathizers similar to the 'many' who prepare Jesus' way in 11:8" (*Mark 8-16*, 742).

116. Mark's central section is structured as a journey; from the north (villages of Caesarea Philippi) to the south (Jerusalem). Like that of the first and second passion prediction, there is a topographical shift in the third passion prediction. Mark also uses the phrase ἐν τῇ ὁδῷ ("on the way") in the third prediction. Collins notes that these two cues (topography and repetition of a phrase) provide the necessary support to view the central section as a journey (*Mark*, 484).

117. France claims there is a change in subject and those that are following (a wider group of followers), that are also afraid, are distinguished from the disciples.

DEATH AND DISCIPLESHIP:
An Analysis of the Predictions of Jesus' Death in the Gospel of Mark

καὶ παραλαβὼν πάλιν[118] τοὺς δώδεκα
ἤρξατο αὐτοῖς λέγειν τὰ μέλλοντα
αὐτῷ συμβαίνειν[119]

33. ὅτι ἰδού[120] ἀναβαίνομεν εἰς Ἱεροσόλυμα,
καὶ ὁ υἱὸς τοῦ ἀνθρώπου παραδοθήσεται[121]

This is seen through Mark's use of the forward placement of δὲ in the construction οἱ δὲ ἀκολουθοῦντες (*The Gospel of Mark*, 412). Gundry argues that Mark's use of the participle construction οἱ δὲ ἀκολουθοῦντες could be attributive. He claims that Mark uses the attributive participle (οἱ ἀκολουθοῦντες) in 11:9 may reveal Mark's intention here; that is, serving as an attribute of those following rather than circumstantial ("[while] following . . .") (*Mark*, 570).

118. Decker claims that Mark's use of πάλιν, a use distinctive to Mark, may be used not as an adverbial indicator of temporal deixis; but as a discourse marker (*Temporal Deixis of the Greek Verb*, 71). Decker uses Randall Buth for support. Buth explains πάλιν as a "cohesion devise [which is used] within the book as a whole and helps to link together different episodes and macro-episodes" (Randall Buth, "Mark's Use of *Palin* and Its Relationship to Discourse and Plot Analysis," *Notes on Translation* 61 [1976], 32). The use of πάλιν therefore, links the three teaching sections of each passion prediction together.

119. The present ptc. μέλλοντα with the present inf. συμβαίνειν "denote an action that necessarily follows a divine decree *is destined, must, will certainly* . . . to be inevitable, *be destined, inevitable*" (BDAG, 628). The present participle construction (10:32) speaks to the certainty of the following actions (10:33-34); for Jesus describes the future suffering that will take place (cf. δεῖ, 8:31 and παραδίδοται, 9:31).

Decker contends that μέλλω may serve as a temporal indicator in Mark, much like that of ἐγγίζω; that is, referring to events coming near (*Temporal Deixis of the Greek Verb*, 84).

120. Mark's use of the exclamatory particle (ἰδού) could serve as a componential tie with Peter's exclamatory emphasis that he has left all to follow Jesus (cf. 10:28). Jesus (10:33) uses it to serve in much the same way as Peter; a marker of strong emphasis (See BDAG, 468). It seems reasonable that Jesus is emphasizing the content or details of the preceding participle clause μέλλοντα . . .; but is doing so to call attention to what he is saying. This exclamatory element is only in the third prediction, not in the preceding two passion predictions.

121. The use of παραδοθήσεται, a future passive, is a reference to the certainty of Jesus' future fate. The passive voice here, ties together the three predictions (cf. δεῖ, 8:31 and παραδίδοται, 9:31); that is, Jesus each time speaks of his death as a divine certainty.

τοῖς ἀρχιερεῦσιν καὶ τοῖς γραμματεῦσιν,
καὶ κατακρινοῦσιν αὐτὸν θανάτῳ
καὶ παραδώσουσιν αὐτὸν τοῖς ἔθνεσιν[122]

34. καὶ   ἐμπαίξουσιν αὐτῷ καὶ ἐμπτύσουσιν αὐτῷ
καὶ μαστιγώσουσιν αὐτὸν καὶ ἀποκτενοῦσιν,[123]
καὶ μετὰ τρεῖς ἡμέρας ἀναστήσεται.[124]

Disciples' Misunderstanding

35. Καὶ   προσπορεύονται αὐτῷ Ἰάκωβος καὶ Ἰωάννης
οἱ υἱοὶ Ζεβεδαίου λέγοντες αὐτῷ διδάσκαλε,

However, each prediction nuances different groups of people attributed with his death.

Marcus also concludes the divine passive is probably in view. However, he links this third prediction of Jesus' death to the Suffering Servant passages in Isaiah (cf. 53:6, 12). Because of this link, he also sees "the divine will probably in view when the Markan Jesus speaks of the Son of Man being turned over to his enemies. Thus, the reverberations of Isaiah 50 and 53 here function in a similar way to the use of *dei* in the first passion prediction, namely, to emphasize that 'it was necessary,' because God willed it, 'that the Son of Man should suffer many things'" (*Mark 8-16*, 745-46).

122. The inclusion of both parties (τοῖς ἀρχιερεῦσιν καὶ τοῖς γραμματεῦσιν, cf. 8:31 and τοῖς ἔθνεσιν, cf. 9:31) speaks to the completeness of the third prediction. France explains the involvement of the different groups. He writes, "here it is specifically the ἔθνη who will kill him, though it is the ἀρχιερεῖς καί γραμματεῖς who will condemn him to death. The Jewish phase of the passion is thus presented by two verbs, first κατακρινοῦσιν, then παραδώσουσιν. This corresponds to what we know of the competence of the Jewish authorities at that time: condemnation could not lead directly to death but must be implemented by handing over to the Romans who had that power" (*The Gospel of Mark*, 413).

123. Each of the future verbs (ἐμπαίξουσιν, ἐμπτύσουσιν, μαστιγώσουσιν, ἀποκτενοῦσιν, 10:34) details the actions of the Romans against Jesus. These details are then repeated in Mark's final section (15:15-25) of his story.

124. The five verbs in 10:33-34 clearly indicate to whom the actions against Jesus are attributed; for the verbs all end in -ουσιν. The two verbs that frame either side of those verbs attributed to various parties end in –εται; thus, indicating that Jesus is the subject, both as the one receiving the punishment (παραδοθήσεται) and the one who rises from the dead (ἀναστήσεται).

DEATH AND DISCIPLESHIP:
An Analysis of the Predictions of Jesus' Death in the Gospel of Mark

θέλομεν ἵνα[125] ὃ ἐὰν αἰτήσωμέν σε ποιήσῃς ἡμιν.

36. δὲ[126]   ὁ εἶπεν αὐτοῖς τί θέλετέ με ποιήσω[127] ὑμῖν

37. δὲ   οἱ εἶπαν αὐτῷ δὸς ἡμῖν ἵνα εἷς σου ἐκ δεξιῶν
καὶ εἷς ἐξ ἀριστερῶν καθίσωμεν ἐν τῇ δόξῃ σου.[128]

38. δὲ   ὁ Ἰησοῦς εἶπεν αὐτοῖς οὐκ οἴδατε τί αἰτεῖσθε.
δύνασθε πιεῖν τὸ ποτήριον ὃ ἐγὼ πίνω ἢ τὸ
βάπτισμα ὃ ἐγὼ βαπτίζομαι βαπτισθῆναι;[129]

39. δὲ   οἱ εἶπαν αὐτῷ δυνάμεθα.[130]

---

125. Content use of ἵνα in 10:35 and 10:37.

126. An adversative use of δέ that Gundry classifies (*Mark*, 577) as a dialogic shift; that is, Mark notes a shift in the dialogue between various characters and their responses by using δέ (cf. vv. 37, 38, 39).

127. Mark's use of the aorist subjunctive of ποιέω, ποιήσω, is a deliberative real subjunctive. It is a "real question [that] expects some kind of answer and is a genuine question. . . . Unlike the interrogative indicative, it does not ask a question of fact, but of *possibility, means, location*, etc" (Wallace, *Greek Grammar Beyond the Basics*, 466). Using the forward position of the interrogative pronoun (τί θέλετε), Jesus asks for clarification while resisting the demand to give James and John whatever they ask.

128. Due to the request of James and John, it is possible that they understood Jesus' identity but not the role that identity entailed. Stein claims that "They recognize correctly that Jesus is indeed the Messiah, as Peter's confession (8:29) . . . and Jesus' teachings concerning his coming glory and the coming of the kingdom (8:38-9:1) indicate. But they refuse to accept Jesus' repeated teaching concerning his coming passion (8:31; 9:31; 10:33-34)" (*Mark*, 484-85). Perhaps Mark's use of the disciples' misunderstanding is to demonstrate to his readers the importance that suffering must precede glory. Recall, each of Jesus' passion predictions and therefore subsequent teachings, explicates a significant contrast to the world's value system; for Jesus' definition of greatness is not prestige and status, but humility and service.

129. Jesus' unexpected answer to James and John reinforces that they do not understand Jesus' role as the suffering Messiah; for they are not expecting that they too must suffer. Gundry also states that his answer "implies that Jesus is able to endure such a fate . . . and that he foreknows his endurance as well as the fate itself" (*Mark*, 577).

130. Mark's use of the adversative δέ along with the disciples' answer of af-

	δὲ ὁ Ἰησοῦς εἶπεν αὐτοῖς τὸ ποτήριον ὃ ἐγὼ πίνω πίεσθε καὶ τὸ βάπτισμα ὃ ἐγὼ βαπτίζομαι βαπτισθήσεσθε,[131]
40. δὲ	τὸ καθίσαι[132] ἐκ δεξιῶν μου ἢ ἐξ εὐωνύμων οὐκ ἔστιν ἐμὸν δοῦναι, ἀλλ'[133] οἷς ἡτοίμασται

Jesus' Instruction on Discipleship

41. Καὶ	ἀκούσαντες οἱ δέκα ἤρξαντο ἀγανακτεῖν περὶ Ἰακώβου καὶ Ἰωάννου.

---

firmation that they indeed *are able* to emulate Jesus in the matters that relate to his suffering further indicates the erroneous understanding of the disciples that is evident following all three of Jesus' passion predictions (cf. 8:32b-33; 9:33-34; 10:35-40).

131. It is important to note that Jesus' response here does not undermine his earlier question (10:38). France claims that "even if they fulfill the 'conditions' he has set down, their request still cannot be granted. The cup and the baptism thus prove not to be qualifying conditions at all, but rather a way of indicating that their whole conception of δόξα and of the way it is to be achieved is misguided. It cannot be earned even by the extreme suffering which he must undergo and which they in their turn will indeed share. He has already warned his disciples in 8:34-38 of the cost of following him, even to the extent of martyrdom, and James and John must reckon with that" (*The Gospel of Mark*, 417).

132. The use of the article τὸ, though it is not in the translation, in the construction τὸ καθίσαι (art. + inf.) functions as a substantive with the infinitive. This use of the article nominalizes the infinitive; that is, the articular infinitive becomes the subject (here, it is the subject of ἔστιν) (Wallace, *Greek Grammar Beyond the Basics*, 234).

133. The use of ἀλλά according to BDAG may carry the nuance of 'except' (45). Gundry claims that Mark may be using ἀλλά to emphasize Jesus' authority and foreknowledge rather than contrasting his authority with God's authority. Gundry writes, ". . . is not mine to give except [that it is mine to give] to those for whom it has been prepared [with the implication that it has not been prepared for James and John]. . . . Mark's characteristic emphases favor this translation . . . the one who prepared the seats of highest honor for others besides James and John, for in all probability the passive obliquely refers to God as the preparer. . . . The strength of ἀλλά as an adversative and the following ellipsis of a subject and verb concentrate attention on 'those for whom it has been prepared'" (*Mark*, 578). Marcus claims that "Jesus does not deny that there will *be* such places, only that there is a simple formula for calculating who will occupy them" (*Mark 8-16*, 754).

DEATH AND DISCIPLESHIP:
An Analysis of the Predictions of Jesus' Death in the Gospel of Mark

42. καὶ   προσκαλεσάμενος αὐτοὺς ὁ Ἰησοῦς
λέγει αὐτοῖς οἴδατε[134] ὅτι οἱ δοκοῦντες ἄρχειν
τῶν ἐθνῶν κατακυριεύουσιν αὐτῶν καὶ
οἱ μεγάλοι αὐτῶν κατεξουσιάζουσιν αὐτῶν.

43. δὲ[135]   οὐχ οὕτως ἐστιν ἐν ὑμῖν, ἀλλ[136] ὃς ἂν θέλῃ[137]
μέγας γενέσθαι ἐν ὑμῖν ἔσται ὑμῶν διάκονος,

44. καὶ   ὃς ἂν θέλῃ ἐν ὑμῖν εἶναι πρῶτος ἔσται πάντων
δοῦλος.[138]

---

134. The use of οἴδατε introduces a subject that is common knowledge, a truism. It is Jesus' use of this truism that makes the οὐχ οὕτως ("not so . . .") even more striking. James and John's request for royal, authoritative privileges does not belong to them; rather the reality and status to rule belongs to the Gentiles; for it is publicly recognized. The disciples' status, therefore, is to serve others; not rule over them.

135. The adversative δέ (10:43) states that the disciples' current position is 'not' one of greatness; for Jesus' truism includes οἱ μεγάλοι ("the great ones," 10:42b) in comparison with the rulers of the Gentiles. This is ironic given the disciples' earlier dispute over τίς μείζων ("who is the greatest," 9:33-34); for current reality suggests that obtaining greatness, as the disciples desired, is not possible.

136. The strong adversative ἀλλά (10:43) emphasizes the responsibility of the disciples in what follows; for Jesus gives them opportunity to be great ὃς ἂν θέλῃ μέγας γενέσθαι ("whoever desires to be great," 10:43). But this greatness comes with a cost that the disciples were not expecting.

137. The use of the present subjunctive (θέλῃ) instead of the indicative (θέλει, 9:35) indicates that the disciples might involve themselves in a similar act as James and John. Mark is not aware of what the disciples might decide; therefore, uses the subjunctive to express a desire rather than fact.

138. Jesus' dialogue continues with his disciples (10:44) and repeats the present subjunctive (θέλῃ) found in 10:43. But these two verses (10:43-44) formulate a striking resemblance to 9:35; it is Jesus' desire to help his disciples understand 'true greatness' and what it entails. Recall that in 9:35, Jesus instructs his disciples because of their selfish understanding about greatness. He turns the disciples' understanding of greatness on its head by indicating that if one desires the position of greatness (τίς μείζων) then he must assume a subordinate position to others; that is, rather than πρῶτος εἶναι ("to be first/most important"), Jesus requires that his followers be ἔσχατος καί διάκονος ("lest significant and an assistant who is subordinate to someone").

45. γὰρ   καὶ¹³⁹ ὁ υἱὸς τοῦ ἀνθρώπου οὐκ ἦλθεν
διακονηθῆναι ἀλλὰ¹⁴⁰ διακονῆσαι
καὶ δοῦναι¹⁴¹ τὴν ψυχὴν αὐτοῦ λύτρον
ἀντὶ¹⁴² πολλῶν.

The summary of Greek text analysis

The Greek text analysis shows Mark's use of repetition of words, phrases, and sentences that point to the prominence and cohesion within Jesus' third

---

It is similar here in 10:43-44. Again, James and John raise the issue of greatness and Jesus instructs his disciples regarding their understanding of greatness. He again redefines their understanding of greatness; for if they θέλῃ μέγας γενέσθαι ("desire to become great") and θέλῃ εἶναι πρῶτος ("desire to be first"), then Jesus requires that his followers be διάκονος ("servants") and δοῦλος ("slaves"). Evans states, "that διάκονος 'service,' . . . clearly denotes a subordinate position, a position to which the world's 'great' do not aspire" (*Mark 8:27-16:20*, 119). Gundry captures Jesus' intent. He states, "Greatness is not achieved in vv 43-44, then. It is only wanted. Being a servant and a slave will not give a new definition of greatness or provide a new avenue to it. It will deny greatness" (*Mark*, 581).

139 The forward position of καί along with γὰρ at the beginning of this verse connects the preceding verse (γὰρ, explanatory) with an emphasis on the Son of Man as the supreme model for service (καί, ascensive). Young's classification of καί here fits best. He states that καί "is a focusing addition that further develops the previous thought. . . . The ascensive idea elaborates on the same thought, bringing it to a climax" (*Intermediate New Testament Greek*, 188). Edwards sees the γὰρ as purposeful; that is, "disciples should adopt the posture of servants and slaves not on the basis of ethical reasoning but *because* it is the posture of the Son of Man" (*The Gospel According to Mark*, 326).

140. The use of ἀλλά strengthens the contrast between διακονηθῆναι ("to be served") and διακονῆσαι ("to serve") emphasizing Jesus' role as the latter.

141. The two infinitives of purpose διακονῆσαι καὶ δοῦναι ("to serve" and "to give") denote Jesus' self-sacrificing attitude that he is asking his disciples also to express. See Young, *Intermediate New Testament Greek*, 168 regarding infinitives of purpose.

142. For the use of ἀντὶ ("in place of") denoting substitutionary atonement of Christ, see Murray J. Harris, "Appendix: Prepositions and Theology in the Greek New Testament," in *Dictionary of New Testament Theology*, ed. Colin Brown (Grand Rapids: Zondervan, 1986), 3:1179-80; Wallace, *Greek Grammar Beyond the Basics*, 365-67; Young, *Intermediate New Testament Greek*, 90.

passion prediction and the central section. The third prediction, like that of Jesus' first and second prediction, complements the intent of Mark's story. It informs the reader of Jesus' identity and the disciples' responsibility as they respond to his identity.

Mark reports Jesus' prediction of his death for a third time, but this third prediction includes three details not found in the first two predictions. They are: (1) details regarding the destination of Jesus' mission (Jerusalem) and the response to it (10:32), (2) details concerning who is responsible for his death (chief priests and scribes) and his suffering (Gentiles, 10:33), and (3) the specifics of his suffering (mocking, scourging, spitting, and killing, 10:34) that are later communicated in Mark's final section of his story (11:1-16:8). Jesus' third prediction, and the disciples' response to it, ultimately point to the climax of Jesus' mission; that is, his substitutionary death in place of many (δοῦναι τὴν ψυχὴν αὐτοῦ λύτρον ἀντὶ πολλῶν, 10:45).

Use of prominence (focus) and cohesion (componential tie)

The first detail Mark adds to Jesus' third prediction is the destination of Jesus' mission for his readers (Ἱεροσόλυμα, v. 32) and the response of those following. The inclusion of the destination is new to Jesus' three descriptions of his death, for the first two predictions simply provide the content of his teaching as it pertains to his death. They do not include the location to which it will occur. Therefore, the inclusion of Jesus' destination shows focus, a level of prominence that grabs the attention of the reader. Also indicating focus is the fact that Jesus leads his disciples toward the destination where "he will be delivered into the hands" of those who will kill him. Stephen Levinsohn proposes that Mark selects Jesus as the main character, the one who is the center of attention moving forward.[143] The reader is to pay attention to Jesus as the central character, though others are present.

---

143. Stephen H. Levinsohn, "Functions of Copula-Participle Combinations ("Periphrastics")" in *The Greek Verb Revisited: A Fresh Approach for Biblical Exegesis* (Bellingham, WA: Lexham Press, 2016), 309. He indicates that Jesus is the character of attention for the reader because Mark presents an event, and while doing so postposes, or selects a character from the cast of characters. The construction that would indicate this is copula + subject + participial clause (καὶ ἦν προάγων αὐτοὺς ὁ Ἰησοῦς, "and Jesus was going ahead of them").

It is not just the location of Jesus' destination, and the fact that Jesus is the central character moving forward, but also the response of the disciples ("they were amazed") and the crowd ("they were afraid") as they follow Jesus. Unlike the first two predictions (8:31; 9:31); Mark here communicates the characters' response (10:32) *prior to* the actual teaching of Jesus' death (10:33-34). This third prediction includes both the crowd and the disciples as they follow Jesus, each are found in the two previous predictions respectively (cf. προσκαλεσάμενος τὸν ὄχλον, 8:34 and ἐφώνησεν τοὺς δώδεκα, 9:35). The two groups following Jesus, therefore are included here to tie the three predictions together (cohesion).

It is not until Jesus leads the way (καὶ ἦν προάγων αὐτοὺς ὁ Ἰησοῦς, 10:32) that the responses of the disciples and crowd are recorded by Mark. Then Jesus once again tells his disciples what will happen to him (τὰ μέλλοντα αὐτῷ συμβαίνειν). Although the present participle construction is not a present divine passive, as found in the first two predictions (cf. δεῖ, 8:31; παραδίδοται, 9:31), this participle construction still speaks to the certainty of the events that follow (10:33b-34). The use of μέλλοντα represents a divine decree, an inevitable and imminent action that is near and certain to happen.

The handing over of Jesus to others (παραδοθήσεται) also points to the certainty of events, for it too is a divine passive speaking to the fact that God is the ultimate agent responsible. Therefore, Mark shows cohesion between the three passion predictions. He does so through the present divine passive (cf. 8:31; 9:31) in the first two predictions and the present participle construction and the future passive (cf. 10:32) in the third prediction. In other words, the three predictions "hang together" to indicate the certainty, that not only will the Son of Man suffer, but also that he can predict the future. And because the ability to predict the future rests in God and God alone; Jesus' three predictions show that he is God. The three predictions then, explicate the formal aspect of Mark's story; that is, Jesus is the Son of God.

The second detail added to the third prediction is the two groups responsible for his death (chief priests and scribes) and suffering (Gentiles). In the first prediction, Jesus makes it clear that he is the object of divine necessity (δεῖ, 8:31) "to suffer many things" and "to be rejected by the elders, chief priests, and scribes." In the second prediction, Jesus makes it clear that he is the object of humility by humanity (παραδίδοται, "he will be delivered into the hands of men," 9:31), likely referring to the Gentiles. Therefore, due to the presence of both groups of people (the chief priests and scribes, and the Gentiles) in Jesus' third prediction, it seems likely that both prominence and cohesion are found in Jesus' third prediction. Perhaps Mark includes both groups in the third prediction ultimately pointing the reader to a climax, for this shows those who are responsible for his death *and* suffering (prominence). Mark has also repeated both groups who are responsible from the first two predictions and placed them in the third prediction to emphatically tie the first two predictions to the third (cohesion), for Mark has just brought clarity to the reader who is responsible for the death *and* the suffering of Jesus. This clarity brings the reader full circle; in other words, Jesus' death is certain to happen through the Jewish (elders, chief priests, and scribes) and Roman (Gentile) authorities.

The third detail added to Jesus' third prediction refers to the specifics of Jesus' suffering. The first two predictions do not include any detail of Jesus' suffering, only that it will happen. The third prediction not only tells us that Jesus will suffer, but how and by whom. The Gentiles will bring incredible shame and ridicule upon Jesus by mocking him (ἐμπαίξουσιν), spitting on him (ἐμπτύσουσιν), whipping him (μαστιγώσουσιν), and killing him (ἀποκτενοῦσιν). But this only occurs because the Jewish authorities will hand Jesus over (παραδώσουσιν) to the Gentiles. Once again, Jesus' teaching points to a radically different Messiah than what is expected by the disciples. This continual redefinition and presentation of the identity of the Messiah, also serves as cohesion; that is, the repetition of Jesus' role as the suffering Messiah ties the central section together. As Mark continues his story, it is clear what the the disciples expect; greatness (τίς μείζων, 9:34; σου ἐκ δεξιῶν καί ἐξ ἀριστερῶν καθίσωμεν, 10:37).

Mark captures the dialogue between James and John and Jesus (10:35-40). The dialogue represents the desire of the disciples, greatness. They want power and prestige. In a similar situation to that of the second passion prediction (cf. 9:33-34), this prediction makes it clear that the disciples have again missed the implications of Jesus' teaching. It is not humility the disciples want; they want to be recognized. Jesus however clarifies that following him entails sacrifice and suffering (10:38-40). Edwards states, "Disciples of Jesus do not decide to accept or reject hardships on the basis of the future rewards accruing from them. They accept suffering on the sole basis that it is the way of Jesus."[144] Perhaps the disciples did know the suffering involved; hence the reason for their amazement when Jesus went out ahead of them on the way to Jerusalem. They did not want to accept their potential fate. Jesus proceeds to instruct his disciples what it takes to be great (10:41-45).

Once again Mark reports that Jesus uses the request of James and John (σου ἐκ δεξιῶν καί ἐξ ἀριστερῶν καθίσωμεν, "may we sit on your right and sit on your left," 10:37) to teach them the importance of sacrificially serving others with humility (10:41-45); the third of three responsibilities required of those who follow Jesus. Mark uses two related concepts regarding authority and status; that is, the request of James and John (σου ἐκ δεξιῶν καί ἐξ ἀριστερῶν καθίσωμεν, 10:37) and Jesus' spoken truism (τῶν ἐθνῶν κατακυριεύουσιν αὐτῶν καί οἱ μεγάλοι αὐτῶν κατεξουσιάζουσιν αὐτῶν) to bring cohesion to the third passion prediction. These two concepts demonstrate that the request of James and John (to have positions of authority, 10:37-40), and Jesus' truism (those who have positions of authority, οἴδατε ὅτι . . ., 10:42), signal that these events are closely related. It is not due to grammar that these two events are related; rather it is the concept of greatness and authority, or power and prestige. Jesus therefore uses a truism "as a negative example of what Christian discipleship should not be. Gentile rulers . . . use their authority to lord it over their subjects, but Christian greatness does not lie in such behavior . . . It does not involve being *master* over others at all; instead, it involves being their servant."[145] Jesus asks something different of his disciples (οὐχ οὕτως δέ ἐστιν ἐν ὑμῖν). Jesus requires humility and sacrifice (ἔσται ὑμῶν διάκονος . . . ἔσται πάντων δοῦλος, 10:43-44).

Jesus' instruction (10:41-45) therefore, emphasizes sacrificially serving others with humility. But his instruction does so not because he introduces a well-known fact about who rightfully has authority, nor is it because of his requirements that he gives to the disciples; rather it is because he comes as the supreme example of humility and sacrifice (ἀλλὰ διακονῆσαι καί δοῦναι

---

144. Edwards, *The Gospel According to Mark*, 323.
145. Stein, *Mark*, 486.

τὴν ψυχὴν αὐτοῦ λύτρον ἀντὶ πολλῶν). Therefore, if one is to truly follow Jesus, he too must exemplify the spirit of humility, service, and sacrifice. France contends,

> We must not forget that this crucial verse, however great its soteriological implications, occurs in context as a model for Jesus' disciples to follow. It is not the λύτρον ἀντὶ πολλῶν that they are expected to reproduce that was Jesus' unique mission. But the spirit of service and self-sacrifice, the priority given to the needs of the πολλοί, are for all disciples. They, too, must serve rather than be served, and it may be that some of them will be called upon, like James and John, to give up their lives. There is no room for quarrels about τίς μείζων.[146]

Mark's point is that whoever desires to follow Jesus must sacrificially submit to serving others (*contra* James and John, v. 37). Greatness is about serving others; it is humble, unrewarded service. Mark's use of language points to both Jesus' identity (τὰ μέλλοντα αὐτῷ συμβαίνειν and παραδοθήσεται) and the significance of this identity, that is, pointing to the disciples' responsibility (ἔσται ὑμῶν διάκονος . . . ἔσται πάντων δοῦλος) as they follow Jesus.

Verb Analysis

Jesus' Third Prediction of His Death

32. δὲ	Ἦσαν ἐν τῇ ὁδῷ	Impf act ind
	ἀναβαίνοντες εἰς Ἱεροςόλυμα	Pres act ptc
	καὶ ἦν	Impf act ind
	προάγων αὐτοὺς	Pres act ptc
	καὶ ἐθαμβοῦντο,	Impf pass ind
	οἱ δὲ ἀκολουθοῦντες	Pres act ptc
	ἐφοβοῦντο.	Impf mid ind
	καὶ παραλαβὼν πάλιν τοὺς δώδεκα	Aor act ptc
	ἤρξατο	Aor mid ind

---

146. France, *The Gospel of Mark*, 421.

	αὐτοῖς λέγειν	Pres act inf
	τὰ μέλλοντα	Pres act ptc
	αὐτῷ συμβαίνειν	Pres act inf
33.	ὅτι ἰδοὺ **ἀναβαίνομεν** εἰς Ἱεροσόλυμα,	Pres act ind
	καὶ ὁ υἱὸς τοῦ ἀνθρώπου παραδοθήσεται	Fut pass ind
	τοῖς ἀρχιερεῦσιν καὶ τοῖς γραμματεῦσιν,	
	καὶ κατακρινοῦσιν αὐτὸν θανάτῳ	Fut act ind
	καὶ παραδώσουσιν αὐτὸν τοῖς ἔθνεσιν	Fut act ind
34. καὶ	ἐμπαίξουσιν αὐτῷ	Fut act ind
	καὶ ἐμπτύσουσιν αὐτῷ	Fut act ind
	καὶ μαστιγώσουσιν αὐτὸν	Fut act ind
	καὶ ἀποκτενοῦσιν,	Fut act ind
	καὶ μετὰ τρεῖς ἡμέρας ἀναστήσεται.	Fut mid ind

Disciples' Misunderstanding

35. Καὶ	προσπορεύονται αὐτῷ Ἰάκωβος καὶ Ἰωάννης	Pres mid ind
	οἱ υἱοὶ Ζεβεδαίου **λέγοντες** αὐτῷ	Pres act ptc
	διδάσκε, θέλομεν ἵνα	Pres act ind
	ὃ ἐὰν αἰτήσωμεν σε	Aor act subj
	ποιήσῃς ἡμῖν.	Aor act subj
36. δὲ	ὁ εἶπεν αὐτοῖς	Aor act ind
	τί θέλετέ με	Pres act ind
	ποιήσω ὑμῖν;	Fut act ind
37. δὲ	οἱ εἶπαν αὐτῷ	Aor act ind
	δὸς ἡμῖν ἵνα	Aor act imper
	εἷς σου ἐκ δεξιῶν καὶ εἷς ἐξ ἀριστερῶν	
	καθίσωμεν ἐν τῇ δόξῃ σου.	Aor act subj
38. δὲ	ὁ Ἰησοῦς εἶπεν αὐτοῖς	Aor act ind

DEATH AND DISCIPLESHIP:
An Analysis of the Predictions of Jesus' Death in the Gospel of Mark

	οὐκ οἴδατε	Perf act ind
	τί αἰτεῖσθε.	Pres mid ind
	δύνασθε	Pres pass ind
	πιεῖν τὸ ποτήριον	Aor act inf
	ὃ ἐγὼ πίνω	Pres act ind
	ἢ τὸ βάπτισμα ὃ ἐγὼ βαπτίζομαι	Pres pass ind
	βαπτισθῆναι;	Aor pass inf
39. δὲ	οἱ εἶπαν αὐτῷ	Aor act ind
	δυνάμεθα.	Pres pass ind
	ὁ δὲ Ἰησοῦς εἶπεν αὐτοῖς	Aor act ind
	τὸ ποτήριον ὃ ἐγὼ πίνω	Pres act ind
	πίεσθε	Fut mid ind
	καὶ τὸ βάπτισμα ὃ ἐγὼ βαπτίζομαι	Pres pass ind
	βαπτισθήσεσθε,	Fut pass ind
40. δὲ	τὸ καθίσαι ἐκ δεξιῶν μου ἢ ἐξ εὐωνύμων	Aor act inf
	οὐκ ἔστιν ἐμὸν	Pres act ind
	δοῦναι, ἀλλ᾽ οἷς	Aor act inf
	ἡτοίμασται.	Perf pass ind

Jesus' Instruction on Discipleship

41. Καὶ	ἀκούσαντες οἱ δέκα	Aor act ptc
	ἤρξαντο	Aor mid ind
	ἀγανακτεῖν περὶ Ἰακώβου καὶ Ἰωάννου.	Pres act inf
42. καὶ	προσκαλεσάμενος αὐτοὺς	Aor mid ptc
	ὁ Ἰησοῦς λέγει αὐτοῖς	Pres act ind
	οἴδατε ὅτι	Perf act ind
	οἱ δοκοῦντες	Pres act ptc
	ἄρχειν τῶν ἐθνῶν	Pres act inf
	κατακυριεύουσιν αὐτῶν	Pres act ind
	καὶ οἱ μεγάλοι αὐτῶν κατεξουσιάζουσιν αὐτῶν.	Pres act ind

Discourse Analysis of the Passion Predictions

43. δὲ	οὐχ οὕτως ἐστιν ἐν ὑμῖν,	Pres act ind
	ἀλλ ὃς ἂν θέλῃ	Pres act subj
	μέγας γενέσθαι ἐν ὑμῖν	Aor mid inf
	ἔσται ὑμῶν διάκονος,	Fut mid ind
44. καὶ	ὃς ἂν θέλῃ ἐν ὑμῖν	Pres act subj
	εἶναι πρῶτος	Pres act inf
	ἔσται πάντων δοῦλος	Fut mid ind
45. γὰρ	καὶ ὁ υἱὸς τοῦ ἀνθρώπου οὐκ ἦλθεν	Aor act ind
	διακονηθῆναι	Aor pass ind
	ἀλλὰ διακονῆσαι	Aor act inf
	καὶ δοῦναι τὴν ψυχὴν αὐτοῦ	Aor act inf
	λύτρον ἀντὶ πολλῶν.	

The summary of verb analysis

The verb analysis examines and explains Mark's verb tense choices as they are communicated through verbal aspect. The analysis then points to levels of prominence. Like the preceding two verb analyses, this verb analysis of Jesus' third passion prediction points to the following conclusions.

Mark uses the aorist tense twenty-three times in the third passion prediction. Unlike the first two passion predictions where the aorist tense is the most frequent tense used, the third passion prediction, however, is different. The present tense is used twenty-nine times and is the most frequent tense used. Although the aorist tense is not the primary tense, its use is like those of the first two predictions; that is, the aorist tense (perfective aspect) indicates Mark's desire to catalogue events from an external summary viewpoint without any detail.

The aorist tense carries the story forward. It provides the reader with the major events within the story. For example, in the third passion prediction Mark uses the aorist participle when he transitions from scene to scene (10:32, 41, 42),[147] the aorist subjunctive in temporal and purpose clauses (a

---

147. The use of the aorist participle include: παραλαβὼν, 10:32; ἀκούσαντες, 10:41; and προσκαλεσάμενος, 10:42. Each of these participles denotes a transition in

DEATH AND DISCIPLESHIP:
An Analysis of the Predictions of Jesus' Death in the Gospel of Mark

future reference, 10:35 and purpose clause, 10:35, 37),[148] the aorist imperative to denote the request of James and John (10:37),[149] the aorist infinitive to note actions or desires not yet realized (10:38 (2x), 40 (2x), 43, 45),[150] and the aorist tense in general noting the beginning of an action (10:32 and 10:41)[151]

---

scenes and serves to carry the narrative forward.

148. Decker notes Mark's use of the aorist subjunctive (ποιήσω, 10:35) as a future reference. He states, "This is again obvious in the context as Jesus responds to a request regarding future action. The subjunctive mood is also significant . . ., reflecting the potential (but as yet unrealized) action. . . . Jesus' query, also framed with an aorist form, asks for a statement of the future action anticipated; he does not request a description of the process, but simply refers to this situation as a whole" (*Temporal Deixis of the Greek Verb*, 37). Although Mark communicates Jesus' reply with a future reference of the aorist subjunctive; it is important to note that Mark does not intend to communicate the details related to Jesus' request; thus, using the aorist, or perfective aspect, to denote an external summary viewpoint.

Mark uses two aorist subjunctives (αἰτήσωμέν, 10:35 and καθίσωμεν, 10:37) with the complementary ἵνα to denote the purpose for the general request of James and John and the request to sit at Jesus' right and left side respectively. There are no unfolding details as to the purpose for the request of James and John, only that they wanted to sit at his right and left sides. The reader is never told by the author any details as to why James and John made a request to Jesus.

149. The aorist imperative (δὸς, 10:37) denotes a specific request/instruction by James and John to Jesus; that is, 'to grant,' or 'allow' them to sit on Jesus' right and left (See BDAG, 243).

150. The aorist infinitives (πιεῖν and βαπτισθῆναι, 10:38; καθίσαι and δοῦναι, 10:40; γενέσθαι, 10:43; διακονῆσαι and δοῦναι, 10:45) are used to communicate uncompleted events, desires. In 10:38, the disciples have not experienced the trials that Jesus is about to go through later in the story. In 10:40, the disciples' position at Jesus' right and left is an unfulfilled desire that Jesus will not attend to; for it is not his to give to them. In 10:43, the disciples' desired position of greatness is also an unfulfilled, unrealized desire at the time of Jesus' dialogue with them. In 10:45, Jesus' service and giving of his life is yet unfulfilled, a future statement not yet realized at the time of the dialogue with his disciples. All these examples employ the aorist infinitive, perfective aspect.

151. The two aorist forms of ἄρχω (ἤρξατο, 10:32; ἤρξαντο, 10:41) are two references "that carry the sense of *begin*" and are used with complementary infinitives (λέγειν and ἀγανακτεῖν) respectively (Decker, *Temporal Deixis of the Greek Verb*, 84). Mark uses the aorist form of ἄρχω following an aorist participle to denote the beginning of a scene, or the transition from the end of one scene to the beginning of another scene (cf. 8:31, 32b).

and noting the actions of various characters throughout the story (10:36, 37, 38, 39, 45 (2x)).[152]

Therefore, Mark's use of the aorist tense (perfective aspect) moves the narrative forward. Mark writes of events in the aorist tense that are not intended to be prominent; that is, they do not serve to grab the reader's attention. On the other hand, the imperfective aspect explicates the internal viewpoint, or the foreground of the narrative. The imperfective aspect includes the imperfect tense, which occurs three times, and the present tense occurring twenty-nine times. Recall that the imperfective aspect highlights the introduction of various characters and/or events to grab the reader's attention; thus, making them prominent.

Mark uses the imperfect tense for offline information. This offline information in the third passion prediction is like the use of the imperfect tense in the first two passion predictions (cf. 8:32; 9:30, 32, 34). Mark's three uses of the imperfect tense (10:32)[153] and the two uses of the imperfect periphrastic participle (10:32)[154] serve to set the scene for the third passion prediction (10:32). Mark's other use of the imperfective aspect, however, the present tense, is used to draw added attention to that which it refers.

Mark uses the present tense twenty-nine times and intends to highlight various events within the third passion prediction. For example, Mark uses the present participle to relate temporal actions to the main verb (10:32b, 35)[155]

---

152. The seven aorist verbs (εἶπεν (3x), 8:36, 38, 39; εἶπαν (2x), 8:37, 39; ἦλθεν, 10:45; and διακονηθῆναι, 10:45) portray actions of various characters without involving any detail; five of which serve to move the dialogue forward between Jesus and James and John.

153. Mark uses the imperfect tense three times (ἦσαν, "they were;" ἐθαμβοῦντο, "they were amazed;" and ἐφοβοῦντο, "they were afraid") to set the scene as the disciples and the crowd follow Jesus and go to Jerusalem. Although this is not the point of the pericope, it does provide the context in which the rest of the events take place.

154. The two imperfect periphrastic participles (ἦσαν . . . ἀναβαίνοντες . . . καί ἦν προάγων αὐτοὺς ὁ Ἰησοῦς) also serve to set the scene for the third passion prediction. The present participles constitute the finite verb tense of the main verb (verb of being) and thus communicate its aspect; here it is the imperfective aspect. See Campbell, *Verbal Aspect and Non-Indicative Verbs: Further Soundings*, 32-33; and Wallace, *Greek Grammar Beyond the Basics*, 648.

155. Mark uses two present participles. One of the present participles (λέγοντες,

and present substantive participles to relate nominal entities engaged in an action that is temporally related to the main verb (10:32, 42).[156] He also uses the present infinitive to highlight the beginning of an action (10:32b),[157] the imminence of an action (10:32c),[158] and the open-endedness of an action (10:42); all from an internal viewpoint.[159] The historic present is used to indicate when a new unit or paragraph begins (10:35, 41),[160] and to highlight Jesus' authoritative

---

"saying," 10:35) portrays contemporaneous action to that of the main verb. Campbell states, "The contemporaneous temporal reference of the present participle in relation to its principal verb is an expected pragmatic implicature of imperfective aspect. Since this aspect views events and activities from the inside, as though unfolding, and without the beginning and end of the action in view, it is inherently capable of portraying events that are occurring at the same time as other events" (*Verbal Aspect and Non-Indicative Verbs: Further Soundings*, 23).

Mark's other use of the present participle (τὰ μέλλοντα, "what was about," 10:32b) may serve a temporal reference. Decker states, "Mark's two uses of μέλλω, both imperfective aspects, are in accord with NT use generally . . . and also correspond to the verb's lexis which is most naturally described as a process rather than with the summary viewpoint of the perfective forms" (*Temporal Deixis of the Greek Verb*, 216 n. 158). In other words, Jesus was describing his impending death as in process rather than from an external summary viewpoint.

156. Mark's two uses of the present substantive participle (οἱ ἀκολουθοῦντες, "the ones who were following," 10:32; and οἱ δοκοῦντες, "the ones who are reputed," 10:42) "express nominal entities. Nevertheless, the verbal side of the substantival participles is evident in that these refer to people who are engaged in some kind of action" (Campbell, *Verbal Aspect and Non-Indicative Verbs: Further Soundings*, 39). These participles typically express contemporaneous action: that is, each of the uses above refer to action occurring simultaneously to their main verbs.

157. Mark's use of the present infinitive construction (ἤρξατο + λέγειν, 10:32b) expresses ingression action.

158. Mark's use of the present infinitive construction (μέλλοντα + συμβαίνειν, 10:32c) "views the action as imminent" (Campbell, *Verbal Aspect and Non-Indicative Verbs: Further Soundings*, 105). Jesus therefore is telling his disciples that the following information related to his suffering and death is imminent (cf. 10:33-34).

159. Mark's use of the present infinitive (ἄρχειν, 10:42) may simply just refer to the portrayal of an action from an internal viewpoint. "The situations to which they contribute are general, and the activities they render are open-ended" (Campbell, *Verbal Aspect and Non-Indicative Verbs: Further Soundings*, 110).

160. The historic present (προσπορεύονται, 10:35 and ἀγανακτεῖν, 10:41) is a

teaching to the disciples (10:42).[161] The futuristic present is used to highlight matters of greater emphasis (10:33, 38, 39).[162] The present subjunctive is used to highlight the willingness of the disciples (10:43, 44),[163] and the present indicative is used to highlight the unfolding nature of Jesus' dialogue with James and John and the other disciples (10:35, 36, 38 (2x), 39, 40, 42 (2x)).[164]

---

shift in verb tense indicating a new paragraph has begun.

161. The historic present (λέγει, 10:42) highlights the beginning of a specific unit of teaching. After Mark reports the dialogue between Jesus and James and John (10:35-40), he uses the historic present for the purpose of drawing the reader into Jesus' teaching. This teaching will revolutionize the disciples' thinking regarding humility and self-sacrifice. Gundry states "the historical present tense of λέγει, 'he says,' emphasizes Jesus' authority. More particularly, λέγει emphasizes the authority of his following statements" (*Mark*, 579).

162. The present tense (ἀναβαίνομεν, 10:33), or futuristic present is the tense used when the speaker, here Mark, "sees an action as carrying over into the future . . . Frequently present and future forms occur in sequence, the matter of greater emphasis occurring in the present tense-form" (Porter, *Idioms of the Greek New Testament*, 32). Mark's point is to communicate that the disciples are not just going to Jerusalem now, but will continue throughout the rest of the story until Jesus' death.

Decker also sees the present tense amidst future tense verbs as future-referring. The present verbs (πίνω, βαπτίζομαι, 10:38; πίνω, βαπτίζομαι, 10:39) likely indicate future events. "Since the reference to Jesus' drinking and being baptized is, in the context, a reference to the cross, it is most likely that a future reference is intended. . . . The present and future forms are thus paralleled, not contrasted. The imperfective aspect of the present is used to present a view of the process of Jesus' drinking and being baptized. The future form is used to depict the expectation of the disciples' similar experience" (*Temporal Deixis of the Greek Verb*, 100).

163. The present subjunctive (ὃς ἂν θέλῃ, (2x) – 10:43, 44) portrays the state of willingness of Jesus' disciples. It is Jesus' intent to present them with an opportunity to act on his teaching. The pres subj portrays therefore imperfective aspect; that is, activities that is personally characteristic and carried out at various times.

164. Mark's use of eight present tense indicatives serves to pull the reader into the dialogue between Jesus and his disciples. The uses express the following: θέλομεν, 10:35, the desire of the disciples to get what they want from Jesus; θέλετέ, 10:36, Jesus' probing response as to how he can help them; αἰτεῖσθε and δύνασθε, 10:38, Jesus' probing response and question to his disciples regarding the seeking of a position that entailed suffering; δυνάμεθα, 10:39, James and John's response to Jesus' question; that is, they too can endure the suffering, κατακυριεύουσιν and κατεξουσιάζουσιν, 10:42,

DEATH AND DISCIPLESHIP:
An Analysis of the Predictions of Jesus' Death in the Gospel of Mark

Mark uses the perfect tense three times. It is the perfect tense-form that portrays frontground prominence. There are two uses of οἴδατε, referring to the present state of affairs of the grammatical subject. The disciples' level of knowledge. The first use refers to Jesus' pointed statement to the disciples' unreasonable request to sit at his right and left ("you do not *know* what you are asking" 10:38). And the second use refers to the disciples' knowledge regarding those who rightly rule and have authority ("You *know* those who rule over the Gentiles . . ." 10:42). Both uses of the perfect tense (stative aspect) bring out more forcefully the status of the disciples; the fact that the disciples *do not know* and *do know* respectively. Mark's use of the perfect tense-form is insightful.

On the one hand, the disciples' claim of knowledge doesn't help them, especially when it comes to understanding the cost of suffering (cf. 10:39). They seek positions of honor, prestige, or rank (10:37). However, they don't know what it takes to obtain these positions – even though they think they know (10:39). Jesus is correct in his assessment; their state of knowledge (οἴδατε) is really no knowledge at all. While on the other hand, their actual state of knowledge (οἴδατε); what they do know (10:42), is what they undoubtedly despised. Yet, the disciples were trying to take advantage of this situation to get what they wanted (positions of authority, honor) only to find out that they're selfishly seeking what they didn't like in the first place. Mark, therefore, uses the perfect tense to vividly communicate the state of affairs of Jesus' followers. It points to the reality of their ignorance when asking Jesus for a position of authority, yet Jesus exposes their knowledge as no knowledge at all.

The third use of the perfect tense refers to a present-perfect.[165] The perfect use of ἡτοίμασται ("*it is* prepared," 10:40) demonstrates the current status which these positions that have already been assigned experience.[166] The perfect tense demonstrates who will eventually be given access to sit with Jesus, for it will be given to those whom God has prepared, not reserved for the most loyal or ambitious of disciples.

Jesus' description of those who have the authority to presently rule.

165. Decker, *Temporal Deixis of the Greek Verb*, 109.

166. Ibid., 232n106. Even though the action is in the past, "The perfect comments only on the state that is, in this instance, presently true as Jesus speaks."

Discourse Analysis of the Passion Predictions

The verb analysis suggests that Mark is emphasizing three events (10:33, 35, and 42). The transition between the three events is marked by two aorist adverbial participles and a historic present. These events are: (1) Jesus' teaching (10:33), (2) the disciples' desire that Jesus fulfill their request (10:35), and (3) Jesus' teaching regarding humility and self-sacrifice (10:42).

Mark writes that Jesus teaches his disciples the certainty and imminence (τὰ μέλλοντα αὐτῷ συμβαίνειν, 10:32) of his death (10:33-34). But the emphasis of his teaching within the third prediction is not found necessarily through the divine passive, like that of the preceding two predictions (cf. 8:31; 9:31). Rather, Mark is emphasizing that it is Jesus *and* his disciples (ἰδοὺ ἀναβαίνομεν, pres, imperfective aspect) that are making the journey to Jerusalem together; thus, serving as event-1. This emphasis for event-1 is seen through two textual clues. They are: (a) the use of the emphatic particle, ἰδοὺ, that calls attention to what Jesus is about to say regarding the certainty of suffering, which will include the disciples, and (b) the use of the present indicative, ἀναβαίνομεν, which occurs with future tense forms that follow (10:34), thus placing greater emphasis on the present tense. The reality of Mark's use of the present tense for emphasis is that the disciples too are on their way to suffering.

Mark transitions from event-1 by using the historic present (προσπορεύονται, 10:35). This shift in verb tense serves to transition from Jesus' teaching (10:33-34) to the dialogue between James and John and Jesus (10:35-40); event-2. The dialogue represents a blatant example of human self-centeredness by James and John. Due to their selective hearing and/or misunderstanding, they hope to receive honor when they get to Jerusalem. Once again, this demonstrates the disciples' misunderstanding regarding status and Jesus' mission.[167] It is not only through this dialogue that the reader sees the misunder-

---

167. Stein explains the potential correct and incorrect understanding of the disciples. He writes, "They recognize correctly that Jesus is indeed the Messiah, as Peter's confession (8:29) . . . and Jesus's teachings concerning his coming glory and the coming kingdom (8:38-9:1) indicate. But they refuse to accept Jesus's repeated teaching concerning his coming passion (8:31; 9:31; 10:33-34). Thus, they are correct on the *who* question: 'Who then is this man?' (4:41). Jesus is the Messiah, who will one day enter his glory and judge the world (8:38). But they are totally wrong on the *what* of his present messianic task. Mark uses this misunderstanding of James and John, that of Peter in 8:32, and that of the disciples in 9:33ff. to teach his readers that suffering

standing of James and John regarding their status (10:35-37), but also their misunderstanding regarding their participation in suffering (10:38-40), for they confidently answer Jesus that they too "can emulate Jesus in matters pertaining to the 'cup' and 'baptism.'"[168] Although Jesus concedes that the disciples will indeed drink of the cup and be baptized with the baptism that he does, Edwards correctly notes that the cup and baptism is in reference to the disciples' persecutions that they will undergo because they have followed Jesus.[169] Mark therefore continues the story only to once again portray Jesus as an authoritative teacher. Jesus summons his disciples to teach them.

The transition to event-3 is marked by an aorist adverbial participle and the use of a historic present (προσκαλεσάμενος ... λέγει, 10:42). Event-3 involves Jesus' response to the disciples' misunderstanding regarding power and prestige. Jesus informs the disciples that they already know of the authorities who rule and how they rule (10:42). But Jesus contrasts (οὐχ οὕτως δέ) this known fact with his own instruction as to what discipleship ought to entail. In fact, Jesus addresses his disciples with their responsibility (10:43-44) and that responsibility includes being a servant and a slave. Mark portrays the priority of humility and self-sacrifice on behalf of others through the present subjunctive (ὃς ἂν θέλῃ (2x), 10:43-44). This demonstrates that the one, who desires to be great *and* first, willingly is a servant *and* slave of others.[170] Jesus then provides the disciples with the ultimate example of service; it is Jesus himself that serves and gives his life for others (10:45).

It is therefore through these three events (10:33, 35, and 42), that Mark emphasizes the necessity of Jesus' followers to experience suffering, the disciples' concern for power and prestige, and Jesus' projected realm for his disciples; to be humble and sacrifice themselves for others. Mark continues to communicate Jesus' identity (10:33-34), as well as the disciples' responsibility (10:41-44). The disciples should not be concerned with themselves (self-interest) or with posi-

---

precedes glory both for the Christ and for his followers" (*Mark*, 484-85).
168. Edwards, *The Gospel According to Mark*, 323.
169. Ibid., 323.
170. Ibid., 326. Edwards notes the absurdity of Jesus' instruction. He writes, "The pronouncement is, of course, an oxymoron, for a slave [δοῦλος], who was inferior even to a servant [διάκονος], was in ancient society that last and least of all."

tions of power and prestige (greatness and first). Rather they are to be slaves, putting and serving others first. The following role analysis is a graphic demonstration of Mark's intent for the third passion prediction (10:32-45).

Role Analysis

Jesus' Third Prediction of His Death

32. δέ	Episode Connector/New Pericope[171]
they were on the way	
going up to Jerusalem	Setting scene
καί	Additive Conjunction
Jesus was going ahead of them	Activity
καί	Additive Conjunction
they were amazed.	Response to Activity
δέ	Shift Conjunction[172]
the ones who were following,	Activity
were afraid.	
καί	
when he took aside the Twelve again,	Transition (Jesus' teaching)
he began to say to them	Activity
what was about to happen to him	
33. "See, we are going up to Jerusalem	EVENT-1 [SAYING]
καί	Additive Conjunction
the Son of Man will be handed over	
to the chief priests and scribes,	
καί	Additive Conjunction
they will condemn him to death	

---

171. Levinsohn states, "Mark practically never uses δέ to introduce a new *episode*; 1:32 and 10:32 are rare exceptions in which καί is not a textual variant. In other words, Mark seldom uses δέ to indicate that one episode develops from the previous one" (*Discourse Features of New Testament Greek*, 80).

172. The discourse function of δέ here denotes a change/shift in characters, from the disciples to the larger crowd who was following Jesus.

DEATH AND DISCIPLESHIP:
An Analysis of the Predictions of Jesus' Death in the Gospel of Mark

καί	Additive Conjunction
will hand him over to the Gentiles	
34. καί	Additive Conjunction
they will mock him	
καί	Additive Conjunction
scourge him	
καί	Additive Conjunction
spit on him	
καί	Additive Conjunction
kill him,	
καί	Additive Conjunction
on the third day he will rise."	

Disciples' Misunderstanding

35. Καί	Episode Connector
James and John, the sons of Zebedee, came up to him saying,	EVENT-2 [SAYING]
"Teacher, we desire that you do for us whatever we may ask."	
36.[173] δέ	Shift Conjunction[174]
he said to them,	
"What do you desire me to do for you?"	Question
37. δέ	Shift Conjunction
they said to him, "Grant to us that we may sit one on your right side	Response (request)

---

173. Verses 36-40 serve as an embedded narrative that provides the reader with background information; that is, the dialogue between James and John and Jesus. This is seen using the aorist forms εἶπεν and εἶπαν.

174. The discourse function of δέ in vv. 36, 37, 38, and 39 denotes a shift between characters within a dialogue.

and one on your left side
in your glory."

38. δέ	Shift Conjunction
Jesus said to them, "You do not know	Saying
What you are asking.	
Are you able to drink the cup	Question
which I will drink and to be baptized	
with the baptism with which I will	
be baptized?"	
39. δέ	Shift Conjunction
they said to him, "We are able."	Response
δέ	Shift Conjunction
Jesus said to them, "The cup which I	Saying
will drink you will drink	
καί	Additive Conjunction
the baptism with which I will be	
baptized you will be baptized,	
40. δέ	Shift Conjunction[175]
to sit on my right side	
καί	Additive Conjunction
on my left side is not mine to give,	
ἀλλά	Adversative Conjunction
to those for whom it has been prepared."	

Jesus' Instruction on Discipleship

41. Καί	Episode Connector

175. Levinsohn proposes a use of δέ that may be used here. He states that δέ can "introduce background material that moves the story to something *distinctive*" (*Discourse Features of New Testament Greek*, 90). The distinctive aspect here may relate to the fact that James and John desire the position to which Jesus states has already been reserved, and it is not for them.

DEATH AND DISCIPLESHIP:
An Analysis of the Predictions of Jesus' Death in the Gospel of Mark

when the Twelve heard this,	Transition (Disciples' response)
[they] began to be indignant about James and John.	Activity
42. καί	Additive Conjunction
when Jesus summoned them	Transition (Jesus' call)
he said to them,	EVENT-3 [SAYING]
"You know that those who are reputed to be rulers the Gentiles lord it over them	
καί	Additive Conjunction
their great ones exercise authority over them.	
43. δέ	Shift Conjunction
it will not be so among you,	
ἀλλά	Adversative Conjunction
whoever desires to become great among you, will be your servant.	
44. καί	Additive Conjunction
whoever among you desires to become first will be slave of all.	
45. γάρ	Supporting Conjunction
καί	Emphasis Conjunction[176]
the Son of Man did not come to be served	
ἀλλά	Adversative Conjunction
to serve	
καί	Additive Conjunction
to give his life as a ransom in the place of many."	

---

176. The discourse function of καί here may be indicating focal prominence; thus, it could be translated as 'even.' Here Mark may be focusing the reader's attention on the fact that Jesus is the supreme example of humble service and self-sacrifice. Young states this use of καί is "ascensive and elaborates on the same thought, bringing it to a climax" (*Intermediate New Testament Greek*, 188).

The summary of role analysis

The role analysis shows three events Mark emphasizes (10:32, 35, and 42). Mark uses verb tense and conjunctions to establish prominence and cohesion. As one reads Jesus' third passion prediction, Mark provides the reader with both an internal and external perspective. When Mark desires to pull his audience into the middle of the conversation (internal perspective), to grab their attention, he utilizes the present tense verb. As the reader transitions between events, and reads the background of the story, Mark utilizes the aorist tense verb (external, summary perspective). The perfect tense, or stative aspect, demonstrates a state of affairs or a condition of existence (e.g., the disciples' knowledge, or lack thereof). The verb tense therefore establishes for the reader what may serve as prominent events throughout the passion prediction.

The conjunctions provide cohesion and demonstrate the logical relationships between the three events throughout the passion prediction. Mark uses καί to connect the various events within the passion predictions. He also uses δέ to introduce movement, or a shift within the dialogue between James and John and Jesus (10:36-39), and to move the story to express something distinctive (10:40). Mark also uses γάρ to support Jesus' preceding teaching regarding the disciples' humble service. These conjunctions provide the reader with ties throughout the third passion prediction to understand the significant turning points and events within the passion prediction. The three events, and their logical relationships, are explained.

Jesus' teaching (event-1, the certainty and imminence of his mission) prompts the open-request of James and John (event-2, 10:35) that is further defined as the desire to sit at Jesus' right and left in glory (10:37). Mark reports that event-2 (dialogue between James and John and Jesus) prompts Jesus to summon the disciples and to teach them (event-3, 10:41-45) the importance of humility and self-sacrifice, for if his disciples choose to humble them and serve others, it will culminate and develop into service for all. Jesus takes the initiative to teach the disciples the significance of the relationship between the certainty and imminence of his identity and mission (10:33-34) and their choice 'to humble and sacrifice themselves for others' or 'not to humble . . . themselves.' Therefore, the two analyses (Greek text and verb) are represented in the final role analysis. The role analysis represents Mark's emphasis in the third of Jesus' three passion predictions.

For the final time within the central section, Mark brings together the formal and functional aspects of his story. The formal aspect is Jesus' identity and mission; that is, the certainty of the Messiah's suffering, death, and resurrection (10:33-34). The functional aspect refers to the responsibilities of the disciples based on the knowledge of Jesus' identity; that is, what are the disciples to do now that they know Jesus (10:41-45)? Mark brings the reader to the final of three passion predictions: the climax. Mark not only adds details regarding Jesus' mission that are not found in the preceding passion predictions (e.g., the destination of Jesus' mission, Jerusalem; the specifics of Jesus' suffering; etc.), but he also exclaims the purpose for Jesus' mission. Jesus loyally follows the will of the Father by leading the disciples to Jerusalem where he will be handed over to be condemned and killed, willingly humbles himself to a level of a servant, and sacrificially suffers in place of all.

Summary of the Passion Predictions

It is the first passion prediction that sets the stage for the central section. At the beginning of the first passion prediction (8:31), Mark links back to the purpose for his story; to communicate Jesus as the Son of God (1:1). Throughout the story, Mark uses events to explicate information regarding Jesus' identity (formal aspect) and responsibilities of the disciples (functional aspect). Mark expresses the formal aspect of his story by further defining Jesus' identity and mission (EVENT-1). He is the suffering, Messiah. Mark also expresses the functional aspect of his story. He does so through Jesus' teaching to the crowd and his disciples. He clarifies what they ought to be now that they know him (EVENT-2, EVENT-3). They must continually follow knowing that death might await them.

Jesus' first passion prediction (8:31-9:1) begins with his foretelling of the necessity of his suffering, death, and resurrection (8:31-32a). Consequently, Peter incorrectly rebukes and therefore improperly follows Jesus. As a matter of fact, he assumes the position of teacher in front of Jesus; not the submissive position reserved for followers (8:32b). Peter's misunderstanding, therefore, results in Jesus' rebuke of him (8:33). It also dictates the content of Jesus' teaching to the crowd and his disciples. A true disciple is one who loyally continues to follow his teacher regardless of the suffering, even if death is involved (8:34-9:1). Jesus illustrates the significance of following him through the command to carry one's cross. This is a significant command, for the crowd and his disciples understand that to carry one's cross means that death might occur because of following.

Mark continues to report Jesus' journey through the central section of his story. In Jesus' second passion prediction he explicates who Jesus is, (formal aspect) and what the disciples ought to do (functional aspect). Mark again reveals the certainty of Jesus' identity and mission; he will suffer. Mark reports Jesus' teaching to his disciples. Jesus clarifies what they ought to do now that they know his identity. They must choose to serve the insignificant, even though society states otherwise.

Jesus' second passion prediction (9:30-37) begins like the first. Jesus foretells of the certainty of his suffering, death, and resurrection (9:30-32). He however adds that it will be at the hands of humanity. None the less, rather than concerning themselves with Jesus' repeated prediction of his death, the disciples argue among themselves who is the greatest (9:33-34). In other words, the concern of the disciples was their status. The disciples' preoccupation with their status results in Jesus' authoritative teaching, for he called his disciples and sits among them (9:35-37). The disciples' concern with status dictates Jesus' teaching. A disciple is one that willingly cares for others regardless of status. Jesus illustrates the significance of caring for others by receiving and embracing an insignificant one, a child. He challenges his disciples to go and do likewise. This is a significant choice the disciples must make, for they understand that to embrace a child means to welcome the lowest one on the social scale of society.

Mark brings the central section to a climax. He once again explains who Jesus is (formal aspect) and what the disciples ought to do (functional aspect). Mark, for the final time, reveals Jesus' identity and the imminence of his mission as the suffering Messiah. Mark also expresses the functional aspect of his story or the significance of Jesus' identity for the disciples. The disciples are to be humble, self-sacrificing servants.

For a third and final time, Mark reports Jesus' passion prediction (10:32-45). However, this time Mark sets the stage for the prediction and includes additional information, the destination of Jesus' journey (10:32). But it is not just that Mark records the destination that serves as a climax to the central section. He also records that Jesus leads the way. After setting the stage, Jesus takes the disciples for a third time and foretells of the certainty and imminence of his suffering, death, and resurrection (10:33-34). Consequently, the realization of the imminence of Jesus' death, James, and John desire for the ultimate positions of authority and honor, Jesus' right and left sides (10:35-37). As a matter of fact, due to their strong desire for these positions and through a dialogue with Jesus, they claim that they too can endure the same suffering as Jesus. The dialogue eventually gives way to a change in scenery with Mark reporting that the rest of the disciples were not pleased with James and John (10:40).

Mark reports that the request of James and John eventually provides the content of Jesus' teaching to the disciples. A great disciple is one who exemplifies humility and sacrificially serves others (10:41-45). The great disciple therefore is not a master *over* others, but a servant *for* others. Jesus uses his strongest illustration yet; himself. The final prediction not only is a climax to Mark's central section, but also gives the disciples the supreme example of service and self-sacrifice. Jesus' illustration is thus purposeful. It is to be so of the disciples; that is, they are also to assume the position of servants and slaves.

Mark captures the reader's attention throughout the central section of his story, and he does so through the expression and example of Jesus. Jesus is the suffering and self-sacrificing Messiah. In other words, the reader knows who Jesus is. Mark also captures the reader's interest by recording the disciples' ignorant, fearful, and prideful response to Jesus' teaching. Nonetheless, through Jesus' teaching and illustrations, ultimately leading to Jesus as the example, the reader knows his responsibility.

Table two shows the relationship between the passion predictions within the central section of Mark's story. The passion predictions are Jesus' first passion prediction (8:30-9:1), second passion prediction (9:30-37), and third passion predictions (10:32-45).

Discourse Analysis of the Passion Predictions

Table 2. Three passion predictions

	Jesus' First Passion Prediction (8:30-9:1)	Jesus' Second Passion Prediction (9:30-37)	Jesus' Third Passion Prediction (10:32-45)
Event 1	*Jesus' Prediction of His Death* "The necessity of Jesus' death"	*Jesus' Prediction of His Death* "Those responsible for Jesus' death"	*Jesus' Prediction of His Death* "The destination of Jesus' death"
Event-2	*Disciples' Misunderstanding* Peter: "Improperly following Jesus"	*Disciples' Misunderstanding* Disciples: "Who is the greatest?"	*Disciples' Misunderstanding* James and John: "Positions of authority and honor"
Event-3	*Jesus' Instruction on Discipleship* "Loyally following" *Jesus' Illustration – Cross*	*Jesus' Instruction on Discipleship* "Willingly caring for the insignificant ones" *Jesus' Illustration – Child*	*Jesus' Instruction on Discipleship* "Humbly serving" *Jesus' Illustration – Christ*

The preceding examination of Jesus' three passion predictions points to the conclusions in table two. Mark's central section 'hangs together' as a section within itself. The following summary provides an explanation of the cohesion within and between each passion prediction. As Mark reports Jesus' journey with his disciples "on the way" to Jerusalem.

Cohesion is shown by the vertical arrows that connect the events. Mark highlights or emphasizes three events within each passion prediction that correspond to the three-fold pattern found in each of the passion predictions. Event-1 highlights the divine necessity, certainty, and immanency of Jesus' death. Jesus teaches that he will suffer, die, and resurrect again. Event-1 refers to Jesus' predictions of his death. Event-3 also highlights the content of Jesus' teaching. However, Jesus' teaching in event-3 possesses a different focus. Event-1 focuses on *Jesus' role* (identity) as the suffering Messiah; whereas event-3 focuses on instruction regarding the *disciples' role* (responsibility) as they follow Jesus.

Event-3 refers to Jesus' instruction on discipleship. The cohesion between the three events is represented in event-2. In event-2, Mark reports the disciples' misunderstanding, thus leading to Jesus' correction/teaching of his disciples. It is the disciples' misunderstanding (event-2) that occurs as a result of Jesus' teaching (event-1) and therefore, the actions of the disciples provide the context for Jesus' teaching on discipleship (event-3). Therefore, it is event-2 that serves as a cohesive tie that holds each of the passion predictions together.

Cohesion is also illustrated by the horizontal arrows that connect events -1 and -3 across the central section. He highlights or emphasizes Jesus' role and the disciples' role, ultimately with the last passion prediction serving as a climax. Mark emphasizes Jesus' role through event-1 of each passion prediction; that role is to serve as the suffering Messiah. Jesus first demonstrates his predictive power (8:31) by telling of the necessity of his death. He also predicts those who will be responsible for his death, the Jewish leaders.

Second, Jesus continues to demonstrate his predictive power (9:31) by teaching his disciples of the certainty of his death. Mark's report of the repetition of Jesus' predictions of his death demonstrates cohesion. Jesus also adds another group responsible for his death; all of humanity. Third, Jesus once again demonstrates his predictive power (10:33-34), for he speaks of the certainty, imminence, and destination of his death. The third passion prediction is the most detailed and serves as a climax to the central section of Mark's story for several reasons. It is in the third passion prediction that Mark (1) adds the details of both preceding predictions; that is, the certainty and the imminence of his death; (2) adds both groups responsible for his death, Jewish leaders and the Gentiles; (3) adds the destination of Jesus' suffering

(Jerusalem), the first time it is mentioned throughout the central section of the story; (4) adds the details regarding the suffering; (5) adds the two groups who follow Jesus (crowd and disciples); and (6) adds Jesus' exclamatory element to include the disciples in his journey to Jerusalem; and therefore they too must suffer.

Mark emphasizes Jesus' expectation for the role of the disciples in event-3 of each passion prediction; that expectation is to follow loyally the suffering Messiah. Jesus first expresses the anticipation for the disciples' role (8:34-9:1) by commanding them to follow continually and loyally. Jesus uses the commands: 'carry one's cross' and 'the losing of one's life' to demonstrate the significance of the disciples' journey. Second, Jesus expresses the disciples' role (9:35-37) by teaching them that to be the greatest, they will have to willingly care for even the insignificant of society. In other words, they must assume a position that is subordinate to another, not try to be the greatest or most prominent/significant. Jesus illustrates 'true greatness' through the receiving of a child. Third, Jesus expresses the disciples' role (10:41-45) by teaching them that they are to aspire a position that the world does not; that is, humbly sacrificing oneself for others. In other words, they must become not just a servant; but a slave of all. Jesus uses the ultimate example for humility and self-sacrifice. He uses himself. Therefore, Mark emphasizes the disciples' role through event-3 of each passion prediction; that role is to exemplify the serving and self-sacrificing Messiah.

Therefore, as the reader moves through the repetition of the three-fold pattern found in each passion prediction (vertical arrows) and as the reader moves through the central section of the story (horizontal arrows), he can see the cohesive ties. Mark has carefully structured his central section of the story so that the reader can see the importance of Jesus' identity and mission ('who is Jesus') and the significance of this identity for the readers ('what they ought to be').

Understanding relationships between the passion predictions within the central section confirms the theme of the story. The passion predictions also explicate Jesus' identity, not only as the Son of God, but as the suffering and self-sacrificing Messiah. The passion predictions portray Jesus' expectations for his disciples; thus, pointing to the importance of these expectations for the reader. These expectations are the theological significance for the reader. He too must adopt a loyal commitment to Christ that is demonstrated through a self-sacrificing servant's heart.

Conclusion

This chapter implements the second of two components of discourse analysis, discourse texture. This component provides the reader with the ability to consider the central section of Mark's story at the level of the text, or micro-structure. The features of the discourse texture of the central section, are examined by using three analyses. These analyses point to Mark's use of language (meta-function of language), relationship of language (cohesion), and the emphasis of language (prominence).

The interpreter uses the Greek text, verb, and role analyses to account for discourse features of the text. It is also necessary to understand how the details of the analyses contribute to the interpreter's understanding of the passion predictions as a unit of information and how the central section is related to what precedes (1:1-8:21) and what follows (11:1-16:20). The purpose of table two was to present an interpretation and illustrate the relationship between the central section and Mark's story as a whole that is based upon the detailed analysis of this chapter. This chapter therefore demonstrated the relationship between the micro-structure, or discourse texture (passion predictions within central section) and macro-structure, or discourse structure (genre and sub-genre).

Chapter Six

Conclusion

This Book has demonstrated the complementary benefit of discourse analysis with New Testament exegesis. Discourse analysis promotes an analysis of language at all levels (e.g., genre, discourse, paragraph, sentence, phrase, and word). In other words, discourse analysis accounts for the relationship of meaning as it pertains to the relationship of the sense of the whole and its parts, and back again. The exegete must begin with the understanding that written texts do not occur in a vacuum. Rather they occur as part of paragraphs, and those paragraphs are a part of discourses, that are ultimately organized with reference to genre.

The contribution of this work pointed to the complementary role of discourse analysis in a suggested interpretation of the Gospel of Mark. The focus was the central section (8:22-10:52); namely, Jesus' three passion predictions. The passion predictions were analyzed, and conclusions were made regarding the meaning, emphasis, and relationship each passion prediction had within the central section and Mark's story.

Chapter two provided the methodological basis, discourse analysis. Four approaches to discourse analysis were reviewed. Due to the objectivity of the method as it pertained to the relationship and function between the genre and central section of Mark, it was concluded that the Systemic-Functional Linguistic (SFL) theory represented the most comprehensive approach. The SFL theory incorporated all the commonalities of discourse analysis. They are: the examination of language above the sentence, the use of language within a given context, and the unity of language, or how a language coheres together. Therefore, the SFL theory, utilizing two components, was applied to both the genre (discourse structure) and the central section (discourse texture) of the Gospel of Mark.

Chapter three implemented the first of two components of discourse analysis: discourse structure. This component analyzed the narrative genre (macro-structure) common to the Gospel accounts. The analysis in chapter three concluded that two categories of genre best represent the Gospel of Mark. They are narrative (genre) and theological narrative biography (sub-genre). The Gospels are narrative because they are comprised of short episodes communicating the life story of a central figure, Jesus Christ. In other words, the Gospel accounts tell a story.

The Gospels also fit into a sub-genre. Sub-genre was defined as a theological narrative biography because this sub-genre category accounts for the literary medium in which the Gospels were written (narrative), the story of the life of Jesus Christ (biography) as the central unifying character, and the application of the story to the life of the reader (theology). The intended purpose of the Gospel accounts is to awaken and subsequently strengthen the faith of the followers of Jesus.

Chapter four concluded that the Gospel of Mark is a theological narrative biography. This analysis of the discourse structure involved a top-down approach to discourse analysis. The top-down approach focused on the larger discourse structure, or genre (macro-structure) of Mark. Therefore, discourse structure made two important contributions to this study. Discourse structure first provided a holistic understanding of Mark's story and second, established a sub-genre necessary to categorize Mark's story.

First, as the elements of Mark's narrative were analyzed it was concluded that he wrote his story to inform the reader of two aspects, formal and functional. These two aspects captured the theme of Mark's story. The formal aspect answered the question, 'who is Jesus?' while the functional aspect answered the question, 'what are his disciples to do?' in light of knowing him.

The analysis of Mark's story concluded that his story is structured into a three-fold identity. In other words, Mark structured his story by the means of three geographical locations (Galilee, on the way to Jerusalem, Jerusalem). Through this structure, Mark communicated his Christological emphasis, the identity of Jesus Christ as the Son of God, and his theological significance, the responsibility of the disciples. Discourse structure pointed to a holistic understanding of Mark's story, for discourse structure not only provided the reader with Mark's two-aspect emphasis, but also the structural means by which his story was told.

Second, the analysis of Mark pointed to the need for a sub-genre. Discourse structure provided the means to explicate the unique nature of Mark's story as theological narrative biography. The analysis demonstrated that Mark's story is more than episodes tied together that communicate the history and biography of Jesus Christ. The information of Mark's story requires the reader to respond regarding his theological emphasis; thus, awakening and subsequently strengthening the reader's faith as a committed follower of Christ.

Chapter five implemented the second of two components of discourse analysis, discourse texture. The central section (8:22-10:52) was analyzed at the level of the text (micro-structure). This analysis demonstrated a bottom-up approach to discourse analysis. The bottom-up approach focused on the smaller units, passion predictions (paragraph).

The passion predictions were analyzed at the level of the word, phrase, sentence, and paragraph to arrive at the meaning. Although discourse analysis must account for the traditional sentence-level grammar, a discourse analysis also explains the relationship of various grammatical structures (e.g., tense and aspect) as part of a larger meaning. It was concluded that each of the passion predictions explicated Mark's Christological and theological emphases, for each explained Jesus' identity as the suffering and self-sacrificing Messiah (formal aspect – 'who is Jesus?') and established that the disciples' too had a role (functional aspect – 'what are they to do?') as they followed Jesus.

Each passion prediction was also analyzed with the other passion predictions; thus, demonstrating how each one related (cohesion) to the others. The analysis went beyond the word-level to incorporate the understanding of the meaning of phrases, sentences, and paragraphs within a given context (the passion predictions) that found its meaning within a larger context (central section). Therefore, discourse texture made two important contributions to this study. Discourse texture first provided the meaning of the central section and second, the relationship and significance of the central section to Mark's story as a whole.

First, the central section was analyzed, and the following meaning obtained. (1) Jesus' identity was explicated as the suffering, self-sacrificing Messiah. (2) The disciples' misunderstood Jesus' role as Messiah. Therefore, they did not demonstrate the characteristics of a follower. (3) The disciples' role was established through Jesus' instruction regarding the characteristics necessary to follow him.

Second, the central section was analyzed, and it was concluded that the central section related to Mark's story. Discourse texture, as it was applied to the central section, explicated the formal (Jesus' identity as the suffering and self-sacrificing Messiah) and functional (the disciples' responsibility) aspects of Mark's story. In other words, discourse texture provided an understanding of Mark's story by accounting for the sense of the whole (Mark's story) as it related to its parts (central section), and its parts (passion predictions) as they related to the whole (Mark's story).

This Book demonstrated that a sub-discipline or complementing method of hermeneutics, discourse analysis, contributed to interpreting, and thus establishing the significance of the passion predictions within the Gospel of Mark. Discourse analysis paid sufficient attention to all the levels of the text beyond the word-level and therefore helped chart the course of the story as it related to its parts and as its parts related to the story. In other words, discourse analysis demonstrated how the story of Mark fits together as a unified whole and how that unified whole accounted for *how* and *why* Mark placed the passion predictions within the central section.

INTERPRETATION

Mark consists of three major sections. A two-section division of Mark does not account for the boundaries of the central section, cohesion between sections, and the prominence within the central section. Mark utilizes the repetition of words and phrases (e.g., Jesus' passion predictions) and the weaving of geography (e.g., on the way to Jerusalem) and theology (e.g., disciples' role as a follower of Jesus) together to closely knit his story together. In other words, the central section provides the reader with *how* each of the other sections

Conclusion

(1:14-8:21 and 11:1-16:8) of his story fit together. Therefore, to consider the Gospel of Mark as two sections (1:14-8:21 and 8:22-16:8) negatively impacts the cohesive nature of the story and therefore points to wrong conclusions. There are two reasons why the reader ought to divide Mark into three sections and not two.

First, Mark appropriately borders the central section using two healing episodes of blind men (8:22-26 and 10:46-52). These episodes serve as discourse boundaries that function to both forecast the coming section (central section) and demonstrate cohesion between sections (central section and the last section). The first healing episode (8:22-26) concludes the blindness theme that occurs with reference to the disciples (cf. 8:18). Since blindness may still be lingering with the disciples (failure to understand Jesus' miracle of the feeding of the four thousand, cf. 6:52), Mark reports that the blind man is able to 'see clearly.' In other words, the blind man can see both physically and spiritually, because of Jesus' multiple touches. There is gradual healing of the blind man. This episode prepares the reader for the central section by comparing the repeated touches of Jesus on the blind man and Jesus' multiple touches (his teaching) on his disciples. This first healing episode therefore sets the stage for the reader noting that the disciples also need to see clearly, both Jesus' identity and mission, as well as their responsibility as followers. They do not understand.

The next healing episode (10:46-52) prepares the reader for the following section (11:1-16:8); thus, demonstrating cohesion. Mark concludes the central section with this healing of the blind man episode. Since an unwillingness to follow faithfully may still be lingering with the disciples, Mark reports that the blind man is able 'to follow faithfully' on the way. In other words, the blind man can see, both physically and spiritually, because of his faith in what he heard from Jesus, not what he had seen. The blind man asked for normalcy, not glory or power (*contra* the disciples). This second episode therefore sets the stage for the disciples to take what they had heard from Jesus and faithfully follow on the way, as the blind man did (10:52). The disciples are to follow even as they enter Jerusalem where their teacher, Jesus, will die. The disciples however do not faithfully follow Jesus in the following section (11:1-16:8).

This demonstrates that even with multiple events of instruction regarding how to follow, they still failed.

Second, Mark's purpose is to declare Jesus' identity and portray the responsibility necessary for the disciples to follow. Mark catalogues episodes to declare Jesus' identity and to portray the actions of the disciples in the first section of his story (1:14-8:21). This section provides the foundation for the rest of the story. In the central section (8:22-10:52) Mark continues to focus on Jesus' identity, while turning his attention to the responsibilities of the disciples; and do so with prominence. In other words, Mark's central section has a prominent place in his story because it highlights the role of Jesus (suffering Messiah) and the role of the disciples. Each of these characters are therefore highlighted through the repetition of Jesus' prediction of his death, and the disciples' continued misunderstanding of his teaching; thus, portraying to the reader that the disciples were unable to follow Jesus correctly.

Each of these characters' roles portrayed by Mark in the central section, not only points back to the first section of his story (1:14-8:21), thus providing overall cohesion to his story, but also forecasts events to occur in the last section (11:1-16:8) of his story, for Jesus and the disciples ultimately affirm their identity. Jesus suffers, dies, and rises again just as he predicted he would. And the disciples show that they are uncommitted to following Jesus faithfully. The central section therefore serves as a cohesive link in the story; a link that provides the reader with essential information for reading Mark.

Further Research

The conclusions of this study are based upon a limited amount of data. It is important not to extrapolate conclusions that go beyond the central section (8:22-10:52) of Mark without further research. This is especially important given the cautious response to discourse analysis. Some question the viability of the methodology. It is necessary to apply the two components of discourse analysis, discourse structure and discourse texture, to other New Testament narratives. Three areas need further exploration.

Conclusion

First, it is necessary to analyze the first section (1:14-8:21) and the third section (11:1-16:8) of Mark's story. Utilizing the three analyses (Greek text, verb, and role) will provide additional support to validate Mark's formal and functional aspect of his story. Second, the analysis of other Gospel accounts, utilizing these same analyses, may also provide support for discourse analysis.

Third, it is also necessary to study all the Gospel accounts to test if they too can be classified as theological narrative biographies. Further examination will help determine if all Gospel accounts are communicated with a similar literary medium about a central unifying character, Jesus Christ; thus, producing a similar intended theological purpose. This will validate the subgenre of narrative for the Gospel accounts, theological narrative biography.

BIBLIOGRAPHY

Achtemeier, Paul J. *Mark*. 2d ed. rev. and exp. Proclamation Commentaries. Philadelphia: Fortress, 1986.

Allen, David L. "The Discourse Structure of Philemon: A Study in Textlinguistics." In *Scribes and Scripture: New Testament Essays in Honor of J. Harold Greenlee*, ed. David Alan Black, 77-96. Winona Lake, Ind: Eisenbrauns, 1992.

Arp, William. Course notes for NT1, Seminar in New Testament Hermeneutics and Exegetical Method. Baptist Bible Seminary, Clarks Summit, Pa, summer 2002.

———. Course notes for NT8, Seminar in Gospel Studies. Baptist Bible Seminary, Clarks Summit, Pa, fall 2005.

Aune, David E. *The New Testament in Its Literary Environment*. Philadelphia, Pa: Westminster Press, 1987.

Bailey. J. L., and L. D. Vander Broek. *Literary Forms in the New Testament*. London: SPCK, 1992.

Bailey, Mark. "Guidelines for Interpreting Jesus' Parables." *Bibliotheca Sacra* 155 (January-March 1998): 29-38.

Banks, Robert J. "Narrative Exegesis." In *Dictionary of Jesus and the Gospels*, ed. Joel B. Green, Scot McKnight, and I. Howard Marshall, 570-71. Downers Grove, Ill: InterVarsity Press, 1992.

Barr, James. *Semantics of Biblical Language*. Oxford: Oxford University Press, 1961.

Barta, Karen A. *The Gospel of Mark*. Wilmington, Del: Glazier, 1988.

Barton, John. *Reading the Old Testament: Method in Biblical Study*. London: Darton, Longman and Todd, 1984.

Bauer, David. *The Structure of Matthew's Gospel: A Study in Literary Design*. Journal for the Study of the New Testament Supplement Series 31. Sheffield: Almond Press, 1988.

Bauer, Walter. *A Greek-English Lexicon of the New Testament and Other Early Christian Literature*, 3d ed. rev. and ed. Frederick William Danker. Chicago: University of Chicago Press, 2000.

Bayer, Hans F. *A Theology of Mark: The Dynamic between Christology and Authentic Discipleship*, Explorations in Biblical Theology series ed. Robert A. Peterson. Phillipsburg, NJ: P&R Publishing, 2012.

Bergen, Robert D. "Text As a Guide to Authorial Intention: An Introduction to Discourse Criticism." *Journal of the Evangelical Theological Society* 30, no. 3 (Sept 1987): 327-36.

Berlin, Adele. *Poetics and Interpretation of Biblical Narrative*. Sheffield: Almond, 1983.

Best, Ernest. "Discipleship in Mark: Mark 8:22-10:52." *Scottish Journal of Theology* 23 (1970): 323-37.

———. *Mark: The Gospel as Story*. Edinburgh: T. & T. Clark, 1983.

Bilezikian, Gilbert G. *The Liberated Gospel: A Comparison of the Gospel of Mark and Greek Tragedy*. Grand Rapids: Baker, 1977.

Black, David A. "Discourse Structure of Philippians: A Study in Textlinguistics." *Novem Testamentum* 37 (1995): 16-49.

———. "Hebrews 1:1-4: A Study in Discourse Analysis." *Westminster Theological Journal* 49 (1987): 175-94.

———. "Introduction." In *Linguistics and New Testament Interpretation: Essays on Discourse Analysis*, ed. David Alan Black with Katharine Barnwell and Stephen Levinsohn, 10-13. Nashville: Broadman and Holman, 1992.

———. *Linguistics for Students of New Testament Greek: A Survey of Basic Concepts and Applications*, 2d ed. Grand Rapids: Baker, 1995.

Black, Stephanie L. *Sentence Conjunctions in the Gospel of Matthew: καί, δέ, τότε, γάρ, οὖν and Asyndeton in Narrative Discourse*. London: Sheffield Academic, 2002.

Blass, F., A. Debrunner, and Robert W. Funk. *A Greek Grammar of the New Testament and Other Early Christian Literature*, 9th-10th ed. Chicago: University of Chicago Press, 1961.

Blomberg, Craig L. "The Diversity of Literary Genres in the New Testament." In *Interpreting the New Testament: Essays on Methods and Issues*, ed. David Alan Black and David S. Dockery, 272-95. Nashville: Broadman and Holman, 2001.

———. *The Historical Reliability of the Gospels*. Downers Grove, Ill: InterVarsity Press, 1985.

———. *Jesus and the Gospels: An Introduction and Survey*, 2d ed. Nashville: Broadman and Holman, 2009.

Blomberg, Craig L. with Jennifer Foutz Markley. *A Handbook of New Testament Exegesis*. Grand Rapids: Baker, 2010.

Bock, Darrell L. "Form Criticism." In *Interpreting the New Testament: Essays on Methods and Issues*, ed. David Alan Black and David S. Dockery, 106-27. Nashville: Broadman and Holman, 2001.

———. *Studying the Historical Jesus: A Guide to Sources and Methods*. Grand Rapids: Baker, 2002.

Bolt, Peter G. *The Cross from a Distance: Atonement in Mark's Gospel*. New Studies in Biblical Theology 18. Downers Grove, Ill: InterVarsity Press, 2004.

———. "Mark's Gospel." In *The Face of New Testament Studies: A Survey of Recent Research*, ed. Scot McKnight and Grant R. Osborne, 391-413. Grand Rapids: Baker, 2004.

Boring, Eugene M. *Mark: A Commentary*. Louisville, Ky: Westminster John Knox, 2006.

———. "Mark 1:1-15 and the Beginning of the Gospel." *Semeia* 52 (1990): 43-81.

Breytenbach, Cilliers. *Nachfolge und Zukunftserwartung nach Markus: Eine Methodenkritische Studie*, Abhandlungen zur Theologie des Alten und Neuen Testaments 71. Zürich: Theologischer Verlag, 1984.

Broadhead, Edwin K. *Mark*. Sheffield, England: Sheffield Academic Press, 2001.

Brooks, James A. *Mark*. New American Commentary 23. Nashville: Broadman and Holman, 1991

Brown, Colin. *Jesus in European Protestant Thought, 1778-1860*. Grand Rapids: Baker, 1988.

Bibliography

Brown, Gillian, and George Yule. *Discourse Analysis*. Cambridge: Cambridge University Press: 1983.

Brown, Jeannine K. "Narrative Criticism." In *Dictionary of Jesus and the Gospels*, 2d ed, eds. Joel B. Green, Jeannine K. Brown, and Nicholas Perrin, 619-24. Downers Grove, IL: InterVarsity Press, 2013.

———. *The Gospels as Stories: A Narrative Approach to Matthew, Mark, Luke, and John*. Grand Rapids: Baker, 2020.

Bultmann, Rudolf. *The History of the Synoptic Tradition*. New York: Harper & Row, 1963.

Burer, Michael H. "Narrative Genre: Studying the Story." In *Interpreting the New Testament Text: Introduction to the Art and Science of Exegesis*, ed. Darrell L. Bock and Buist M. Fanning, 197-219. Wheaton, Ill: Crossway, 2006.

Burridge, Richard A. *What Are the Gospels? A Comparison with Graeco-Roman Biography*. Society for New Testament Studies Monograph Series 70. Cambridge University Press, 1992.

Buth, Randall. "Mark's Use of the Historical Present." *Notes on Translation* 65 (1977): 7-13.

———. "Mark's Use of *Palin* and Its Relationship to Discourse and Plot Analysis." *Notes on Translation* 61 (1976): 32-6.

Callow, Kathleen. *Discourse Considerations in Translating the Word of God*. Grand Rapids: Zondervan, 1974.

———. "Patterns of Thematic Development in 1 Corinthians 5:1-13." In *Linguistics and New Testament Interpretation: Essays on Discourse Analysis*, ed. David Alan Black with Katharine Barnwell and Stephen Levinsohn, 194-206. Nashville: Broadman and Holman, 1992.

Campbell, Constantine R. *Advances in the Study of Greek: New Insights for Reading the New Testament*. Grand Rapids, Zondervan: 2015.

———. *Basics of Verbal Aspect in Biblical Greek*. Grand Rapids: Zondervan, 2008.

———. *Verbal Aspect, the Indicative Mood, and Narrative: Soundings in the Greek of the New Testament*. Studies in Biblical Greek 13. New York: Peter Lang, 2007.

———. *Verbal Aspect, and Non-Indicative Verbs: Further Soundings in the Greek of the New Testament*. Studies in Biblical Greek 15. New York: Peter Lang, 2008.

Campbell, Constantine R. and Jonathan T. Pennington. *Reading the New Testament as Christian Scripture: A Literary, Canonical, and Theological Survey*. Grand Rapids: Baker, 2020.

Carson, D. A. "Systematic Theology and Biblical Theology." In *New Dictionary of Biblical Theology: Exploring the Unity & Diversity of Scripture*, ed. Brian S. Rosner, T. Desmond Alexander, and Carson Goldsworthy, 89-103. Downers Grove, Ill: InterVarsity Press, 2001.

Carson, D. A., and Douglas J. Moo. *An Introduction to the New Testament*, 2d ed. Grand Rapids: Zondervan, 2005.

Chapman, Siobhan, and Christopher Routledge, eds. *Key Thinkers in Linguistics and the Philosophy of Language*. Edinburgh: Edinburgh University Press, 2005.

Christopher, Gregory T. "A Discourse Analysis of Colossians 2:16-3:17." *Grace Theological Journal* 11 (1990): 205-20.

———. "Linguistics and Literary Theory: Redefining the Disciplinary Boundaries." PhD diss., University of Texas at Arlington, 2000.

Church, Forrester F. F. "Rhetorical Structure and Design in Paul's Letter to Philemon," *Harvard Theological Review* 71 (Jan-April 1978): 17-33.

Clark, Greg. "General Hermeneutics." In *The Face of New Testament Studies: A Survey of Recent Research*, ed. Scot McKnight and Grant R. Osborne, 104-17. Grand Rapids: Baker, 2004.

Cole, R. Alan. *Mark*. Tyndale New Testament Commentaries, rev. ed. Grand Rapids: Eerdmans, 1989.

Collins, Adela Yarbro. "Establishing the Text: Mark 1:1." In *Text and Contexts: The Function of Biblical Texts in their Textual and Situational Contexts*, ed. Lars Hartman, Tord Fornberg and David Hellholm, 111-27. Oslo: Scandinavian University Press, 1995.

———. *Mark*. Hermeneia: A Critical and Historical Commentary on the Bible. Minneapolis: Fortress, 2007.

Collins, John J. "Introduction: Towards the Morphology of a Genre." *Semeia* 14 (1979): 1-20.

Cook, John G. *The Structure and Persuasive Power of Mark: A Linguistic Approach*. Semeia Studies. Atlanta: Scholars Press, 1995.

Cotterell, Peter, and Max Turner. *Linguistics and Biblical Interpretation*. Downers Grove, Ill: InterVarsity Press, 1989.

Coulthard, Malcolm. *An Introduction to Discourse Analysis*, 2d ed. London: Longman, 1985.

Coulthard, Malcolm, and Martin Montgomery, ed. *Studies in Discourse Analysis*. London: Routledge and Kegan Paul, 1981.

Cross, Anthony R. "Genres of the New Testament." In *Dictionary of New Testament Background*, ed. Craig A. Evans and Stanley E. Porter, 402-11. Downers Grove, Ill: IVP, 2000.

Culpepper, R. Alan. *Mark*. Smyth and Helwys Bible Commentary. Macon, Ga: Smyth and Helwys, 2007.

Dahood, Mitchell. *Psalms: Introduction, Translation, and Notes*. Anchor Bible 1. Garden City, NY: Doubleday, 1966.

Danker, Frederick William. *The Concise Greek-English Lexicon of the New Testament*. Chicago, Ill: University of Chicago Press, 2009.

de Beaugrande, Robert-Alain, and Wolfgang Ulrich Dressler. *Introduction to Text Linguistics*. London: Longman, 1981.

Decker, Rodney J. *Mark 1-8: A Handbook on the Greek Text*. Waco, TX: Baylor U. Press, 2014.

———. "The Function(s) of the Imperfect Tense in Mark's Gospel." Society of Biblical Literature Annual Meeting, Biblical Greek Language and Linguistics Section, New Orleans, La, Nov 2009.

———. *Temporal Deixis of the Greek Verb in the Gospel of Mark with Reference to Verbal Aspect*. Studies in Biblical Greek 10. New York: Peter Lang, 2001.

DeSilva, David A. *An Introduction to the New Testament: Contexts, Methods and Ministry Formation*. Downers Grove, Ill: InterVarsity Press, 2004.

Devitt, Amy. "Generalizing about Genre: New Conceptions of an Old Concept." *College Composition and Communication* 44 (Dec. 1993): 573-86.

Dibelius, Martin. *Die Formgeschichte des Evangeliums.* Tübingen: Mohr Siebeck, 1919.

———. *From Tradition to Gospel.* Library of Theological Translations. New York: Scribner, 1971.

Donahue, John R., and Daniel J. Harrington. *The Gospel of Mark.* The Sacra Pagina Series. Collegeville, Minn: Liturgical Press, 2002.

Dooley, Robert A., and Stephen H. Levinsohn. *Analyzing Discourse: A Manual of Basic Concepts.* Dallas: SIL International, 2001.

Doty, William G. *Letters in Primitive Christianity.* Philadelphia: Fortress Press, 1973.

Dunn, James D. G. *The Epistles to the Colossians and to Philemon.* The New International Greek Testament Commentary. Grand Rapids: Eerdmans, 1996.

du Toit, A. B. "The Significance of Discourse Analysis for New Testament Interpretation and Translation: Introductory Remarks with Special Reference to 1 Peter 1:3-13." *Neotestamentica* 8 (1974): 54-80.

Duvall, J. Scott and J. Daniel Hays. *Grasping God's Word: A Hands-On Approach to Reading, Interpreting, and Applying the Bible,* 4th ed. Grand Rapids: Zondervan, 2020.

Edwards, James R. *The Gospel According to Mark.* The Pillar New Testament Commentary Series. Grand Rapids: Eerdmans, 2002.

Epp, Eldon J. "Textual Criticism in the Exegesis of the New Testament, with an Excursus on Canon." In *A Handbook to the Exegesis of the New Testament,* ed. Stanley E. Porter, 45-97. Leiden: Brill, 2002.

Evans, Craig A. *Mark 8:27-16:20*. Word Biblical Commentary 34B. Dallas: Thomas Nelson, 2001.

Fairclough, Norman. *Discourse and Social Change*. Cambridge: Polity Press, 1992.

Fanning, Buist M. *Verbal Aspect in New Testament Greek*. Oxford Theological Monographs. Oxford: Clarendon, 1990.

Fantin, Joseph D. *The Greek Imperative Mood in the New Testament: A Cognitive and Communicative Approach*. Studies in Biblical Greek 12. New York: Peter Lang, 2010.

Firth, John R. *Papers in Linguistics, 1934-51*. Oxford: Oxford University Press, 1951.

Fowler, Robert M. "Using Literary Criticism on the Gospels." *Christian Century* 26 (May 1982): 87-95.

France, R. T. *The Gospel of Mark*. The New International Greek Testament Commentary Series. Grand Rapids: Eerdmans, 2002.

Frei, Hans. *Eclipse of Biblical Narrative*. New Haven, Conn: Yale University Press, 1974.

Funk, Robert W. *The Poetics of Biblical Narrative*. Sonoma, Calif: Polebridge Press, 1988.

Garland, David E. *A Theology of Mark's Gospel: Good News About the Messiah, the Son of God*, Biblical Theology of the New Testament, gen. ed. Andreas J. Köstenberger. Grand Rapids: Zondervan, 2015.

———. *Mark*. NIV Application Commentary. Grand Rapids: Zondervan, 1996.

Givón, Talmy. *Syntax and Semantics, 12: Discourse and Syntax*, ed. Talmy Givón. New York: Academic, 1979.

Gladd, Benjamin L. *Handbook on the Gospels: Matthew, Mark, Luke, John*. Grand Rapids: Baker, 2021.

Gleason, H. A. *Contrastive Analysis in Discourse Structure*. Georgetown University Monograph Series on Languages and Linguistics 21 (1968): 39-64.

Globe, Alexander. "The Caesarean Omission of the Phrase 'Son of God' in Mark 1:1." *Harvard Theological Review* 75 no, 2 (April 1982): 209-18.

Green, Joel B. "Discourse Analysis and New Testament Interpretation." In *Hearing the New Testament: Strategies for Interpretation*, ed. Joel B. Green, 175-96. Grand Rapids: Eerdmans, 1995.

———. *The Way of the Cross: Following Jesus in the Gospel of Mark*. Eugene, OR: Wipf & Stock, 1991.

Greidanus, Sydney. *The Modern Preacher and the Ancient Text: Interpreting and Preaching Biblical Literature*. Grand Rapids: Eerdmans, 1988.

Grimes, Joseph E. *The Thread of Discourse*. Janua Linguarum 207. Hague: Mouton, 1975.

Guelich, Robert A. "The Gospel Genre." In *The Gospel and the Gospels*, ed. Peter Stuhlmacher, 173-208. Grand Rapids: Eerdmans, 1991.

———. *Mark 1-8:26*, Word Biblical Commentary 34a. Nashville: Thomas Nelson, 1989.

———. "Mark, Gospel of." In *Dictionary of Jesus and the Gospels*, ed. Joel B. Green, Scot McKnight, and I. Howard Marshall, 512-25. Downers Grove, Ill: InterVarsity Press, 1992.

———. "The Gospels: Portraits of Jesus and His Ministry." *Journal of Evangelical Theological Society* 24 (1982): 117-125.

Gundry, Robert H. "Recent Investigations into the Literary Genre 'Gospel.'" In *New Dimensions in New Testament Study*, ed. Richard N. Longenecker and Merrill C. Tenney, 97-114. Grand Rapids: Zondervan, 1974.

———. *Mark: A Commentary on His Apology for the Cross*. Grand Rapids: Eerdmans, 1993.

Gunn, David M. "Narrative Criticism." In *To Each Its Own Meaning: An Introduction to Biblical Criticisms and Their Application*, ed. Steven L. McKenzie and Stephen R. Haynes, 171-95. Louisville, Ky: Westminster John Knox Press, 1993.

Guthrie, Donald. *New Testament Introduction*. rev. ed. Downers Grove, Ill: InterVarsity Press, 1990.

Guthrie, George H. "Discourse Analysis." In *Interpreting the New Testament: Essays on Methods and Issues*," ed. David Alan Black and David S. Dockery, 253-71. Nashville: Broadman and Holman, 2001.

Halliday, M. A. K. "Dimensions of Discourse Analysis: Grammar." In *Handbook of Discourse Analysis. Vol. 2, Dimensions of Discourse*, ed. T. A. van Dijk, 29-56. London: Academic Press, 1985.

———. *An Introduction to Functional Grammar*. London: Edward Arnold, 1985.

———. *Language as Social Semiotic: The Social Interpretation of Language and Meaning*. London: Edward Arnold, 1978.

Halliday, M. A. K., and Robin P. Fawcett, ed. *New Developments in Systemic Linguistics*. Vol. 1, *Theory and Description*. London: Pinter, 1987.

Halliday, M. A. K., and R. Hasan. *Cohesion in English*. London: Longman, 1976.

———. *Language, Context, and Text: Aspects of Language in a Social-Semiotic Perspective*. Geelong, Australia: Deakon University, 1985.

———. "Text and Context: Aspects of Language in a Social-Semiotic Perspective." *Sophia Linguistica* 6 (1980): 4-91.

Halliday, M. A. K. and Christian M. I. M. Matthiessen. *Halliday's Introduction to Functional Grammar*, 4th rev. ed. London: Routledge, 2014.

Hare, Douglas R. A. *Mark*. Louisville, Ky: Westminster John Knox, 1996.

Harris, Murray J. "Appendix: Prepositions and Theology in the Greek New Testament." In *Dictionary of New Testament Theology*, ed. Colin Brown, 3:1171-1215. Grand Rapids: Zondervan, 1986.

Harris, Zellig S. "Discourse Analysis." *Language* 28, no. 1 (1952): 1-30.

Hartmann, Peter. *Theorie der Grammatik*. Hague: Mouton, 1963.

———. *Zur Theorie der Sprachwissenschaft*. Assen: Van Gorcum, 1961.

Head, Peter M. "A Text-Critical Study of Mark 1:1: 'The Beginning of the Gospel of Jesus Christ.'" *New Testament Studies* 37 (1991): 621-29.

Healy, Mary. *The Gospel of Mark*. Grand Rapids: Baker, 2008.

Hellholm, David. "Amplificatio in the Macro-Structure of Romans." In *Rhetoric and the New Testament: Essays from the 1992 Heidelberg Conference*. Journal for the Study of the New Testament Supplement Series 90, ed. Stanley E. Porter and Thomas H. Olbricht, 123-51. Sheffield: JSOT 1993.

———. *Das Visionenbuch des Hermas als Apokalypse: Formgeschichtliche und texttheoretische Studien zu einer literarischen Gattung. I. Methodologische Vorüberlegungen und makrostrukturelle Textanalyse*. ConBNT 13.1; Lund: Gleerup, 1980.

Hill, Andrew E. and John H. Walton. *A Survey of the Old Testament*, 3d ed. Grand Rapids: Zondervan, 2009.

Hirsch, E. D., Jr. *Validity in Interpretation*. New Haven, Conn: Yale University Press, 1967.

Hooker, Morna D. *The Gospel According to Saint Mark*, Black's New Testament Commentaries 2. Peabody, Mass: Hendrickson, 1991.

———. "Who Can This Be?" In *Contours of Christology in the New Testament*, ed. Richard N. Longenecker, 79-99. Grand Rapids: Eerdmans, 2005.

Humphrey, Robert L. *Narrative Structure and Message in Mark: A Rhetorical Analysis*. Studies in the Bible and Early Christianity 60. Lewiston: Edwin Mellen Press, 2003.

Hurtado, Larry W. "Gospel (Genre)." In *Dictionary of Jesus and the Gospels*, ed. Joel B. Green, Scot McKnight, and I. Howard Marshall, 276-82. Downers Grove, Ill: InterVarsity Press, 1992.

Johanson, Bruce C. *To All the Brethren: A Text-Linguistic and Rhetorical Approach to 1 Thessalonians*. Coniectanea Biblica. Stockholm: Almqvist & Wiksell, 1987.

Johnson, Elliott E. "Author's Intention and Biblical Interpretation." In *Hermeneutics, Inerrancy and the Bible: Papers from ICBI Summit II*, eds. Earl D. Radmacher and Robert D. Preus, 409-29. Grand Rapids: Zondervan, 1984.

———. *Expository Hermeneutics: An Introduction*. Grand Rapids: Zondervan, 1990.

Johnson, Sherman E. *A Commentary on the Gospel According to St. Mark*. Harper's New Testament Commentary 2. Peabody, Mass: Hendrickson, 1972.

Kähler, Martin. *The So-Called Historical Jesus and the Historic, Biblical Christ*. Philadephia: Fortress Press, 1964.

Kaiser, Walter C., Jr. "I Will Remember the Deeds of the Lord: The Meaning of Narrative." In *An Introduction to Biblical Hermeneutics: The Search for Meaning*, rev. & exp. ed., ed. Walter C. Kaiser Jr. and Moisés Silva, 123-37. Grand Rapids: Zondervan, 2007.

———. *Toward an Exegetical Theology: Biblical Exegesis for Preaching and Teaching*. Grand Rapids: Baker, 1981.

Kaiser, Walter C., Jr. and Moisés Silva. *Introduction to Biblical Hermeneutics: The Search for Meaning*, rev. and exp. ed. Grand Rapids: Zondervan, 2007.

Kernaghan, Robert J. *Mark*. IVP New Testament Commentary 2. Downers Grove, Ill: InterVarsity Press, 2007.

Kilgallen, John J. *A Brief Commentary on the Gospel of Mark*. New York: Paulist, 1989.

Kingsbury, Jack D. *The Christology of Mark's Gospel*. Philadelphia: Fortress Press, 1983.

———. *Conflict in Mark: Jesus, Authorities, Disciples*. Minneapolis: Fortress Press, 1989.

Klein, William, Craig Blomberg, and Robert Hubbard. *Introduction to Biblical Interpretation*. Nashville: Word, 1993.

Koester, Helmut. "From the Kerygma-Gospel to Written Gospels." *New Testament Studies* 35 (1989): 361-81.

Köstenberger, Andreas J., Benjamin L. Merkle, and Robert L. Plummer. *Going Deeper with New Testament Greek*, rev. ed. Nashville, TN: Broadman & Holman, 2020.

Kudasiewicz, Joseph. *The Synoptic Gospels Today*. Translated by Sergius Wroblewski. New York: Alba House, 1996.

Lamb, Sydney M. *Outline of Stratificational Grammar*. Washington, D.C.: Georgetown University Press, 1966.

Lane, William L. *The Gospel of Mark*. The New International Commentary on the New Testament. Grand Rapids: Eerdmans, 1974.

Larsen, Kevin W. "The Structure of Mark's Gospel: Current Proposals." *Currents in Biblical Research* 3, no.1 (2004): 140-60.

Lemke, J. L. "Semantics and Social Values." *Word* 40 (1989): 37-50.

Levinsohn, Stephen H. *Discourse Features of New Testament Greek: A Coursebook*, 2d ed. Dallas: Summer Institute of Linguistics, 2000.

———. "A Discourse Study of Constituent Order and the Article in Philippians." In *Discourse Analysis and Other Topics in Biblical Greek*, ed. Stanley E. Porter and D. A. Carson, 60-74. Journal for the Study of the New Testament Supplement Series. Sheffield: Sheffield Academic Press, 1995.

———. "Functions of Copula-Participle Combinations ("Periphrastics")." In *The Greek Verb Revisited: A Fresh Approach for Biblical Exegesis*, ed. Steven E. Runge and Christopher J. Fresch. Bellingham, WA: Lexham Press, 2016.

———. "Preliminary Observations on the Use of the Historic Present in Mark." *Notes on Translation* 65 (1977): 13-28.

Long, Philips V. "The Art of Biblical History." In *Foundations of Contemporary Interpretation*, ed. Moisés Silva, 287-429. Grand Rapids: Zondervan, 1996.

Longacre, Robert E. "Building for the Worship of God: Exodus 25:1-30:10." In *Discourse Analysis of Biblical Literature*, ed. Walter Bodine, 21-49. The Society of Biblical Literature Semeia Studies. Atlanta, Ga: Scholars, 1995.

———. "Discourse Perspective on the Hebrew Verb: Affirmation and Restatement." In *Linguistics and Biblical Hebrew*, ed. Walter R. Bodine, 177-89. Winona Lake, Ind: Eisenbrauns, 1992.

———. *The Grammar of Discourse*, 2d ed. New York and London: Plenum, 1996.

———. *Joseph, A Story of Divine Providence: A Text Theoretical and Textlinguistic Analysis of Genesis 37 and 39-48*. Winona Lake, Ind: Eisenbrauns, 1989.

———. "The Paragraph as a Grammatical Unit." *Syntax and Semantics, 12: Discourse and Syntax*, ed. Talmy Givón, 115-34. New York: Academic Press, 1979.

———. "Why We Need a Vertical Revolution in Linguistics." In *The Fifth LACUS Forum*, ed. Wolfgang Wölck and Paul Garvin, 247-70. Columbia, S.C.: Hornbeam, 1978.

Longman, Tremper, III. *Foundations of Contemporary Interpretation*, ed. Moisés Silva. Grand Rapids: Zondervan, 1996.

Louw, Johannes P. "Discourse Analysis and the Greek New Testament." *Bible Translator* 24, no. 1 (Jan 1973): 101-18.

———. "Reading A Text as Discourse." In *Linguistics and New Testament Interpretation: Essays on Discourse Analysis*, ed. David Alan Black with Katharine Barnwell and Stephen Levinsohn, 17-30. Nashville: Broadman and Holman, 1992.

———. *A Semantic Discourse Anlysis of Romans*. 2 vols. Pretoria: University of Pretoria, 1987.

———. *Semantics of New Testament Greek*. Philadelphia: Fortress Press, 1982.

———. "A Semiotic Approach to Discourse Analysis with Reference to Translation Theory." *Bible Translator* 39 (1988): 329-35.

———. "South African Discourse Analysis in Theory and Practice." *Verbum et Ecclesia* 29, no. 2 (2008): 387-406.

Mann, C. S. *Mark: A New Translation with Introduction and Commentary*. The Anchor Bible 27. New York: Doubleday, 1986.

Marcus, Joel. *Mark 1-8: A New Translation with Introduction and Commentary.* The Anchor Yale Bible Commentaries 27. New York: Doubleday, 2002.

———. *Mark 8-16: A New Translation with Introduction and Commentary.* The Anchor Yale Bible Commentaries 27a. New Haven, Conn: Yale University Press, 2009.

Martin, George. *The Gospel According to Mark: Meaning and Message.* Chicago: Loyola Press, 2005.

Martin, J. R. *English Text: System and Structure.* Philadelphia: John Benjamins, 1992.

Martin, Ralph P. *Mark: Evangelist and Theologian.* Exeter: Paternoster Press, 1972.

Martín-Asensio, Gustavo. "Participant Reference and Foregrounded Syntax in the Stephen Episode." In Discourse Analysis and the New Testament: Approaches and Results, ed. Stanley E. Porter and Jeffrey T. Reed, 235-57. Journal for the Study of the New Testament Supplement Series 170. Sheffield: Sheffield Academic Press, 1999.

———. *Transitivity-Based Foregrounding in the Acts of the Apostles: A Functional-Grammatical Approach to the Lucan Perspective*, Journal for the Study of the New Testament Supplement Series 202. Sheffield: Sheffield Academic Press, 2000.

Marxsen, Willi. *Mark the Evangelist.* Nashville: Abingdon, 1969.

Matthews, P. H. *Syntax.* Cambridge: Cambridge University Press, 1981.

Mathewson, David L. and Elodie Ballantine Emig. *Intermediate Greek Grammar: Syntax for Students of the New Testament.* Grand Rapids: Baker, 2016.

McKenzie, Steven L., and Stephen R. Haynes, eds. *To Each Its Own Meaning: An Introduction to Biblical Criticisms and Their Application.* Louisville, Ky: Westminster John Knox Press, 1993.

McKnight, Edgar V. "Literary Criticism." In *Dictionary of Jesus and the Gospels*, ed. Joel B. Green, Scot McKnight, and I. Howard Marshall, 473-81. Downers Grove, Ill: InterVarsity Press, 1992.

———. *What Is Form Criticism?* Philadelphia: Fortress Press, 1969.

McKnight, Scot. *Interpreting the Synoptic Gospels.* Grand Rapids: Baker, 1988.

Merkle, Benjamin L. *Exegetical Gems from Biblical Greek: A Refreshing Guide to Grammar and Interpretation.* Grand Rapids: Baker, 2019.

Moloney, Francis J. *The Gospel of Mark: A Commentary.* Peabody, Mass: Hendrickson, 2002.

———. *A Hard Saying: The Gospel and Culture.* Collegeville, Minn: Liturgical Press, 2001.

———. *Mark: Storyteller, Interpreter, Evangelist.* Peabody, Mass: Hendrickson, 2004.

Neely, Linda L. "A Discourse Analysis of Hebrews." *Occasional Papers in Translation and Textlinguistics* 3-4 (1987): 1-146.

Nida, Eugene A. *Componential Analysis of Meaning: An Introduction to Semantic Structures.* Hague: Mouton, 1975.

———. *Toward a Science of Translating: With Special Reference to Principles and Procedures Involved in Bible Translating.* Leiden: Brill, 1964.

Nida, Eugene A., et.al. *Style and Discourse: With Special Reference to the Text of the Greek New Testament*. Roggebaai, South Africa: Bible Society, 1983.

Nineham, D. E. *The Gospel of Saint Mark*. Pelican Gospel Commentaries. Baltimore, Md: Penguin, 1963.

Oden, Thomas C., and Christopher A. Hall. *Mark*. Ancient Christian Commentary on Scripture: New Testament 2. Downers Grove, Ill: InterVarsity Press, 1998.

Olsson, Birger. "A Decade of Text-Linguistic Analyses of Biblical Texts at Uppsala." *Studia Theologica* 39 (1985): 107-26.

———. *Structure and Meaning in the Fourth Gospel: A Text-Linguistic Analysis of John 2:1-11 and 4:1-42*. Coniectanea Biblica. Lund, Sweden: Gleerup, 1974.

Osborne, Grant R. "Genre Criticism—Sensus Literalis." *Trinity Journal* 4, no. 2 (1983): 1-27.

———. *The Hermeneutical Spiral: A Comprehensive Introduction to Biblical Interpretation*, rev. and exp. Downers Grove, Ill: InterVarsity Press, 2006.

———. "Redaction Criticism." In *Interpreting the New Testament: Essays on Methods and Issues*, ed. David Alan Black and David S. Dockery, 128-49. Nashville: Broadman and Holman, 2001.

Palmer, F. R., ed. *Selected Papers of J. R. Firth 1952-59*. London: Longman, 1968.

Pearson, Brook W. R., and Stanley E. Porter. "The Genres of the New Testament." In *A Handbook to the Exegesis of the New Testament*, ed. Stanley E. Porter, 131-65. Leiden: Brill, 2002.

Pennington, Jonathan T. *Reading the Gospels Wisely: A Narrative and Theological Introduction*. Grand Rapids: Baker, 2012.

Perrin, Norman. *The New Testament: An Introduction*. New York: Harcourt Brace Jovanovich, 1974.

———. *What Is Redaction Criticism*? Philadelphia: Fortress Press, 1970.

Perrin, Norman, and Dennis Duling. *The New Testament: An Introduction*, 2d ed. New York: Harcourt, Brace, Jovanovich, 1982.

Peterson, Norman R. "Point of View in Mark's Narrative." *Semeia* 12 (1978): 97-121.

Pike, Kenneth L. *Language in Relation to a Unified Theory of the Structure of Human Behavior*. Hague: Mouton, 1967.

Polhill, John B. "Interpreting the Book of Acts." In *Interpreting the New Testament: Essays on Methods and Issues* eds. David Alan Black and David S. Dockery, 391-411. Nashville: Broadman and Holman, 2001.

Porter, Stanley E. "Discourse Analysis and New Testament Studies: An Introductory Survey." In *Discourse Analysis and Other Topics in Biblical Greek*, ed. Stanley E. Porter and D. A. Carson, 14-35. Journal for the Study of the New Testament Supplement Series, 113. Sheffield: Sheffield Academic Press, 1995.

———. "Exegesis of the Pauline Letters, Including the Deutero-Pauline Letters." In *A Handbook to the Exegesis of the New Testament*, ed. Stanley E. Porter, 503-53. Leiden: Brill, 2002.

———. "Greek Grammar and Syntax." In *The Face of New Testament Studies: A Survey of Recent Research*, ed. Scot McKnight and Grant R. Osborne, 76-103. Grand Rapids: Baker, 2004.

———. "How Can Biblical Discourse Be Analyzed? A Response to Several Attempts." In *Discourse Analysis and Other Topics in Biblical Greek*, ed. Stanley E. Porter and D. A. Carson, 107-16. Journal for the Study of the New Testament Supplement Series 113, Sheffield: Sheffield Academic Press, 1995.

———. *Idioms of the Greek New Testament*, 2d ed. Biblical Languages: Greek 2. Sheffield: Sheffield Academic Press, 1999.

———. *Letter to the Romans: A Literary and Linguistic Commentary*. Sheffield: Sheffield Phoenix Press, 2016.

———. "Linguistic Schools." In *Linguistics and New Testament Greek: Key Issues in the Current Debate*, eds. David Alan Black and Benjamin L. Merkle, 11-36. Grand Rapids: Baker, 2020.

———. *Verbal Aspect in the Greek of the New Testament with Reference to Tense and Mood*. Studies in Biblical Greek 1. New York: Peter Lang, 1989.

Porter, Stanley E., and Andrew W. Pitts. "New Testament Greek Language and Linguistics in Recent Research." *Currents in Biblical Research* 6, no. 2 (Feb 2008): 214-55.

Porter, Stanley E. and Jeffrey T. Reed. "Greek Grammar Since BDF: A Retrospective and Prospective Analysis." *Filología Neotestamentaria* 4, no. 8 (1991): 143-64.

Porter, Stanley E., and Matthew Brook O'Donnell. *Discourse Analysis and the Greek New Testament: Theory, Application and Results*. Leiden: Brill, forthcoming.

Powell, Mark Alan. "Toward A Narrative-Critical Understanding of Mark." *Interpretation* 47, no. 4 (Oct 1993): 341-46.

―――. *What Is Narrative Criticism?* Minneapolis: Fortress Press, 1990.

Reed, Jeffrey T. "The Cohesiveness of Discourse: Towards A Model of Linguistic Criteria for Analyzing New Testament Discourse." In *Discourse Analysis and the New Testament*, ed. Stanley E. Porter and Jeffrey T. Reed, 28-46. Journal for the Study of the New Testament Supplement Series 170. Sheffield: Sheffield Academic Press, 1999.

―――. "Cohesive Ties in 1 Timothy: In Defense of the Epistle's Unity." *Neotestamentica* 26 (1992): 131-47.

―――. "Discourse Analysis." In *A Handbook to the Exegesis of the New Testament*, ed. Stanley E. Porter, 189-217. Leiden: Brill, 2002.

―――. "Discourse Analysis as New Testament Hermeneutic: A Retrospective and Prospective Appraisal." *Journal of The Evangelical Theological Society* 39, no. 2 (1996): 223-40.

―――. *A Discourse Analysis of Philippians: Method and Rhetoric in the Debate over Literary Integrity*. Journal for the Study of the New Testament Supplement Series 136. Sheffield: Sheffield, 1997.

―――. "Identifying Theme in the New Testament: Insights from Discourse Analysis." In *Discourse Analysis and Other Topics in Biblical Greek*, ed. Stanley E. Porter and D. A. Carson, 75-101. Journal for the Study of the New Testament Supplement Series 113. Sheffield: Sheffield Academic Press, 1995.

―――. "Modern Linguistics and Historical Criticism: Using the Former for Doing the Latter." In *Linguistics and the New Testament: Critical Junctures*, ed. Stanley E. Porter and D. A. Carson, 36-62. Journal for the Study of the New Testament Supplement Series 168. Sheffield: Sheffield Academic Press, 1999.

———. "To Timothy or Not? A Discourse Analysis of 1 Timothy." In *Biblical Greek Language and Linguistics: Open Questions in Current Research*, ed. Stanley E. Porter and D. A. Carson, 90-118. Journal for the Study of the New Testament Supplement Series 80. Sheffield: JSOT, 1993.

Resseguie, James L. *Narrative Criticism of the New Testament: An Introduction*. Grand Rapids: Baker, 2005.

Rhoads, David, Joanna Dewey, and Donald Michie. *Mark as Story: An Introduction to the Narrative of a Gospel*, 2d ed. Minneapolis: Fortress Press, 1999.

Robbins, Vernon K. *The Composition of Mark's Gospel: Selected Studies from Novum Testamentum*. Brill's Readers in Biblical Studies 3. Leiden: Brill, 1999.

Robertson, A. T. *A Grammar of the Greek New Testament in the Light of Historical Research*. Nashville: Broadman Press, 1934.

Rodd, Cyril S. *The Gospel of Mark*. Epworth Commentaries. Peterborough, UK: Epworth Press, 2005.

Runge, Steven E. *Discourse Grammar of the Greek New Testament: A Practical Introduction for Teaching and Exegesis*. Nashville: Peabody, Mass: Hendrickson Publishers, 2010.

Ryken, Leland. *How to Read the Bible As Literature*. Grand Rapids: Zondervan, 1984.

Sandy, D. Brent, and Ronald L. Giese Jr. *Cracking Old Testament Codes: A Guide to Interpreting the Literary Genres of the Old Testament*. Nashville: Broadman and Holman, 1995.

Scacewater, Todd A. "Introduction – Discourse Analysis: History, Topics, and Applications." In *Discourse Analysis of the New Testament Writings* ed. Todd A. Scacewater, 1-11. Dallas, TX: Fontes Press, 2020.

Schenk, Wolfgang. "The Testamental Disciple-Instruction of the Markan Jesus (Mark 13): Its Levels of Communication and its Rhetorical Structures." In *Discourse Analysis and the New Testament: Approaches and Results*, ed. Stanley E. Porter and Jeffrey T. Reed, 197-222. Journal for the Study of the New Testament Supplement Series 170. Sheffield: Sheffield Academic Press, 1999.

Schiffrin, Deborah. *Approaches to Discourse*. Oxford: Blackwell, 1994.

Schmidt, Karl Ludwig. *Der Rahmen der Geschichte Jesu: Literarkritische Untersuchungen zur ältesten Jesusüberlieferung*. Berlin: Trowitzsch, 1919.

Schürer, Emil. *The History of the Jewish People in the Age of Jesus Christ (175 B.C.-A.D. 135)*. rev. and ed. G. Vermes and F. Millar. 3 vols. Edinburgh: T. & T. Clark, 1973-87.

Schweitzer, Albert. *The Quest for the Historical Jesus*. Grand Rapids: Eerdmans, 1969.

Schweizer, Eduard. "Mark's Theological Achievement." In *The Interpretation of Mark*, ed. W. R. Telford. Edinburgh: T&T Clark, 1995.

Silva, Moisés. "But These Are Written That You May Believe: The Meaning of the Gospels." In *Introduction To Biblical Hermeneutics: The Search for Meaning*, ed. Walter C. Kaiser Jr. and Moisés Silva, 157-71. Grand Rapids: Zondervan, 2007.

———. "Discourse Analysis and Philippians." In *Discourse Analysis and Other Topics in Biblical Greek*, ed. Stanley E. Porter and D. A. Carson,

102-06. Journal for the Study of the New Testament Supplement Series 113. Sheffield: Sheffield Academic Press, 1995.

Shuler, Philip L. *A Genre for the Gospels: The Biographical Character of Matthew*. Philadelphia: Fortress, 1982.

Slomp, Jan. "Are the Words 'Son of God' in Mark 1:1 Original?" *Biblical Translator* 28 (1977): 143-50.

Small, Russell. "Mark." In *Approaching the New Testament: A Guide for Students*, gen. eds. Adam McClendon and John Cartwright, 40-41. Nashville, TN: Broadman & Holman, 2022.

Snodgrass, Klyne. "Parable." In *Dictionary of Jesus and the Gospels*, ed. by Joel B. Green, Scot McKnight, and I. Howard Marshall, 591-601. Downers Grove, Ill: InterVarsity Press, 1992.

Snyman, Andries H. "Discourse Analysis: A Semantic Discourse Analysis of the Letter to Philemon." In *Text and Interpretation: New Approaches in the Criticism of the New Testament*, ed. P. J. Hartin and J. H. Petzer, 83-99. Leiden: Brill, 1991.

———. "Hebrews 6:4-6: From A Semiotic Discourse Perspective." In *Discourse Analysis and the New Testament: Approaches and Results*, ed. Stanley E. Porter and Jeffrey T. Reed, 354-68. Journal for the Study of the New Testament Supplement Series 170. Sheffield: Sheffield Academic Press, 1999.

Stamps, Dennis L. "Rhetorical and Narratological Criticism." In *A Handbook to the Exegesis of the New Testament*, ed. Stanley E. Porter, 219-39. Leiden: Brill, 2002.

Stanton, Graham N. *The Gospels and Jesus*, 2d ed. New York: Oxford University Press, 2002.

Stein, Robert H. *Mark*. Baker Exegetical Commentary on the New Testament. Grand Rapids: Baker, 2008.

———. *Studying the Synoptic Gospels: Origin and Interpretation*, 2d ed. Grand Rapids: Baker, 2001.

Sternberg, Meir. *The Poetics of Biblical Narrative, Ideological Literature and the Drama of Reading*. Bloomington, Ind: Indiana University Press, 1985.

Strauss, Mark L. *Four Portraits, One Jesus: A Survey of Jesus and the Gospels*, 2d ed. Grand Rapids: Zondervan, 2020.

———. *Introducing Jesus: a short guide to the gospels' history and message*. Grand Rapids: Zondervan, 2018.

———. *Mark: An Exegetical Commentary on the New Testament*. Grand Rapids: Zondervan, 2014.

Stubbs, Michael. *Discourse Analysis: The Sociolinguistic Analysis of Natural Language*. Oxford: Basil Blackwell, 1983.

Summer Institute of Linguistics. http://www.sil.org/sil (accessed July 19, 2011).

Sweetland, Dennis. *Mark: From Death to Life*. Hyde Park, N.Y.: New City Press, 2007.

———. *Our Journey with Jesus: Discipleship According to Mark*. Wilmington, Del: Michael Glazier, 1987.

Talbert, Charles H. *Literary Patterns, Theological Themes and the Genres of Luke-Acts*. Society of Biblical Literature Monograph Series, 20; Missoula, Mont: Scholars Press, 1974.

———. *What Is a Gospel? The Genre of the Canonical Gospels*. Philadelphia: Fortress, 1984.

Tannell, Robert C. "The Disciples in Mark: The Function of a Narrative Role." *Journal of Religion* 57 (1977): 386-405.

———. "The Gospel of Mark as Narrative Christology." *Semeia* 16 (1979): 57-95.

Taylor, Vincent. *The Formation of the Gospel Tradition*. London: Macmillan, 1933.

——— *The Gospel According to St. Mark*. London: Macmillan, 1957.

Thiemann, Ronald F. "Radiance and Obscurity in Biblical Narrative." In *Scriptural Authority and Narrative Interpretation*, ed. Garrett Green, 21-41. Philadelphia: Fortress Press, 1987.

Thomas, Robert L. *Evangelical Hermeneutics: The New Versus the Old*. Grand Rapids: Kregel, 2002.

Titrud, Kermit. "The Function of καί in the Greek New Testament and An Application to 2 Peter." In *Linguistics and New Testament Interpretation: Essays on Discourse Analysis*, ed. David Alan Black with Katharine Barnwell and Stephen Levinsohn, 240-70. Nashville: Broadman and Holman, 1992.

Tolbert, Mary Ann. *Sowing the Gospel: Mark's World in Literary-Historical Perspective*. Minneapolis: Fortress, 1989.

Turner, David L. *Interpreting the Gospels and Acts: An Exegetical Handbook*, series ed. John D. Harvey, Handbooks for New Testament Exegesis. Grand Rapids: Kregel, 2019.

Twelftree, Graham. "Discipleship in Mark's Gospel." *St. Mark's Review* 141 (1990): 5-11.

van Dijk, T. A. *Text and Context: Explorations in the Semantics and Pragmatics of Discourse*. London: Longman, 1977.

Vanhoozer, Kevin J. *Is There A Meaning in This Text?* Grand Rapids: Zondervan, 1998.

———. "The Semantics of Biblical Literature: Truth and Scripture's Diverse Literary Forms." In *Hermeneutics, Authority, and Canon*, ed. D. A. Carson and John D. Woodbridge, 49-104. Grand Rapids: Zondervan, 1986.

Van Iersel, Bas M. F. *Mark: A Reader-Response Commentary*. Translated by W. H. Bisscheroux. Edinburgh: T. & T. Clark, 1998.

———. *Reading Mark*. Translated by W. H. Bisscheroux. Edinburgh: T. & T. Clark, 1989.

Van Neste, Ray. *Cohesion and Structure in the Pastoral Epistles*. London: T&T Clark, 2004.

Votaw, Clyde Weber. *The Gospels and Contemporary Biographies in the Greco-Roman World*. Philadelphia: Fortress, 1970.

Wallace, Daniel B. *Greek Grammar Beyond the Basics: An Exegetical Syntax of the New Testament*. Grand Rapids: Zondervan, 1996.

Wanamaker, Charles A. *The Epistles to the Thessalonians*, The New International Greek Testament Commentary. Grand Rapids: Eerdmans, 1990.

Wasserman, Tommy. "The 'Son of God' Was in the Beginning (Mark 1:1)." *Journal of Theological Studies* 61, pt. 1 (April 2011): 20-50.

Watson, Duane F. "Roman Social Classes." In *Dictionary of New Testament Background*, ed. Craig A. Evans and Stanley E. Porter, 999-1004. Downers Grove, Ill: InterVarsity Press, 2000.

Watts, Rikki E. *Isaiah's New Exodus in Mark*. Biblical Studies Library. Grand Rapids: Baker, 1997.

Webster's New World College Dictionary, 3d ed. New York: Macmillan, 1997.

Weima, Jeffrey A. D. "Literary Criticism." In *Interpreting the New Testament: Essays on Methods and Issues*, ed. David Alan Black and David S. Dockery, 150-69. Nashville: Broadman and Holman, 2001.

Weiss, Johannes. *Jesus' Proclamation of the Kingdom of God*. Philadelphia: Fortress Press, 1971.

Wellek, René, and Austin Warren. *Theory of Literature*, 3d ed. New York: Harcourt, Brace and World, 1956.

Westfall, Cynthia Long. *Discourse Analysis of the Letter to the Hebrews: The Relationship Between Form and Meaning*. Library of New Testament Studies. London: T & T Clark, 2006.

Young, Richard A. *Intermediate New Testament Greek: A Linguistic and Exegetical Approach*. Nashville: Broadman and Holman, 1994.

Zuck, Roy B. *Basic Bible Interpretation: A Practical Guide to Discovering Biblical Truth*. Colorado Springs, Colo: Victor Books, 1991.

www.ingramcontent.com/pod-product-compliance
Lightning Source LLC
Chambersburg PA
CBHW050252010526
44107CB00003B/296